Betty Crocker's

quick&easy

COOKBOOK

30 minutes
or less to dinner every night

Wiley Publishing, Inc.

Published by Wiley Publishing, Inc.,
New York, NY

For general information on our other products and services or to obtain technical support please contact our Customer Care Department within the U.S. at 800-762-2974, outside the U.S. at 317-572-3993 or fax 317-572-4002.

Wiley also publishes its books in a variety of electronic formats. Some content that appears in print may not be available in electronic books.

ISBN: 0-7645-3930-2

Cataloging-in-Publication Data is available upon request from the Library of Congress.

General Mills, Inc.

DIRECTOR, BOOK AND ELECTRONIC PUBLISHING: Kim Walter

MANAGER, BOOK PUBLISHING: Lois L. Tlusty

EDITOR: Cheri Olerud

RECIPE DEVELOPMENT AND TESTING: Betty Crocker Kitchens

FOOD STYLISTS: Betty Crocker Kitchens

PHOTOGRAPHY: General Mills Photo Studios and General Mills Image Library

Wiley Publishing, Inc.

PUBLISHER: Natalie Chapman

EXECUTIVE EDITOR: Anne Ficklen

MANAGING EDITOR: S. Kristi Hart

EDITOR: Caroline Schleifer

ASSISTING EDITOR: Pamela Adler

PRODUCTION EDITOR: Donna Wright

COVER AND BOOK DESIGN: Edwin Kuo

INTERIOR LAYOUT: Holly Wittenberg

MANUFACTURING BUYER: Kevin Watt

For consistent baking results, the Betty Crocker Kitchens recommend Gold Medal Flour.

Manufactured in China

10 9 8 7 6 5 4 3 2 1

Cover photo and photo page 4: Stove-Top Lasagna (page 94)

For more great ideas visit www.bettycrocker.com

Dear Friends,

"What's for dinner tonight?" If that's a question you hear everyday, your dinner solution is right here with *Betty Crocker's Quick & Easy Cookbook.*

This book is full of great dinner ideas, with over 300 easy-to-make recipes that can be prepared in 30 minutes or less. On those evenings when you're really pressed for time, look for **super express** recipes that can be ready in 20 minutes or less. They make the next question— "Is dinner ready?"—one that you can answer "yes!" to a whole lot faster.

How can these recipes be so quick to make? Lasagna usually takes hours to assemble and bake. The solution? Savvy shortcuts, like quick-cooking noodles, mean you'll be able to enjoy it for a weeknight meal anytime. You may love chicken in cream sauce, but who has time to make sauce from scratch? The answer? Try Alfredo Chicken and Mushrooms with a refrigerated sauce that you can buy. Fudge Pudding Cake looks and tastes like it took hours to make but is ready in minutes. The secret? Use your microwave to "bake" dessert.

Don't have time to grocery shop before dinner? Stock your kitchen with basics from the **Pantry Planner,** then just turn to **Pantry Recipes** that use ingredients you're sure to have on hand. Or glance at **1-Step Recipes**—these oh-so-simple ideas are handy when you want easy inspiration for new ways to prepare pasta, chicken breasts or other dinner staples.

Need more information about a recipe? Turn to the sidebar tips that accompany each one. IT'S **a snap!** tells you about the ingredients and suggests tasty substitutions or time-saving tactics. Look to **COME & eat!** tips for quick ideas to round out your meal or simple additions that make dinner extra special.

Dinnertime is a great time for family and friends once you've solved the what's-for-dinner dilemma. Here are plenty of super ideas to keep you and your family cooking—and enjoying—dinner together.

Betty Crocker

P.S. Your delicious dinner solution is right here!

quick&easy
Table of Contents

Pantry Planner

Stocking Your Pantry for Quick Cooking

Having a wide variety of food and ingredients at hand in your cupboard, refrigerator and freezer offers tremendous flexibility when you are asked the everyday "What's for dinner?" question. This pantry list covers all the basics of quick cooking; add your own favorites to it. And check out Pantry Recipes in every chapter. If you have a well-stocked pantry, you'll be able to prepare all of these easy recipes, even when you don't have time to shop.

Produce

Fruits:
• apples, bananas, grapes
• citrus fruits (lemons, oranges)

Vegetables:
• carrots
• onions
• potatoes
• ready-to-use coleslaw mix
• ready-to-use salad mix

Refrigerated

Breads and Dough Products:
• pita breads
• prepared doughs (biscuit, breadsticks)
• ready-to-use pizza crust
• ready-to-use garlic or cheese breads
• tortillas (corn, flour)

Condiments:
• chopped garlic
• prepared horseradish
• prepared pesto

Dairy:
• butter or margarine
• cheese (shredded, sliced)
• cream cheese
• eggs or egg substitutes
• milk
• sour cream
• yogurt (plain, flavored)

Meat, Poultry and Fish

• boneless, skinless chicken breasts or thighs
• fresh or frozen fish steaks
• ground beef
• sausage (smoked, hot dogs, bratwurst)
• ready-to-cook seasoned meat and poultry products

Frozen Foods

• desserts and whipped topping
• dough (bread, pizza)
• fruits (blueberries, peaches)
• ice cream and frozen yogurt
• juice concentrate
• pancakes, waffles
• pizza
• ravioli (cheese- or beef-filled)
• vegetables (corn, green beans, favorite combination)

Bakery

• breads (sandwich bread, rolls, bagels)
• cookies

Shelf-Stable Products

Baking Basics:
- Bisquick® baking mix
- cake mix
- chips (semisweet chocolate, butterscotch or peanut butter)
- flour
- frosting
- nuts (walnuts, peanuts)
- sugar (granulated, brown, powdered)

Canned Basics:
- beans (kidney, black)
- broth (chicken, vegetable)
- canned tuna and chicken
- fruits (pears, peaches, cocktail)
- gravy
- green chilies
- mushrooms
- pasta, pizza sauces
- soups
- tomato products (sauce, paste, stewed, diced, seasoned)

Cereals and Snacks:
- bread crumbs
- cereals
- chips, popcorn, pretzels
- crackers
- croutons
- taco shells

Condiments and Sauces:
- Asian (hoisin, oyster, peanut and sweet-and-sour sauces)
- barbecue sauce
- chutney
- honey
- ice-cream toppings
- ketchup
- maple syrup
- mustards (Dijon, spicy brown, yellow)
- peanut butter
- preserves (jam, jelly, marmalade)
- relishes (olives, peppers, pickles)
- salsa, picante sauce
- soy sauce, teriyaki sauce

Dressings, Oils and Vinegars:
- cooking spray
- marinades
- mayonnaise, salad dressing
- oils (vegetable, olive)
- salad dressings
- vinegars (cider, white and red wine)

Herbs, Spices and Dry Mixes:
- Basil
- bouillon granules or cubes
- chili powder
- cumin
- dry sauce mixes (cheese, gravy, white)

- dry seasoning mixes (meat loaf, sloppy joe, spaghetti, taco)
- dry soup mixes
- garlic and onion powder or salt
- herb or seasoning blends, regular or salt-free (Italian seasoning, lemon)
- oregano
- parsley flakes
- pepper seasoning
- salad dressing mix
- tarragon
- thyme

Pasta, Rice, Grains and Potatoes:
- barley (quick-cooking)
- couscous
- instant potatoes
- noodle and pasta mixes
- pasta (long, short and tube types)
- potato mixes
- rice (white, brown and quick-cooking)
- rice mixes

Streamline Kitchen Time

No need to feel frazzled in the kitchen. Speeding up your cooking is easy when you follow these make-it-easier strategies and tips.

1 Get organized

Locate your kitchen equipment at the point of first use: Store equipment and serving pieces so they're easily accessible: skillets and pot holders next to the stove, the coffee maker and mugs next to the sink, etc.

2 Clear the cupboard

Move kitchen equipment that you don't use often, such as items for holiday cooking, to a high cupboard or store in a "seasonal" cupboard.

3 Bring to a boil

Jump-start boiling water, by starting with hot water. Cover saucepan with a lid so it will come to a boil faster.

4 Mash it faster

Mash potatoes in minutes by cutting potatoes into small pieces (1 to 1 1/2 inches) to cut cooking time by half. This works great for other veggies, too!

5 Pasta pronto

For promptly prepared pasta, toss frozen or fresh vegetables into the pasta cooking water during the last few minutes of cooking instead of cooking the pasta and vegetables separately.

6 Quicken chicken

For faster-cooking chicken, pound boneless, skinless chicken breast halves between sheets of waxed paper with a meat mallet or the bottom of a heavy pan to about 1/4-inch thickness.

7 Nonstick in no time

For easy cleanup when measuring honey, syrup or other sticky stuff, spray measuring spoons and cups with cooking spray; the sticky stuff will slide right out!

8 Butter secrets

Need softened butter in a hurry? Get out the cheese grater, and grate the stick of butter or margarine against the holes! Keep rolling up the paper or foil on the stick as you go to avoid greasy hands.

9 Make it mini

Cut meat loaf bake time in half by pressing the uncooked meat loaf mixture into muffin cups instead of a loaf pan.

10 Skip the pan

Save cleanup time by using aluminum foil instead of a baking pan. Bake fish sticks, chicken fingers and other foods on a piece that's large enough to hold the food, with extra to hang on to.

Timesaving Gadgets

It's true, having the "right gadget" can shave off minutes when time really matters. Purchase these handy kitchen helpers in discount stores, large supermarkets or the kitchenware section of department or hardware stores.

Garlic press

Crushes a whole clove of garlic right into the pan or bowl; you don't have to peel the clove or even dirty a cutting board! Presses with nonstick surfaces are easiest to clean.

Kitchen knives

For ultra convenience, get the permanently sharpened set. They make paring, slicing and chopping vegetables and fruits a breeze.

Microplane cheese grater-zester

Easily grates cheese, butter, chocolate and cheese. Also makes short work of grating lemon, lime and orange peels without removing the bitter white part below the skin.

Kitchen scissors

This handy helper speeds through multiple tasks: quickly trims fat from chicken, and cuts up herbs, dried fruit, canned whole tomatoes, green onions, marshmallows and even pizza.

Citrus juicer

Squeezes juice easily and quickly from fresh lemons, limes and oranges.

Pizza cutter

Works great for pizza, right? Did you know that you can also use this handy gadget to slice garlic toast, focaccia bread, waffles and pancakes? Try it the next time you serve one of these.

Scoop

This multipurpose tool scoops ice cream and frozen yogurt, and forms cookie dough into perfect rounds. For a dripless way to fill muffin and cupcake pans, use it for batters, too. Choose a smaller scoop for making melon balls and meatballs.

Vegetable brush and peeler

Here's a handy two-in-one gadget. Use the brush to clean carrots, apples and potatoes, then just turn the utensil to quickly remove the peel from cucumbers, zucchini, apples and pears.

Shaker canister

Fill a super-convenient canister with your favorite seasoning mix and keep close to the grill to shake on meats, poultry and fish. Keep several filled with spice mixes, pepper blends and cinnamon-sugar.

Wire whisk

Reach for this kitchen essential to save time as you blend and whip egg mixtures, sauces and pancake, waffle and cake batters.

Delicious Do-Aheads

Taking just a little extra time to prepare a few items ahead really saves you time in the long run. And on one of those nights when you'd rather not cook and you're reaching into the freezer, you'll thank yourself for thinking ahead!

Make burgers or meatballs

Mix extra ground beef and seasonings; shape into patties or balls. Freeze individually in plastic wrap, so you can cook just what you need.

Cook ground beef

Cook and drain ground beef. Freeze in freezer bags or containers in 2-cup amounts (which equals about 1 pound cooked). Then just pop out and use for chili, meat sauce or tacos.

Cut-up uncooked meat

Cut chicken or turkey breasts, steaks or pork tenderloin into strips or cubes. Freeze in resealable freezer bags or containers with lids for up to 9 months. Thaw in refrigerator before cooking in stir-fries or skillet meals.

Cook extra chicken

Cook more than you need and cut up. Freeze in 1-cup amounts in small freezer bags up to 4 months. Use in casseroles and pot pies.

Cook extra pasta, couscous and rice

After draining hot pasta or rice, toss extras with oil to keep it from sticking together. Refrigerate in resealable plastic bags for up to 5 days or freeze in freezer containers up to 6 months. To reheat, microwave covered on High for 1 to 3 minutes or until heated through; or simply place in colander and pour boiling water over it until heated through. Drain and serve immediately.

Dice vegetables

Chop or slice more fresh vegetables, such as onions, bell peppers, celery and carrots, than you need for one meal. Freeze in resealable plastic freezer bags or containers with lids. No need to thaw them before using in stir-fries or skillet meals.

Shred cheese

Use for pizza, pasta and casseroles. When you're pressed for time, purchase already-shredded or grated cheese.

Cut up fruit

Freeze in resealable plastic freezer bags. Use directly from freezer for smoothies or fruit sauces.

Wash salad

Rinse sturdy lettuce leaves such as romaine and iceberg and blot dry with paper towels. Store in perforated vegetable bags or regular plastic bags until ready to use. When you're really pressed for time, purchase bagged salad.

Grate ginger and mince garlic

Use for seasoning stir-fries and other dishes. When you're really pressed for time, purchase bottled grated ginger and minced garlic.

1 Appetizers and Super-Easy Snacks

🕐 = *super express* ready in 20 minutes or less

1-Step Recipes

Super-Easy Snacks and Dips
Need some really easy snacks that quiet grumbling tummies but still leave room for dinner? Combine a few ingredients to make:

1 Stuffed Celery Sticks
Stir chili powder and Worcestershire sauce into cream cheese and fill celery sticks; sprinkle with crushed corn or oat cereal.

2 Savory Popcorn Mix
Drizzle popcorn, pretzels and fish-shaped crackers with melted butter; sprinkle with garlic and onion powders, and dried basil and oregano leaves.

3 Quick Fruit Dip
Stir brown sugar and ground cinnamon into plain yogurt. Use as dip for sliced apples, strawberry slices, grapes or other fresh fruit.

4 Zippy Vegetable Dip
Blend cottage cheese, plain yogurt or sour cream and an envelope of ranch dressing mix in blender. Use as dip for baby-cut carrots, celery sticks, pepper strips, broccoli or cauliflower pieces.

5 So-Simple Salsa Dip
Mix equal parts salsa and softened cream cheese; use as dip for tortilla chips.

6 Yogonanas
Poke end of wooden stick into banana half; roll banana in plain or flavored yogurt and sprinkle with crushed cereal. Eat right away, or freeze 1 hour.

7 Bell Pepper Nachos
Sprinkle shredded mozzarella or Monterey Jack cheese over slices of green, red and yellow peppers; melt cheese in microwave.

8 Cucumber Open-Face Sandwiches
Top cucumber slices with mayonnaise or salad dressing; top with imitation crabmeat or smoked turkey slices.

9 Filled Mini-Muffins
Slice mini-muffins; fill with cream cheese and smoked salmon, or turkey slices and cranberry-orange relish.

10 Applesauce Yogurt
Mix equal parts of vanilla yogurt and applesauce; stir in honey and pumpkin pie spice and sprinkle with chopped nuts.

Creamy Pesto Dip

1 cup sour cream or plain yogurt

1/4 cup pesto

Chopped tomato, if desired

Assorted fresh vegetables, if desired

1 Mix sour cream and pesto until well blended. Sprinkle with tomato. Serve with vegetables.

IT'S **a**
snap!

There's a great selection of already cut-up vegetables in the produce section of the grocery store. Try baby-cut carrots, celery sticks and broccoli and cauliflower flowerets for delicious dip dunkers.

1/4 CUP: Calories 150 (Calories from Fat 135); Fat 15g (Saturated 7g); Cholesterol 30mg; Sodium 125mg; Carbohydrate 2g (Dietary Fiber 0g); Protein 2g • **% DAILY VALUE:** Vitamin A 8%; Vitamin C 0%; Calcium 8%; Iron 2% • **DIET EXCHANGES:** 3 Fat

Pantry Recipes

If you have a well-stocked pantry (see pages 6–7), you'll
be able to make this recipe anytime, even when there's
no time to shop.

Salsa and Black Bean Dip

2/3 cup thick-and-chunky salsa

1/2 teaspoon chili powder

1 can (15 1/4 ounces) whole kernel corn, drained

1 can (15 ounces) black beans, rinsed and drained

Mix all ingredients. MAKE 3 CUPS DIP IN 5 MINUTES

serve it 3 ways!

1 Appetizer
Stir in 1/2 teaspoon ground cumin; use tortilla chips
for dipping.

2 Light Meal
Heat salsa and bean mixture in 2-quart saucepan. Spoon
about 3 tablespoons mixture into warmed soft tortillas
for a fast snack or dinner. Sprinkle with chopped fresh
cilantro, and serve with sour cream.

3 Main Course
Serve over baked chicken breasts, or any cooked meat as a
salsa for a quick and easy dinner.

10 SERVINGS (2 TABLESPOONS EACH)

Caesar Vegetable Dip

1/2 cup sour cream

1/4 cup mayonnaise or
salad dressing

1/4 cup creamy Caesar dressing

2 tablespoons shredded
Parmesan cheese

2 tablespoons chopped
red bell pepper

1 hard-cooked egg, chopped

Assorted raw vegetables,
if desired

1 Mix sour cream, mayonnaise and Caesar dressing until
smooth. Stir in cheese. Serve immediately, or cover and
refrigerate 30 minutes to blend flavors, if desired.

2 Spoon into serving bowl. Sprinkle with bell pepper and
egg. Serve with vegetables.

super
express

prep: 10 min

IT'S a
snap!
Want a quick dress-
up for this dip? Serve
it in a hollowed-out
red, yellow or green
bell pepper half.

1 TABLESPOON: Calories 50 (Calories from Fat 45); Fat 5g (Saturated 1g); Cholesterol 15mg;
Sodium 65mg; Carbohydrate 0 (Dietary Fiber 0g); Protein 1g • % DAILY VALUE:
Vitamin A 2%; Vitamin C 2%; Calcium 2%; Iron 0% • DIET EXCHANGES: 1 Fat

Chapter 1: Appetizers and Super-Easy Snacks

13

4 SERVINGS (1/4 CUP EACH)

Gingered Caramel and Yogurt Dip with Fruit

1/2 package (8-ounce size) cream cheese, softened

1/2 cup vanilla low-fat yogurt

1/4 cup caramel topping, plus 1 to 2 teaspoons more for drizzling

1 tablespoon finely chopped crystallized ginger, if desired

1 medium apple, sliced

1 medium pear, sliced

1 medium banana, sliced

1 Beat cream cheese in medium bowl with electric mixer on medium speed until creamy. Beat in yogurt and 1/4 cup caramel topping until smooth. Cover and refrigerate at least 20 minutes until chilled.

2 Spoon dip into small serving bowl. Drizzle with 1 to 2 teaspoons caramel topping; swirl into dip with tip of knife. Sprinkle with ginger. Serve with apple, pear and banana slices.

1 SERVING: Calories 270 (Calories from Fat 100); Fat 11g (Saturated 7g); Cholesterol 30mg; Sodium 190mg; Carbohydrate 42g (Dietary Fiber 3g); Protein 4g • **% DAILY VALUE:** Vitamin A 10%; Vitamin C 10%; Calcium 8%; Iron 4% • **DIET EXCHANGES:** 2 Fruit, 1 Skim Milk, 1 1/2 Fat

Gingered Caramel and Yogurt Dip with Fruit

Quick Guacamole

2 large avocados, pitted, peeled and mashed

1/3 cup thick-and-chunky salsa

1 tablespoon lime juice

Tortilla chips, if desired

1 Mix avocados, salsa and lime juice in glass or plastic bowl. Serve with tortilla chips.

IT'S **a**
snap!

To quickly and easily mash the avocados for this super-quick dip, make certain they are fully ripe and use a fork or pastry blender.

1 TABLESPOON: Calories 10 (Calories from Fat 10); Fat 1g (Saturated 0g); Cholesterol 0mg; Sodium 20mg; Carbohydrate 1g (Dietary Fiber 0g); Protein 0g • % **DAILY VALUE:** Vitamin A 0%; Vitamin C 2%; Calcium 0%; Iron 0% • **DIET EXCHANGES:** 1 Serving is Free

Five-Layer Mexican Dip

1 can (15 to 16 ounces) refried beans

2 tablespoons salsa

1 1/2 cups sour cream

1 cup guacamole

1 cup shredded Cheddar cheese (4 ounces)

2 medium green onions, chopped (2 tablespoons)

Tortilla chips, if desired

1 Mix refried beans and salsa. Spread in thin layer on 12- or 13-inch serving plate or pizza pan.

2 Spread sour cream over beans, leaving about 1-inch border of beans around edge. Spread guacamole over sour cream, leaving border of sour cream showing.

3 Sprinkle cheese over guacamole. Sprinkle onions over cheese. Serve immediately, or cover and refrigerate until serving. Serve with tortilla chips.

IT'S **a**

snap!

Save time and buy guacamole. You'll find it in the dairy or frozen section of the supermarket and may be labeled "avocado dip" instead of "guacamole."

1 SERVING: Calories 120 (Calories from Fat 80); Fat 9g (Saturated 5g); Cholesterol 25mg; Sodium 220mg; Carbohydrate 8g (Dietary Fiber 2g); Protein 4g • % **DAILY VALUE:** Vitamin A 6%; Vitamin C 14%; Calcium 6%; Iron 4% • **DIET EXCHANGES:** 1/2 Starch, 2 Fat

prep: **15 min**

COME
&eat!

This is an easy dip to
use for entertaining.
Purchase cubed
honeydew melon
from the salad bar
or produce area and
it's ready in no time!
Or use any com-
bination of fruits you
like. Strawberries,
kiwifruit, pears and
grapes are good
choices.

10 SERVINGS

Easy Sugar 'n Spice Dip

1 tablespoon packed brown sugar or honey	2 cups cubed honeydew melon or cantaloupe
1/4 teaspoon ground cinnamon	1 pint (2 cups) red raspberries
Dash of ground nutmeg	
1 1/3 cups vanilla thick-and-creamy low-fat yogurt	

1 Mix brown sugar, cinnamon and nutmeg in small bowl.
Stir in yogurt.

2 Spoon yogurt mixture into small serving bowl. Sprinkle
with additional ground cinnamon. Serve with melon and
raspberries.

1 SERVING: Calories 95 (Calories from Fat 10); Fat 1g (Saturated 0g); Cholesterol 0mg;
Sodium 20mg; Carbohydrate 13g (Dietary Fiber 2g); Protein 2g • **% DAILY VALUE:**
Vitamin A 18%; Vitamin C 32%; Calcium 2%; Iron 0% • **DIET EXCHANGES:** 1 Fruit;
1/2 Fat

Easy Sugar 'n Spice Dip

ABOUT 4 CUPS SPREAD

Corn and Olive Spread

IT'S **a**
snap!

You can easily cut
this recipe in half,
using about 2 table-
spoons of the ranch
dressing mix. It's
ready even faster!

2 packages (8 ounces each) cream cheese, softened

I envelope (I ounce) ranch dressing mix

I medium red bell pepper, chopped (I cup)

I can (4 1/4 ounces each) chopped ripe olives, drained

I can (II ounces) whole kernel corn, drained

I can (4 ounces) chopped green chilies, drained

Tortilla chips, if desired

1 Beat cream cheese and dressing mix (dry) in large bowl with spoon until smooth.

2 Stir in remaining ingredients except tortilla chips. Serve with tortilla chips. Refrigerate leftovers.

1 TABLESPOON: Calories 40 (Calories from Fat 25); Fat 3g (Saturated 2g); Cholesterol 5mg; Sodium 95mg; Carbohydrate 2g (Dietary Fiber 0g); Protein 1g • **% DAILY VALUE:** Vitamin A 4%; Vitamin C 8%; Calcium 0%; Iron 0% • **DIET EXCHANGES:** 1 Fat

Tropical Prosciutto Bites

1/4 pound thinly sliced prosciutto or fully cooked ham, cut into 1-inch strips

1 large mango or papaya, peeled and cut into 12 pieces

6 medium strawberries

1 Wrap some strips of prosciutto around mango pieces and some strips around strawberries. Secure with toothpicks.

IT'S **a**
snap!

To tote these bites, arrange them in a single layer in a shallow plastic storage container. Add a layer of waxed paper, and arrange remaining bites on top. Let the container double as a serving tray.

1 SERVING: Calories 65 (Calories from Fat 20); Fat 2g (Saturated 1g); Cholesterol 10mg; Sodium 280mg; Carbohydrate 8g (Dietary Fiber 1g); Protein 5g • **% DAILY VALUE:** Vitamin A 4%; Vitamin C 38%; Calcium 0%; Iron 2% • **DIET EXCHANGES:** 1 Very Lean Meat, 1/2 Fruit

13 SERVINGS (1/2 CUP EACH)

Sweet and Crunchy Snack

3 cups miniature pretzel twists

1 cup honey-roasted peanuts

1 cup Frosted Cheerios® cereal

1 cup dried banana chips

1 cup candy-coated chocolate candies

1 Mix all ingredients. Store in airtight container.

IT'S **a**
snap!

This snack mix freezes great! Make a double batch, and freeze half. Use for last-minute picnics, as a sports snack or on the way to soccer practice.

1/2 CUP: Calories 220 (Calories from Fat 100); Fat 11g (Saturated 5g); Cholesterol 0mg; Sodium 270mg; Carbohydrate 27g (Dietary Fiber 2g); Protein 5g • **% DAILY VALUE:** Vitamin A 2%; Vitamin C 2%; Calcium 2%; Iron 6% • **DIET EXCHANGES:** 1 Starch, 1 Fruit, 2 Fat

Sweet and Crunchy Snack

prep: **5 min**
bake: **10 min**

IT'S **a**
snap!

A little time-saver
when using nuts:
be sure to taste
them before you use
them. Because of
their high oil con-
tent, nuts tend to
go rancid rather
quickly. You can
prepare the pecans
up to 3 weeks
ahead; store in
a tightly covered
container at room
temperature.

8 SERVINGS (1/4 CUP EACH)

Savory Pecans

2 cups pecan halves

**2 tablespoons butter
or margarine, melted**

1 tablespoon soy sauce

**1/4 to 1/2 teaspoon ground
red pepper (cayenne)**

1 Heat oven to 300°. Mix all ingredients. Spread pecan mixture in ungreased jelly roll pan, 15 1/2 × 10 1/2 × 1 inch.

2 Bake about 10 minutes or until pecans are toasted. Serve
warm, or cool completely.

1/4 CUP: Calories 230 (Calories from Fat 190); Fat 21g (Saturated 3g); Cholesterol 10mg;
Sodium 135mg; Carbohydrate 5g (Dietary Fiber 2g); Protein 2g • % **DAILY VALUE:**
Vitamin A 2%; Vitamin C 0%; Calcium 0%; Iron 2% • **DIET EXCHANGES:** 5 Fat

super
express

prep: **5 min**
bake: **15 min**

Chili and Garlic Snack Mix

3 cups Cheerios® cereal

**3 cups corn chips
(broken in half, if desired)**

1 cup unsalted peanuts

1 cup thin pretzel sticks

1/3 cup butter or margarine, melted

1/2 teaspoon chili powder

1/2 teaspoon garlic powder

IT'S **a**
snap!
For an anytime snack, prepare this tasty mix up to 1 week before serving, and store in an airtight container.

1 Heat oven to 300°. Mix cereal, corn chips, peanuts and pretzels in large bowl. Mix remaining ingredients; pour over cereal mixture. Toss until evenly coated. Spread in ungreased jelly roll pan, 15 1/2 × 10 1/2 × 1 inch.

2 Bake uncovered 15 minutes, stirring once. Cool completely. Store in airtight container.

1/2 CUP: Calories 190 (Calories from Fat 110); Fat 12g (Saturated 4g); Cholesterol 10mg; Sodium 290mg; Carbohydrate 17g (Dietary Fiber 2g); Protein 5g • % DAILY VALUE: Vitamin A 6%; Vitamin C 0%; Calcium 2%; Iron 14% • DIET EXCHANGES: 1 Starch, 1 1/2 Fat

24 APPETIZERS

Beef and Provolone Pinwheels

1/4 cup mayonnaise or salad dressing

2 cloves garlic, finely chopped

2 flour tortillas (8 to 10 inches in diameter)

1 cup fresh spinach

1/4 pound thinly sliced cooked roast beef

6 slices (3/4 ounce each) provolone cheese

1 medium tomato, thinly sliced

1 Mix mayonnaise and garlic in small bowl. Spread mixture evenly over tortillas.

2 Top tortillas with layers of spinach, beef, cheese and tomato; roll up tightly. Cut each tortilla into 12 pieces; secure with toothpicks. Serve immediately or refrigerate until serving.

IT'S **a**

snap!

For a quick do-ahead, assemble and wrap the tortillas individually in plastic wrap and refrigerate for up to 24 hours.

1 APPETIZER: Calories 55 (Calories from Fat 35); Fat 4g (Saturated 2g); Cholesterol 10mg; Sodium 85mg; Carbohydrate 2g (Dietary Fiber 0g); Protein 3g • **% DAILY VALUE:** Vitamin A 4%; Vitamin C 2%; Calcium 4%; Iron 2% • **DIET EXCHANGES:** 1 Fat

Hot Reuben Dip

1 package (8 ounces) cream cheese, softened

1 1/2 cups shredded Swiss cheese (6 ounces)

1/2 cup Thousand Island dressing

4 ounces deli sliced corned beef, chopped

1/2 cup drained sauerkraut

Cocktail rye bread slices, vegetables or pretzels, if desired

prep: 10 min
bake: 15 min

1 Heat oven to 400°. Mix cream cheese, 1 cup of the Swiss cheese, the dressing and corned beef. Spread in ungreased pie plate, 9 × 1 1/4 inches, or quiche dish, 9 × 1 1/2 inches. Top with sauerkraut and remaining 1/2 cup Swiss cheese.

2 Bake about 15 minutes or until bubbly around edge. Serve hot with cocktail rye bread, vegetables or pretzels.

COME
&eat!

Make your own quick mini-version of the world-famous deli sandwich by spreading this dip on toasted slices of rye bread. Serve with spicy brown mustard and extra Thousand Island dressing on the side.

1/4 CUP: Calories 200 (Calories from Fat 150); Fat 17g (Saturated 9g); Cholesterol 50mg; Sodium 470mg; Carbohydrate 3g (Dietary Fiber 0g); Protein 9g • % DAILY VALUE: Vitamin A 10%; Vitamin C 0%; Calcium 18%; Iron 4% • DIET EXCHANGES: 1 1/2 High-Fat Meat, 1 Fat

24 SERVINGS (2 TABLESPOONS EACH)

Baked Spinach–Artichoke Dip

IT'S **a**
snap!
**For a quick
do-ahead, make
and refrigerate
this sensational,
simple-to-prepare
dip up to 24 hours
ahead; bake as
directed.**

1 cup mayonnaise or salad dressing

1 cup grated Parmesan cheese

1 can (14 ounces) artichoke hearts, drained and coarsely chopped

1 package (10 ounces) frozen chopped spinach, thawed and squeezed to drain

1/2 cup chopped red bell pepper

1/4 cup shredded Monterey Jack or mozzarella cheese (1 ounce)

Toasted baguette slices or assorted crackers, if desired

1 Heat oven to 350°. Mix mayonnaise and Parmesan cheese. Stir in artichokes, spinach and bell pepper.

2 Spoon mixture into 1-quart casserole. Sprinkle with Monterey Jack cheese.

3 Cover and bake about 20 minutes or until cheese is melted. Serve warm with baguette slices.

2 TABLESPOONS: Calories 100 (Calories from Fat 80); Fat 9g (Saturated 2g); Cholesterol 10mg; Sodium 190mg; Carbohydrate 3g (Dietary Fiber 1g); Protein 3g • **% DAILY VALUE:** Vitamin A 8%; Vitamin C 2%; Calcium 8%; Iron 2% • **DIET EXCHANGES:** 1 Vegetable, 1 1/2 Fat

Crunchy Chicken Chunks

prep: **10 min**
microwave: **8 min**

1 1/2 cups **Country® Corn Flakes cereal, crushed (1/2 cup)**

1/2 cup **Original Bisquick®**

3/4 teaspoon **paprika**

1/4 teaspoon **salt**

1/4 teaspoon **pepper**

1 pound **boneless, skinless chicken breasts, cut into 1-inch pieces**

1 tablespoon **vegetable oil**

1 Mix all ingredients except chicken and oil in 2-quart resealable plastic food-storage bag. Mix chicken and oil.

2 Shake about 6 chicken pieces at a time in bag until coated. Shake off any extra crumbs. Place chicken pieces in single layer on microwavable rack in microwavable dish.

3 Cover with waxed paper. Microwave on High 3 minutes. Turn dish 1/2 turn. Microwave 4 to 5 minutes longer or until chicken is no longer pink in center.

COME
& eat!

Enjoy these tender chicken chunks with barbecue sauce or honey-mustard sauce. For a super-quick honey-mustard sauce, mix equal amounts of honey and your favorite prepared mustard.

1 SERVING: Calories 180 (Calories from Fat 55); Fat 6g (Saturated 1g); Cholesterol 45mg; Sodium 390mg; Carbohydrate 13g (Dietary Fiber 0g); Protein 18g • % DAILY VALUE: Vitamin A 4%; Vitamin C 2%; Calcium 4%; Iron 16% • DIET EXCHANGES: 1 Starch, 2 Lean Meat

16 APPETIZERS

Ham and Gouda Quesadillas

COME
&eat!

For an easy special touch, cut 2 or 3 oil-packed sun-dried tomatoes into small wedges. Spread about 1/4 teaspoon cream cheese onto each quesadilla wedge, and top with tomato piece and parsley sprig. Secure each wedge with a toothpick if desired.

2 tablespoons soft cream cheese with roasted garlic or garlic-and-herb spreadable cheese

4 flour tortillas (8 inches in diameter)

6 ounces thinly sliced cooked ham

2 tablespoons chopped drained oil-packed sun-dried tomatoes

1/2 cup shredded Gouda cheese (2 ounces)

2 tablespoons chopped fresh parsley

2 tablespoons olive or vegetable oil

1 Spread cream cheese over 2 of the tortillas. Layer tortillas with ham, tomatoes, cheese and parsley. Top with remaining 2 tortillas.

2 Heat 1 tablespoon of the oil in 10-inch nonstick skillet over medium heat. Add one quesadilla; brush top with more oil. Cook 2 to 3 minutes on each side or until golden brown and cheese is melted. Remove from skillet; keep warm. Repeat with remaining 1 tablespoon oil and second quesadilla.

3 Cut each quesadilla into 8 wedges. Serve immediately.

1 APPETIZER: Calories 75 (Calories from Fat 35); Fat 4g (Saturated 1g); Cholesterol 10mg; Sodium 220mg; Carbohydrate 6g (Dietary Fiber 0g); Protein 4g • **% DAILY VALUE:** Vitamin A 2%; Vitamin C 0%; Calcium 4%; Iron 2% • **DIET EXCHANGES:** 1/2 Starch, 1 Fat

Ham and Gouda Quesadillas

prep: **10 min**
broil: **5 min**

IT'S **a**
snap!
To save even more
time, make a plate
of nachos instead.
Just spread the chips
on the cookie sheet
and randomly top
with remaining
ingredients. Broil
as directed.

24 APPETIZERS

Shrimp Nacho Bites

24 large corn tortilla chips

**1/2 cup black bean dip
(from 9-ounce can)**

1/4 cup thick-and-chunky salsa

**24 cooked peeled deveined
medium shrimp (about
1/2 pound)**

**1 avocado, pitted, peeled
and cut into 24 slices**

**1/2 cup shredded
Colby-Monterey Jack
cheese (2 ounces)**

**24 fresh cilantro leaves,
if desired**

1 Top each tortilla chip with about 1 teaspoon bean dip,
1/2 teaspoon salsa, 1 shrimp, 1 avocado slice and about
1 teaspoon cheese. Place on cookie sheet.

2 Set oven control to broil. Broil with tops about 5 inches
from heat 2 to 3 minutes or just until cheese is melted.
Garnish with cilantro leaves. Serve immediately.

1 APPETIZER: Calories 40 (Calories from Fat 25); Fat 3g (Saturated 1g); Cholesterol 15mg;
Sodium 85mg; Carbohydrate 2g (Dietary Fiber 1g); Protein 2g • **% DAILY VALUE:**
Vitamin A 2%; Vitamin C 2%; Calcium 2%; Iron 2% • **DIET EXCHANGES:** 1 Fat

Shrimp Nacho Bites

prep: **8 min**
cook: **16 min**

Shrimp Quesadillas

8 flour tortillas (8 to 10 inches in diameter)

2 cups shredded Monterey Jack cheese with jalapeño peppers (8 ounces)

1 large tomato, chopped (1 cup)

1/2 cup real bacon pieces (from 2-ounce jar)

1 package (4 ounces) frozen cooked salad shrimp, rinsed and thawed

1 Heat 10-inch nonstick skillet over medium-high heat. Place 1 tortilla in skillet. Sprinkle with 1/4 cup of the cheese, 1/4 cup of the tomato, 2 tablespoons of the bacon and 1/4 of the shrimp. Sprinkle with additional 1/4 cup of the cheese. Top with another tortilla.

2 Cook 1 to 2 minutes or until bottom is golden brown; turn. Cook 1 to 2 minutes longer or until bottom is golden brown.

3 Repeat 3 more times with remaining ingredients. Cut each quesadilla into wedges.

COME

&eat!

Want to serve something more than chips and dip before dinner? Here's a quick and easy recipe for just that occasion! Change the flavors by making a few quesadillas with Monterey Jack cheese, several with Cheddar and some with mozzarella.

1 SERVING: Calories 240 (Calories from Fat 115); Fat 13g (Saturated 7g); Cholesterol 60mg; Sodium 640mg; Carbohydrate 25g (Dietary Fiber 2g); Protein 17g • **% DAILY VALUE:** Vitamin A 10%; Vitamin C 4%; Calcium 26%; Iron 12% • **DIET EXCHANGES:** 1 Starch, 1 1/2 Medium-Fat Meat, 2 Vegetables

Avocado-Seafood Appetizer Bites

super express

prep: 20 min

1 avocado, pitted, peeled and cut into chunks

3 tablespoons mayonnaise or salad dressing

2 teaspoons lime juice

Dash of ground red pepper (cayenne)

Dash of salt

2 large cucumbers, cut into 3/8-inch slices (24 slices)

1 package (8 ounces) refrigerated flake-style imitation crabmeat

Fresh cilantro leaves, if desired

1 Place avocado, mayonnaise, lime juice, red pepper and salt in food processor or blender. Cover and process until smooth. Or, if you prefer, blend by hand.

2 Spread avocado mixture on each cucumber slice. Top with crabmeat. Sprinkle with cilantro. Serve immediately.

IT'S a snap!

For an easy way to pit an avocado, cut the avocado lengthwise in half around the pit and pull apart the halves. The pit will stay in one of the halves. Firmly and carefully strike the pit with the sharp edge of a knife. While holding the avocado, twist the knife to loosen and remove the pit.

1 APPETIZER: Calories 40 (Calories from Fat 25); Fat 3g (Saturated 0g); Cholesterol 5mg; Sodium 90mg; Carbohydrate 2g (Dietary Fiber 1g); Protein 2g • % DAILY VALUE: Vitamin A 0%; Vitamin C 2%; Calcium 0%; Iron 0% • DIET EXCHANGES: 1 Fat

24 APPETIZERS

Blue Cheese and Pear Triangles

C O M E
& eat!

For a terrific quick
hot appetizer, omit
step 1; assemble the
triangles and bake
on an ungreased
cookie sheet at 425°
for 3 to 5 minutes
or until hot and
cheese is melted.

**12 slices pumpernickel cocktail
bread, cut diagonally in half**

**3 tablespoons mayonnaise or
salad dressing**

**1 medium unpeeled red or
green pear, thinly sliced and
slices cut in half**

**2 tablespoons chopped drained
roasted red bell peppers
(from 7-ounce jar)**

1/3 cup crumbled blue cheese

1/3 cup chopped walnuts

**Fresh marjoram leaves or
chopped fresh chives, if desired**

1 Heat oven to 400°. Place bread on ungreased cookie sheet. Bake 4 to 5 minutes or until lightly toasted.

2 Spread mayonnaise over bread. Top with pear slices, bell pepper pieces, cheese, walnuts and marjoram. Serve immediately.

1 APPETIZER: Calories 45 (Calories from Fat 25); Fat 3g (Saturated 1g); Cholesterol 5mg; Sodium 60mg; Carbohydrate 3g (Dietary Fiber 0g); Protein 1g • **% DAILY VALUE:** Vitamin A 0%; Vitamin C 2%; Calcium 2%; Iron 0% • **DIET EXCHANGES:** 1 Fat

Blue Cheese and Pear Triangles

Roasted Pepper–Tomato Crostini

IT'S **a**
snap!
You can prepare the tomato topping and bake the bread several hours ahead. Just before serving, spread the topping on the bread and bake as directed.

18 slices Italian bread, 1/2 inch thick

2 large tomatoes, diced (2 cups)

1 jar (7 ounces) roasted red bell peppers, drained and chopped

1/4 cup chopped fresh basil leaves

1 tablespoon balsamic vinegar

1/4 teaspoon salt

1/3 cup shredded mozzarella cheese

1 Heat oven to 375°. Place bread on cookie sheet. Bake about 5 minutes or until toasted.

2 Mix tomatoes, bell peppers, basil, vinegar and salt. Spread tomato mixture on bread. Top each slice with about 1 teaspoon cheese.

3 Bake about 5 minutes or until cheese is melted. Serve hot.

1 APPETIZER: Calories 65 (Calories from Fat 10); Fat 1g (Saturated 0g); Cholesterol 0mg; Sodium 160mg; Carbohydrate 12g (Dietary Fiber 1g); Protein 3g • **% DAILY VALUE:** Vitamin A 4%; Vitamin C 14%; Calcium 2%; Iron 4% • **DIET EXCHANGES:** 1/2 Starch, 1 Vegetable

Roasted Pepper–Tomato Crostini

prep: **10 min**
broil: **6 min**

COME
&eat!

For a change of
pace, top these
taters with black
beans and salsa and
Monterey Jack
cheese instead
of chicken, cheese
and bacon.

4 SERVINGS (2 POTATO SKINS EACH)

Cheesy Ranch Potato Skins

2 medium unpeeled baking potatoes

Butter-flavored cooking spray

1/2 teaspoon garlic powder

1/4 cup finely chopped cooked chicken or turkey

1/4 cup shredded reduced-fat Cheddar cheese (1 ounce)

2 tablespoons bacon-flavor bits

Reduced-calorie ranch dressing, if desired

1 Pierce potatoes with fork. Arrange potatoes about 1 inch apart in circle on microwavable paper towel. Microwave uncovered on High 8 to 10 minutes or until tender. Cut potatoes lengthwise into fourths. Carefully scoop out pulp, leaving 1/4-inch shells. Cover and refrigerate potato pulp for another use.

2 Set oven control to broil. Place potato shells, skin sides down, on rack in broiler pan. Spray with cooking spray. Sprinkle with garlic powder. Broil with tops 4 to 5 inches from heat about 5 minutes or until crisp and brown.

3 Sprinkle chicken and cheese over potato shells. Broil about 30 seconds or until cheese is melted. Sprinkle with bacon bits. Serve hot with ranch dressing.

1 SERVING: Calories 105 (Calories from Fat 10); Fat 1g (Saturated 1g); Cholesterol 10mg; Sodium 120mg; Carbohydrate 14g (Dietary Fiber 2g); Protein 7g • **% DAILY VALUE:** Vitamin A 0%; Vitamin C 4%; Calcium 4%; Iron 6% • **DIET EXCHANGES:** 1 Starch, 1/2 Lean Meat

Onion and Rosemary Focaccia Squares

prep: **15 min**
bake: **12 min**

Olive oil-flavored cooking spray

1 can (10 ounces) refrigerated pizza crust dough

3 cloves garlic, finely chopped

1/2 teaspoon dried rosemary leaves, crumbled

1 large sweet onion (Bermuda, Maui, Spanish or Vidalia), thinly sliced and separated into rings

3/4 cup grated Parmesan cheese

1/4 teaspoon salt, if desired

IT'S **a**
snap!

Fresh or dried basil in place of the rosemary makes a nice substitution in these flavorful wedges.

1 Heat oven to 400°. Spray cookie sheet with cooking spray. Roll or pat pizza dough into 13 × 9-inch rectangle on cookie sheet. Sprinkle with garlic and rosemary. Arrange onion rings evenly over dough. Sprinkle with cheese.

2 Bake about 12 minutes or until cheese just begins to brown. Lightly spray focaccia with cooking spray and sprinkle with salt if desired. Cut into 6 squares. Serve immediately.

1 SQUARE: Calories 190 (Calories from Fat 55); Fat 6g (Saturated 3g); Cholesterol 10mg; Sodium 460mg; Carbohydrate 26g (Dietary Fiber 1g); Protein 9g • % DAILY VALUE: Vitamin A 2%; Vitamin C 0%; Calcium 18%; Iron 8% • DIET EXCHANGE: 2 Starch, 1/2 High-Fat Meat

prep: **10 min**
bake: **10 min**

4 SERVINGS (2 CHEESE STICKS EACH)

String Cheese Sticks with Dipping Sauce

IT'S **a**

snap!

If you don't have
pizza sauce on
hand, you can warm
spaghetti sauce or
salsa for dipping.

2 1/4 cups Original Bisquick

2/3 cup milk

1 package (8 ounces) plain or smoked string cheese

1 tablespoon butter or margarine, melted

1/4 teaspoon garlic powder

1 can (8 ounces) pizza sauce, heated

1 Heat oven to 450°. Stir Bisquick and milk until soft dough forms; beat 30 seconds with spoon. Place dough on surface sprinkled with Bisquick; gently roll in Bisquick to coat. Shape into a ball; knead 10 times.

2 Roll dough 1/4 inch thick. Cut into eight 6 × 2-inch rectangles. Roll each rectangle around 1 piece of cheese. Pinch edge into roll to seal; seal ends. Roll on surface to completely enclose cheese sticks. Place seam sides down on ungreased cookie sheet.

3 Bake 8 to 10 minutes or until golden brown. Mix butter and garlic powder; brush over warm cheese sticks before removing from cookie sheet. Serve warm with pizza sauce for dipping.

1 STICK: Calories 250 (Calories from Fat 115); Fat 13g (Saturated 6g); Cholesterol 20mg; Sodium 730mg; Carbohydrate 24g (Dietary Fiber 1g); Protein 11g • **% DAILY VALUE:** Vitamin A 8%; Vitamin C 4%; Calcium 30%; Iron 6% • **DIET EXCHANGES:** 1 1/2 Starch, 1 Med-Fat Meat, 1 Fat

String Cheese Sticks with Dipping Sauce

prep: **5** min
bake: **10** min

COME
&eat!

Rather than serving
a traditional dinner,
try serving several
appetizers together
and let the family
"graze" on them.

10 SERVINGS

Mozzarella and Basil with Marinara Sauce

8 ounces fresh mozzarella cheese, cubed

2 tablespoons chopped fresh basil leaves

2 cups chunky marinara sauce

Baguette slices, if desired

1 Heat oven to 350°. Place cheese in shallow 2-quart casserole. Sprinkle with basil. Spoon marinara sauce around cheese.

2 Bake 8 to 10 minutes or until cheese is hot and bubbly. Serve with baguette slices.

1 SERVING: Calories 120 (Calories from Fat 55); Fat 6g (Saturated 3g); Cholesterol 10mg; Sodium 370mg; Carbohydrate 10g (Dietary Fiber 1g); Protein 7g • **% DAILY VALUE:** Vitamin A 10%; Vitamin C 6%; Calcium 18%; Iron 2% • **DIET EXCHANGES:** 1 Vegetable, 1 Fat, 1/2 Skim Milk

Mozzarella and Basil with Marinara Sauce

prep: **10 min**
bake: **10 min**

IT'S **a**
snap!

Want an easy way to add extra flavor to foods? Just add the grated peel, or zest, of citrus fruits to spreads, marinades, dips, dressings, sauces and baked goods. For an additional flavor boost, combine grated peel with the juice of the same fruit.

6 SERVINGS (8 CHIPS EACH)

Lime Tortilla Chips

1/2 teaspoon grated lime peel

2 tablespoons lime juice

2 teaspoons olive or vegetable oil

2 teaspoons honey

Dash of salt

4 flour tortillas (8 inches in diameter)

Salsa, if desired

1 Heat oven to 350°. Spray large cookie sheet with cooking spray. Mix all ingredients except tortillas. Brush lime mixture on both sides of each tortilla. Cut each tortilla into 12 wedges. Place in single layer on cookie sheet.

2 Bake 8 to 10 minutes or until crisp and light golden brown; cool. Serve with salsa. Store remaining chips in airtight container at room temperature.

1 SERVING: Calories 115 (Calories from Fat 35); Fat 4g (Saturated 1g); Cholesterol 0mg; Sodium 140mg; Carbohydrate 18g (Dietary Fiber 1g); Protein 3g • **% DAILY VALUE:** Vitamin A 0%; Vitamin C 2%; Calcium 4%; Iron 4% • **DIET EXCHANGES:** 1 Starch, 1 Fat

2 Speedy Soups, Salads and Sandwiches

🌙 = *super express* ready in 20 minutes or less

1-Step Recipes

Quick Sandwiches and Spreads For the quickest of all dinners, the sandwich, try these "familiar-with-a-twist" sandwiches and sandwich spreads. They're all good to go!

1 Italian Turkey Burgers

Spread pasta sauce and chopped onion over cooked turkey burgers on an Italian roll; top with provolone cheese and lettuce.

2 French Vegetable Sandwiches

Fill focaccia bread, French or Italian rolls with deli-marinated vegetables and shredded mozzarella cheese.

3 Barbecued Beef Sandwiches

Top English muffin or buns with warmed barbecued beef; sprinkle with shredded Cheddar cheese.

4 Nachoburgers

Top cooked burgers in buns with nacho cheese sauce; sprinkle with chopped green onions and garlic pepper seasoning.

5 Honey-Mustard Chicken Sandwiches

Mix honey and Dijon or regular yellow mustard; spread over cooked chicken breast halves and place in toasted English muffin; top with romaine and roasted red peppers.

6 Cheesy Beef Pockets

Wrap sliced roast beef, spinach leaves and bell pepper in pocket or pita bread; dip into warm sauce made of melted process cheese, milk and green onions.

7 Mexican Layered Sandwich

Layer cooked turkey, guacamole, shredded cheese, sliced olives, bell pepper strips, chopped green onions and sour cream on tortillas.

8 Creamy Maple-Nut Spread

Mix vanilla custard yogurt and maple syrup; stir in chopped nuts and spread over bread, pancakes or waffles, bagels, crackers, apples or pears.

9 Creamy Tuna Spread

Blend ricotta cheese, lemon juice, sour cream and drained canned tuna in blender; stuff into pita halves with shredded lettuce.

10 Easy Cheese Spread

Mix whipped cream cheese, shredded Cheddar cheese, yellow mustard and Worcestershire sauce. Spread on rye or wheat bread.

Oriental Chicken Noodle Soup

super
express

prep: **10 min**
cook: **8 min**

3 cups water

1 package (3 ounces) chicken-flavor ramen noodle soup mix

2 cups cut-up cooked chicken

2 medium stalks bok choy (with leaves), cut into 1/4-inch slices

1 medium carrot, sliced (1/2 cup)

1 teaspoon sesame oil, if desired

IT'S a
snap!

To make this quick soup easier to eat, break the block of dry noodles into pieces. That way, the noodles won't be as long and unwieldy.

1 Heat water to boiling in 3-quart saucepan. Break block of noodles (reserve seasoning packet). Stir noodles, chicken, bok choy and carrot into water. Heat to boiling; reduce heat. Simmer uncovered 3 minutes, stirring occasionally.

2 Stir in contents of seasoning packet and sesame oil.

1 SERVING: Calories 205 (Calories from Fat 70); Fat 8g (Saturated 2g); Cholesterol 60mg; Sodium 340mg; Carbohydrate 12g (Dietary Fiber 1g); Protein 22g • **% DAILY VALUE:** Vitamin A 68%; Vitamin C 6%; Calcium 2%; Iron 8% • **DIET EXCHANGES:** 1/2 Starch, 2 1/2 Lean Meat, 1 Vegetable

6 SERVINGS

Italian Sausage and Mostaccioli Soup

IT'S **a**

snap!

For a hint of
licorice flavor, use
dried tarragon
in this soup if you
don't have fennel.

**1 pound turkey Italian sausage
links, cut into 1-inch pieces**

2 cups broccoli flowerets

**1 cup uncooked mostaccioli or
penne pasta (3 ounces)**

2 1/2 cups water

1/2 teaspoon dried basil leaves

**1/4 teaspoon fennel seed,
crushed**

1/4 teaspoon pepper

**1 medium onion, chopped
(1/2 cup)**

1 clove garlic, finely chopped

**1 can (28 ounces) roma (plum)
tomatoes, undrained**

**1 can (10 1/2 ounces)
condensed beef broth**

1 Cook sausage in 4-quart Dutch oven over medium-high
heat, stirring occasionally, until brown; drain.

2 Stir in remaining ingredients, breaking up tomatoes. Heat
to boiling; reduce heat to medium-low. Cover and cook
about 15 minutes, stirring occasionally, until pasta is tender.

1 SERVING: Calories 265 (Calories from Fat 90); Fat 10g (Saturated 3g); Cholesterol 45mg;
Sodium 910mg; Carbohydrate 22g (Dietary Fiber 3g); Protein 17g • **% DAILY VALUE:**
Vitamin A 16%; Vitamin C 34%; Calcium 6%; Iron 12% • **DIET EXCHANGES:** 1 Starch,
1 1/2 High-Fat Meat, 2 Vegetable

Italian Sausage and Mostaccioli Soup

prep: **10 min**
cook: **10 min**

6 SERVINGS

Black Beans and Salsa Noodle Soup

3 cans (14 1/2 ounces each) vegetable broth

1 jar (16 ounces) salsa

1 can (15 ounces) black beans, rinsed and drained

1 can (11 ounces) whole kernel corn, drained

1 package (5 ounces) Japanese curly noodles or 5 ounces uncooked spaghetti

1/3 cup chopped fresh cilantro

1 tablespoon lime juice

1 teaspoon chili powder

1/4 teaspoon ground cumin

1/4 teaspoon pepper

2 tablespoons shredded Parmesan cheese

1 Heat broth to boiling in 4-quart Dutch oven. Stir in remaining ingredients except cheese; reduce heat to medium.

2 Cook 5 to 6 minutes, stirring occasionally, until noodles are tender. Sprinkle with cheese.

1 SERVING: Calories 220 (Calories from Fat 20); Fat 2g (Saturated 1g); Cholesterol 0mg; Sodium 1660mg; Carbohydrate 48g (Dietary Fiber 8g); Protein 10g • **% DAILY VALUE:** Vitamin A 30%; Vitamin C 14%; Calcium 12%; Iron 22% • **DIET EXCHANGES:** 2 Starch, 2 Vegetable

Black Beans and Salsa Noodle Soup

prep: **5 min**
cook: **15 min**

6 SERVINGS

Rio Grande Turkey Soup

1 can (14 1/2 ounces) chicken broth

1 can (28 ounces) whole tomatoes, undrained

1 jar (16 ounces) thick-and-chunky salsa

2 to 3 teaspoons chili powder

1/2 bag (1-pound size) frozen corn, broccoli and red peppers (or other combination)

1 cup uncooked cavatappi or shell pasta (3 ounces)

2 cups cut-up cooked turkey or chicken

1/4 cup chopped fresh parsley

1 Heat broth, tomatoes, salsa and chili powder to boiling in 4-quart Dutch oven, breaking up tomatoes. Stir in frozen vegetables and pasta. Heat to boiling; reduce heat.

2 Simmer uncovered about 12 minutes, stirring occasionally, until pasta and vegetables are tender. Stir in turkey and parsley; cook until hot.

1 SERVING: Calories 215 (Calories from Fat 45); Fat 5g (Saturated 1g); Cholesterol 40mg; Sodium 940mg; Carbohydrate 27g (Dietary Fiber 4g); Protein 20g • **% DAILY VALUE:** Vitamin A 34%; Vitamin C 34%; Calcium 8%; Iron 16% • **DIET EXCHANGES:** 1 Starch, 1 1/2 Lean Meat, 3 Vegetable

Ham 'n Corn Chowder

prep: **10 min**
cook: **10 min**

1/2 cup chopped thinly sliced
fully cooked ham

1 1/2 cups milk

1 bag (1 pound) frozen
whole kernel corn

1 can (10 3/4 ounces)
condensed cream of celery
soup

2 medium green onions, sliced
(2 tablespoons)

1 Mix ham, milk, frozen corn and soup in 3-quart saucepan.
Heat to boiling, stirring occasionally; reduce heat.

2 Simmer uncovered 10 minutes, stirring occasionally.
Sprinkle with onions.

IT'S **a**
snap!
Want a tasty warm
bread to serve with
this creamy soup?
Sprinkle a 1-pound
round focaccia bread
with 1/3 cup shredded
cheese, and heat in
the microwave on
High 1 to 2 minutes
until the cheese is
melted. Cut into
wedges, and serve
immediately.

1 SERVING: Calories 230 (Calories from Fat 75); Fat 8g (Saturated 3g); Cholesterol 20mg;
Sodium 860mg; Carbohydrate 32g (Dietary Fiber 3g); Protein 11g • **% DAILY VALUE:**
Vitamin A 12%; Vitamin C 4%; Calcium 16%; Iron 6% • **DIET EXCHANGES:** 1 Starch,
1 Vegetable, 1 Skim Milk, 1 Fat

prep: **5 min**
cook: **10 min**

4 SERVINGS

Easy Cheesy Vegetable Soup

4 ounces reduced-fat process cheese spread loaf, cubed

3 1/2 cups fat-free (skim) milk

1/2 teaspoon chili powder

2 cups cooked brown or white rice

1 bag (1 pound) frozen cauliflower, carrots and asparagus (or other combination), thawed and drained

1 Heat cheese and milk in 3-quart saucepan over low heat, stirring occasionally, until cheese is melted.

2 Stir in chili powder. Stir in rice and vegetables; cook until hot.

IT'S **a**
snap!

Be ready to make this soup anytime by cooking your favorite rice ahead of time. Store cooked rice in an airtight container or resealable plastic food-storage bag and refrigerate up to 5 days or freeze up to 6 months.

1 SERVING: Calories 210 (Calories from Fat 35); Fat 2g (Saturated 4g); Cholesterol 15mg; Sodium 580mg; Carbohydrate 33g (Dietary Fiber 4g); Protein 15g • **% DAILY VALUE:** Vitamin A 100%; Vitamin C 18%; Calcium 42%; Iron 4% • **DIET EXCHANGES:** 1 Starch, 2 Vegetable

Easy Cheesy Vegetable Soup

4 SERVINGS

Cream of Broccoli Soup

2 tablespoons butter or margarine

1 medium onion, chopped (1/2 cup)

2 medium carrots, thinly sliced (1 cup)

2 teaspoons mustard seed

1/2 teaspoon salt

1/4 teaspoon pepper

3/4 pound broccoli, coarsely chopped (3 1/2 cups)

1 can (14 1/2 ounces) chicken broth

1 cup water

2 teaspoons lemon juice

1/4 cup sour cream

1 Melt butter in 3-quart saucepan over medium heat. Cook onion and carrots in butter about 5 minutes, stirring occasionally, until onion is tender. Stir in mustard seed, salt and pepper. Stir in broccoli, broth and water. Heat to boiling; reduce heat. Cover and simmer about 10 minutes or until broccoli is tender.

2 Place one-third of the broccoli mixture in blender. Cover and blend on high speed until smooth; pour into bowl. Continue to blend in small batches until all soup is pureed.

3 Return soup to saucepan. Stir in lemon juice. Heat over low heat just until hot. Stir in sour cream.

1 SERVING: Calories 140 (Calories from Fat 90); Fat 10g (Saturated 6g); Cholesterol 25mg; Sodium 840mg; Carbohydrate 11g (Dietary Fiber 4g); Protein 6g • **% DAILY VALUE:** Vitamin A 100%; Vitamin C 70%; Calcium 8%; Iron 6% • **DIET EXCHANGES:** 2 Vegetable, 2 Fat

prep: **5 min**
cook: **20 min**

Cincinnati-Style Chili

1 pound ground beef

2 large onions, chopped (2 cups)

2 cans (14 1/2 ounces each) whole tomatoes, undrained

2 cans (15 to 16 ounces each) kidney beans, undrained

2 cans (8 ounces each) tomato sauce

2 tablespoons chili powder

1 package (7 ounces) spaghetti

1 1/4 cups shredded Cheddar cheese (5 ounces)

1 Cook beef and about 1 1/2 cups of the onion in 4-quart Dutch oven over medium heat 8 to 10 minutes, stirring occasionally, until beef is brown and onion is tender; drain.

2 Stir in tomatoes, beans, tomato sauce and chili powder, breaking up tomatoes. Cook uncovered over medium heat about 10 minutes, stirring occasionally, until desired consistency. Meanwhile, cook and drain spaghetti as directed on package.

3 Cover and refrigerate half of chili for another meal. Spoon remaining chili over hot spaghetti; sprinkle with cheese and remaining onion.

COME
&eat!

Want a great way to make two meals out of one cook time? Serve one meal as suggested above. Later on in the week, heat leftover chili and serve with corn bread or tortilla chips.

1 SERVING: Calories 495 (Calories from Fat 160); Fat 18g (Saturated 9g); Cholesterol 55mg; Sodium 830mg; Carbohydrate 62g (Dietary Fiber 9g); Protein 30g • **% DAILY VALUE:** Vitamin A 30%; Vitamin C 18%; Calcium 22%; Iron 34% • **DIET EXCHANGES:** 3 Starch, 2 High-Fat Meat, 3 Vegetable

COME
&eat!

New England baked
beans traditionally
simmer in the oven
for many hours.
But this range-top
version can be on
your table in 30 min-
utes! Serve with a
crusty Italian bread
and Raspberry Stirred
Custard (page 402)
for dessert.

4 SERVINGS

New England Baked Bean Stew

1/2 pound boneless, skinless chicken breasts, cut into 1/2-inch pieces

1/2 pound fully cooked Polish sausage, cut into 1/2-inch slices

1 can (15 to 16 ounces) great northern beans, rinsed and drained

1 can (15 to 16 ounces) dark red kidney beans, rinsed and drained

1 can (14 1/2 ounces) diced tomatoes with olive oil, garlic and spices, undrained

1 tablespoon packed brown sugar

4 medium green onions, sliced (1/4 cup)

1 Spray 12-inch nonstick skillet with cooking spray; heat over medium-high heat. Cook chicken in skillet 3 to 5 minutes, stirring occasionally, until brown.

2 Stir in remaining ingredients except onions. Cook uncovered over medium-low heat 8 to 10 minutes, stirring occasionally, until chicken is no longer pink in center.

3 Stir in onions. Cook 3 to 5 minutes, stirring occasionally, until onions are crisp-tender.

1 SERVING: Calories 525 (Calories from Fat 170); Fat 19g (Saturated 6g); Cholesterol 65mg; Sodium 1150mg; Carbohydrate 64g (Dietary Fiber 15g); Protein 40g • **% DAILY VALUE:** Vitamin A 6%; Vitamin C 12%; Calcium 18%; Iron 48% • **DIET EXCHANGES:** 4 Starch, 3 1/2 Lean Meat, 1 Vegetable

New England Baked Bean Stew

6 SERVINGS

Cantaloupe and Chicken Salad

1/4 cup plain yogurt

1/4 cup mayonnaise or
salad dressing

1 tablespoon lemon juice

1 tablespoon chopped
fresh chives

1/4 teaspoon salt

5 cups cantaloupe,
cut into 1 1/2-inch pieces

2 1/2 cups cut-up cooked
chicken

1 cup red or green grapes,
cut in half

1 medium cucumber,
cut into 1 × 1/4-inch strips

1 Mix yogurt and mayonnaise in large bowl. Stir in lemon juice, chives and salt.

2 Stir in remaining ingredients. Serve immediately, or refrigerate at least 2 hours until chilled but no longer than 24 hours.

1 SERVING: Calories 250 (Calories from Fat 110); Fat 12g (Saturated 2g); Cholesterol 5mg; Sodium 220mg; Carbohydrate 18g (Dietary Fiber 2g); Protein 19g • **% DAILY VALUE:** Vitamin A 74%; Vitamin C 100%; Calcium 4%; Iron 6% • **DIET EXCHANGES:** 2 1/2 Lean Meat, 1 Vegetable, 1 Fruit, 1/2 Fat

super
express

prep: **20 min**

Caribbean Chicken and Vegetables Salad

Spicy Lime Dressing (below)

2 cups cut-up cooked chicken

1/4 cup chopped fresh cilantro

1 large tomato, chopped (1 cup)

1 medium avocado, pitted, peeled and chopped

1 small yellow summer squash, chopped

1 can (15 ounces) black beans, rinsed and drained

Leaf lettuce

1 Make Spicy Lime Dressing.

2 Toss remaining ingredients except lettuce in large bowl.
Pour dressing over salad; toss. Serve on lettuce.

IT'S **a**

snap!

You'll get the most juice from a lime or lemon if you roll it on the counter or microwave it on High for 10 seconds before cutting.

Spicy Lime Dressing

1/4 cup lime juice

2 tablespoons olive or vegetable oil

1 tablespoon honey

1/2 teaspoon chili powder

1/4 teaspoon ground cumin

1/4 teaspoon salt

2 or 3 drops red pepper sauce

Shake all ingredients in tightly covered container.

1 SERVING: Calories 410 (Calories from Fat 170); Fat 19g (Saturated 4g); Cholesterol 60mg; Sodium 630mg; Carbohydrate 40g (Dietary Fiber 10g); Protein 30g • % DAILY VALUE: Vitamin A 12%; Vitamin C 36%; Calcium 10%; Iron 24% • DIET EXCHANGES: 2 Starch, 3 Medium-Fat Meat, 2 Vegetable, 1 Fat

4 SERVINGS

Chicken Salad with Pea Pods and Almonds

1/4 cup vegetable oil

3 tablespoons sugar

2 tablespoons red wine vinegar or seasoned rice vinegar

1 tablespoon soy sauce

1/4 pound snow (Chinese) pea pods, strings removed (1 cup), cut diagonally in half

3 cups coleslaw mix

1 can (10 ounces) chunk light chicken, drained

1/2 cup sliced almonds, toasted*

1 Mix oil, sugar, vinegar and soy sauce in large bowl.

2 Add remaining ingredients; toss. Serve immediately.

***HOW TO toast nuts:** Cook nuts in ungreased heavy skillet over medium-low heat 5 to 7 minutes, stirring frequently until browning begins, then stirring constantly until golden brown. Or bake uncovered in ungreased shallow pan in 350° oven about 10 minutes, stirring occasionally, until golden brown.

1 SERVING: Calories 310 (Calories from Fat 190); Fat 21g (Saturated 3g); Cholesterol 30mg; Sodium 480mg; Carbohydrate 18g (Dietary Fiber 3g); Protein 15g • **% DAILY VALUE:** Vitamin A 2%; Vitamin C 46%; Calcium 6%; Iron 10% • **DIET EXCHANGES:** 1 Lean Meat, 3 Vegetable, 4 Fat

6 SERVINGS

Italian Ham and Pasta Salad

prep: **20 min**

5 cups cooked penne pasta

2 cups broccoli flowerets

1/2 cup coarsely chopped bell pepper

2 tablespoons finely chopped onion

1 pound fully cooked ham, cut into julienne strips

1/2 cup Italian dressing

1 Mix all ingredients except dressing in large bowl.

2 Pour dressing over mixture; toss.

IT'S **a**
snap!

Cubes of cooked chicken breast or turkey ham could easily be used in place of the ham in this herbed pasta salad. A drizzle of bottled zesty or creamy Italian dressing makes this a flavorful salad.

1 SERVING: Calories 380 (Calories from Fat 145); Fat 16g (Saturated 3g); Cholesterol 45mg; Sodium 1320mg; Carbohydrate 38g (Dietary Fiber 3g); Protein 24g • **% DAILY VALUE:** Vitamin A 8%; Vitamin C 64%; Calcium 4%; Iron 16% • **DIET EXCHANGES:** 2 Starch, 2 Medium-Fat Meat, 2 Vegetable, 1/2 Fat

5 SERVINGS

Fiesta Taco Salad

I pound ground beef	**1/2 cup pitted ripe olives, drained**
1/2 cup taco sauce	**I cup corn chips**
6 cups bite-size pieces lettuce	**I cup shredded Cheddar cheese (4 ounces)**
I medium green bell pepper, cut into strips	**1/2 cup Thousand Island dressing**
2 medium tomatoes, cut into wedges	

1 Cook beef in 10-inch skillet over medium heat 8 to 10 minutes, stirring occasionally, until brown; drain. Stir in taco sauce. Cook 2 to 3 minutes, stirring occasionally, until heated.

2 Toss lettuce, bell pepper, tomatoes, olives and corn chips in large bowl. Spoon hot beef mixture over lettuce mixture; toss. Sprinkle with cheese. Serve immediately with dressing.

IT'S **a**

snap!

To save cooking time in any recipe that calls for cooked ground beef, you can brown the beef ahead of time. Just drain and keep in a covered container in the refrigerator for up to 3 days, or freeze for later use.

1 SERVING: Calories 465 (Calories from Fat 290); Fat 32g (Saturated 12g); Cholesterol 80mg; Sodium 700mg; Carbohydrate 12g (Dietary Fiber 3g); Protein 25g • **% DAILY VALUE:** Vitamin A 24%; Vitamin C 62%; Calcium 18%; Iron 16% • **DIET EXCHANGES:** 2 Starch, 1/2 High-Fat Meat, I Vegetable, 5 Fat

Fiesta Taco Salad

prep: **8** min
cook: **10** min

IT'S **a**
snap!
Buy fresh uncooked shrimp to cook yourself, or purchase freshly cooked shrimp. Frozen shrimp can save even more time because it is available already peeled and cooked, and it needs only to be thawed before tossing in the salad.

4 SERVINGS

Spinach-Shrimp Salad with Hot Bacon Dressing

4 slices bacon, cut into 1-inch pieces

1/4 cup white vinegar

1 tablespoon sugar

1/4 teaspoon ground mustard (dry)

4 cups lightly packed bite-size pieces spinach leaves

1 cup sliced mushrooms (3 ounces)

1 cup crumbled feta cheese (4 ounces)

1/2 pound cooked peeled deveined medium shrimp

1 Cook bacon in 10-inch skillet over medium-high heat, stirring occasionally, until crisp. Stir in vinegar, sugar and mustard; continue stirring until sugar is dissolved.

2 Toss spinach, mushrooms, cheese and shrimp in large bowl. Drizzle hot bacon dressing over spinach mixture; toss. Serve immediately.

1 SERVING: Calories 200 (Calories from Fat 110); Fat 12g (Saturated 7g); Cholesterol 150mg; Sodium 670mg; Carbohydrate 7g (Dietary Fiber 1g); Protein 20g • **% DAILY VALUE:** Vitamin A 62%; Vitamin C 8%; Calcium 24%; Iron 18% • **DIET EXCHANGES:** 2 1/2 Medium-Fat Meat, 1 Vegetable

Chutney-Salmon Salad

2 cans (6 ounces each) skinless boneless salmon, drained and flaked

3 cups broccoli slaw

2/3 cup mayonnaise or salad dressing

1/3 cup chutney

1/4 cup dry-roasted peanuts, chopped

1 Mix salmon, broccoli slaw, mayonnaise and chutney in glass or plastic bowl.

2 Stir in peanuts just before serving.

prep: **10 min**

IT'S **a**
snap!

For some tasty variations on this recipe, use canned crabmeat in place of the salmon and try different kinds of chutney. Sprinkle with chopped soy nuts, sunflower nuts or toasted walnuts or pecans.

1 SERVING: Calories 480 (Calories from Fat 350); Fat 39g (Saturated 6g); Cholesterol 70mg; Sodium 750mg; Carbohydrate 14g (Dietary Fiber 3g); Protein 22g • **% DAILY VALUE:** Vitamin A 20%; Vitamin C 100%; Calcium 22%; Iron 10% • **DIET EXCHANGES:** 2 High-Fat Meat, 3 Vegetable, 4 1/2 Fat

IT'S **a**

snap!

To get a head start on dinner, chop the papaya and bell pepper, wrap separately and refrigerate. You can also make the dressing a day ahead and refrigerate it.

4 SERVINGS

Chopped Vegetable and Crabmeat Salad

Lime Dressing (below)

2 cups chopped escarole

2 cans (6 ounces each) crabmeat, drained and flaked, or 2 cups chopped cooked turkey or chicken

1 small jicama, peeled and chopped (1 cup)

1 large papaya, peeled, seeded and chopped (1 cup)

1 medium yellow or red bell pepper, chopped (1 cup)

1/2 cup dry-roasted peanuts

1/4 cup chopped fresh cilantro

1 Make Lime Dressing.

2 Place remaining ingredients except peanuts and cilantro in large bowl. Pour dressing over salad; toss. Top with peanuts and cilantro.

Lime Dressing

1/3 cup frozen (thawed) limeade concentrate

1/4 cup vegetable oil

1 tablespoon rice or white vinegar

1 teaspoon grated gingerroot

1/4 teaspoon salt

Shake all ingredients in tightly covered container.

1 SERVING: Calories 430 (Calories from Fat 215); Fat 24g (Saturated 3g); Cholesterol 75mg; Sodium 520mg; Carbohydrate 37g (Dietary Fiber 9g); Protein 25g • **% DAILY VALUE:** Vitamin A 41%; Vitamin C 100%; Calcium 14%; Iron 12% • **DIET EXCHANGES:** 3 High-Fat Meat, 1 Vegetable, 2 Fruit

Chopped Vegetable and Crabmeat Salad

prep: **15 min**

8 SERVINGS

Key Lime Fruit Salad

1 container (6 ounces) Key lime pie yogurt

2 tablespoons orange juice

2 cups fresh pineapple chunks

1 cup strawberry halves

2 cups green grapes

1 cup blueberries

2 cups cubed cantaloupe

1/4 cup flaked or shredded coconut, toasted*

1 Mix yogurt and orange juice.

2 Layer fruit in order listed in 2 1/2-quart clear glass bowl. Pour yogurt mixture over fruit. Sprinkle with coconut. Serve immediately.

***HOW TO toast coconut:** Bake coconut uncovered in ungreased shallow pan in 350° oven 5 to 7 minutes, stirring occasionally, until golden brown.

IT'S a **snap!**

For a quicker preparation, use a 20-ounce can of pineapple chunks, drained. For a similar tangy taste, use lemon instead of Key lime pie flavored yogurt.

1 SERVING: Calories 120 (Calories from Fat 20); Fat 2g (Saturated 1g); Cholesterol 0mg; Sodium 25mg; Carbohydrate 25g (Dietary Fiber 2g); Protein 2g • **% DAILY VALUE:** Vitamin A 12%; Vitamin C 70%; Calcium 4%; Iron 2% • **DIET EXCHANGES:** 2 Fruit

Key Lime Fruit Salad

8 SERVINGS

Italian New Potato Salad

3/4 pound green beans

10 to 12 new potatoes
(1 1/2 pounds), cut into
fourths

1/4 cup water

1/2 cup Italian dressing or
balsamic vinaigrette

1/4 cup chopped red onion

1 can (2 1/4 ounces) sliced
ripe olives, drained

IT'S a
snap!

It's easy to tell when
the potatoes are
done: you should be
able to just pierce
them with a fork.

1 Cut beans in half if desired. Place beans, potatoes and water in 2-quart microwavable casserole. Cover and microwave on High 10 to 12 minutes, rotating dish 1/2 turn every 4 minutes, until potatoes are tender; drain.

2 Place beans and potatoes in large glass or plastic bowl. Pour dressing over vegetables; toss. Add onion and olives; toss.

1 SERVING: Calories 125 (Calories from Fat 65); Fat 7g (Saturated 1g); Cholesterol 0mg; Sodium 210mg; Carbohydrate 17g (Dietary Fiber 3g); Protein 2g • **% DAILY VALUE:** Vitamin A 6%; Vitamin C 14%; Calcium 4%; Iron 6% • **DIET EXCHANGES:** 1 Starch, 1 Fat

Italian New Potato Salad

prep: **5 min**
chill: **15 min**

IT'S **a**
snap!

If you can make
this salad ahead of
time, the flavors
blend and become
tastier after a couple
hours of chilling.
If you're short on
time, though, you can
enjoy it right away.

6 SERVINGS

Corn and Black Bean Salad

1 can (15 ounces) black beans, rinsed and drained

1 can (about 8 ounces) whole kernel corn, drained

1 can (4 ounces) chopped green chilies, drained

1/2 cup medium salsa

1/4 cup chopped onion

2 tablespoons chopped fresh cilantro

1 Mix all ingredients in medium bowl.

2 Cover and refrigerate 15 minutes.

1 SERVING: Calories 135 (Calories from Fat 10); Fat 1g (Saturated 0g); Cholesterol 0mg; Sodium 760mg; Carbohydrate 29g (Dietary Fiber 6g); Protein 8g • **% DAILY VALUE:** Vitamin A 8%; Vitamin C 16%; Calcium 6%; Iron 14% • **DIET EXCHANGES:** 2 Starch

Chicken-Pesto Panini

prep: **8 min**
cook: **5 min**

super express

**8 slices Italian bread,
1/2 inch thick**

**2 tablespoons butter or
margarine, softened**

**1/2 pound thinly sliced cooked
deli chicken or turkey**

4 tablespoons basil pesto

**4 slices (1 ounce each)
mozzarella cheese**

**Spaghetti sauce, warmed,
if desired**

1 Spread one side of each bread slice with butter. Place 4 bread slices with butter sides down; top with chicken, pesto and cheese. Top with remaining bread slices, butter sides up.

2 Cover and cook sandwiches in 12-inch skillet over medium heat 4 to 5 minutes, turning once, until bread is crisp and cheese is melted. Serve with spaghetti sauce.

IT'S **a**
snap!

**Instead of Italian
bread, try onion or
herb focaccia. Slice
focaccia horizontally
in half; spread cut
sides with butter.
Cut into 4 wedges.
Layer chicken, pesto
and cheese on bottom
wedges and place on
large cookie sheet.
Place tops of wedges,
butter sides up, on
cookie sheet, next
to sandwiches. Broil
4 to 6 inches from
heat for 3 minutes.**

1 SERVING: Calories 490 (Calories from Fat 215); Fat 24g (Saturated 10g); Cholesterol 85mg; Sodium 610mg; Carbohydrate 22g (Dietary Fiber 1g); Protein 30g • % DAILY VALUE: Vitamin A 10%; Vitamin C 0%; Calcium 30%; Iron 12% • DIET EXCHANGES: 1 1/2 Starch, 2 Lean Meat, 4 Fat

6 SERVINGS

Thai Chicken Wraps

I cup Oriental dressing

1/4 cup creamy peanut butter

1/8 teaspoon ground red pepper (cayenne)

I pound boneless, skinless chicken breasts, cut into 1/2-inch strips

1/2 teaspoon finely chopped gingerroot

3 cups coleslaw mix (8 ounces)

I medium red bell pepper, cut into thin strips

2 tablespoons chopped peanuts

1/4 cup chopped fresh cilantro

6 flour tortillas (8 to 10 inches in diameter)

1 Mix dressing, peanut butter and red pepper until smooth. Set aside half of mixture to serve with wraps.

2 Spray 10-inch nonstick skillet with cooking spray; heat over medium-high heat. Cook chicken and gingerroot in skillet, stirring occasionally, until chicken is brown. Reserve about 1/4 cup of remaining dressing mixture. Stir remaining dressing mixture into chicken. Cover and cook over medium-low heat 3 to 4 minutes, stirring occasionally, until chicken is no longer pink in center. Remove chicken from skillet.

3 Add reserved 1/4 cup dressing mixture, the coleslaw mix, bell pepper, peanuts and cilantro to skillet. Toss to coat mixture well. Spread about 1/3 cup each coleslaw mixture and chicken down center of each tortilla; roll up. Serve with remaining dressing mixture.

1 SERVING: Calories 505 (Calories from Fat 250); Fat 28g (Saturated 5g); Cholesterol 45mg; Sodium 560mg; Carbohydrate 43g (Dietary Fiber 4g); Protein 25g • **% DAILY VALUE:** Vitamin A 26%; Vitamin C 44%; Calcium 8%; Iron 14% • **DIET EXCHANGES:** 2 Starch, 3 Lean Meat, 3 Vegetable, 2 Fat

Thai Chicken Wraps

Pantry Recipes

If you have a well-stocked pantry (see pages 6–7), you'll be able to make this recipe anytime, even when there's no time to shop.

Tortilla Wrap 'em Ups

1/4 cup canned diced green chilies

4 flour tortillas (8 to 10 inches in diameter)

1/2 cup shredded Cheddar cheese

Heat oven to 350°. Spread **chilies** on **tortillas** and sprinkle with **cheese**. Roll up tightly (secure with toothpicks if necessary) and place seam sides down in ungreased square pan, $9 \times 9 \times 2$ inches. Cover and bake about 10 minutes or until warm. MAKES 4 WRAPS IN 15 MINUTES

serve it 3 ways!

1 Appetizer

Cut each wrap into 1-inch slices. Serve with a bowl of salsa for dipping.

2 Light Meal

Cut each wrap diagonally into 3 pieces. Place on a bed of shredded lettuce or salad greens. Drizzle with ranch dressing.

3 Main Course

Heat a can of chili and spoon over each heated wrap. Top with spoonfuls of sour cream and salsa.

prep: **5 min**
cook: **20 min**

Salsa Chicken Sandwiches

4 frozen breaded chicken breast patties

4 whole wheat sandwich buns, split

8 teaspoons purchased black bean dip

1/4 cup thick-and-chunky salsa

1/2 cup shredded lettuce

1 Cook chicken in oven as directed on package, adding buns, cut sides up, the last 3 to 4 minutes of cooking time until lightly toasted.

2 Spread bottom half of each bun with 2 teaspoons of the bean dip. Top each with chicken patty; spread with 1 tablespoon of the salsa. Add lettuce and tops of buns.

IT'S **a**
snap!

Look for the black bean dip in the snacks and chips aisle or refrigerated dip section in your grocery store. If you prefer, use guacamole dip instead.

1 SANDWICH: Calories 350 (Calories from Fat 165); Fat 18g (Saturated 5g); Cholesterol 50mg; Sodium 880mg; Carbohydrate 30g (Dietary Fiber 3g); Protein 20g • **% DAILY VALUE:** Vitamin A 4%; Vitamin C 4%; Calcium 4%; Iron 12% • **DIET EXCHANGES:** 2 Starch, 2 Medium-Fat Meat, 1 Fat

prep: **5 min**
cook: **6 min**

4 SERVINGS

Open-Face Garden Turkey Sandwiches

4 cups frozen stir-fry bell peppers and onions (from 1-pound bag)

1 pound uncooked turkey breast slices, about 1/4 inch thick

1/2 cup shredded Cheddar cheese (2 ounces)

4 tablespoons sandwich spread, mayonnaise or salad dressing

4 slices pumpernickel bread, toasted

1 Spray 12-inch nonstick skillet with cooking spray; heat over medium-high heat. Cook frozen stir-fry vegetables in skillet 3 to 5 minutes, stirring frequently, until tender. Remove vegetables from skillet.

2 Cook turkey as directed on package in same skillet until light golden brown and no longer pink in center. Remove from heat.

3 Top each turkey slice with vegetables and cheese. Cover and let stand 1 to 2 minutes or until cheese is melted. Spread sandwich spread on bread. Top each slice with turkey topped with vegetables and cheese.

1 SANDWICH: Calories 330 (Calories from Fat 100); Fat 11g (Saturated 4g); Cholesterol 95mg; Sodium 410mg; Carbohydrate 28g (Dietary Fiber 4g); Protein 34g • **% DAILY VALUE:** Vitamin A 10%; Vitamin C 100%; Calcium 12%; Iron 16% • **DIET EXCHANGES:** 1 Starch, 3 1/2 Lean Meat, 3 Vegetable

4 SERVINGS

Philly Beef Sandwiches

2 tablespoons butter or margarine

1 medium onion, coarsely chopped (1/2 cup)

1 1/2 cups sliced mushrooms (4 ounces)

1/3 cup chopped green bell pepper

4 kaiser rolls, split

3/4 pound thinly sliced cooked roast beef

4 slices (1 ounce each) provolone cheese

1 Melt butter in 10-inch skillet over medium-high heat. Cook onion, mushrooms and bell pepper in butter about 5 minutes, stirring occasionally, until vegetables are tender.

2 Set oven control to broil. Place bottom halves of rolls on ungreased cookie sheet. Top with vegetable mixture, beef and cheese. Broil with tops 4 to 6 inches from heat 2 to 3 minutes or just until cheese is melted. Add tops of rolls.

IT'S **a**

snap!

Looking for ways to spend less time in the kitchen? Stop and pick up part of dinner at the deli on your way home. While you're there, purchase a pound of sliced roast beef. Use 3/4 pound in this recipe, and save the rest for later in the week.

1 SERVING: Calories 520 (Calories from Fat 260); Fat 29g (Saturated 14g); Cholesterol 110mg; Sodium 640mg; Carbohydrate 31g (Dietary Fiber 2g); Protein 36g • **% DAILY VALUE:** Vitamin A 12%; Vitamin C 10%; Calcium 26%; Iron 26% • **DIET EXCHANGES:** 2 Starch, 4 Medium-Fat Meat, 1 1/2 Fat

prep: **5 min**
broil: **7 min**

IT'S **a**
snap!

You're in luck with this easy sandwich— fresh spinach is usually available prewashed and packaged in the produce section of large supermarkets.

4 SERVINGS

Canadian Bacon and Spinach Sandwiches

4 slices French bread, cut diagonally 1 inch thick

1 cup bite-size pieces spinach leaves

2 tablespoons ranch dressing

4 slices (2 ounces each) Canadian-style bacon

4 slices (1 ounce each) Swiss cheese

1 Set oven control to broil. Place bread on rack in broiler pan or on cookie sheet. Broil with tops 4 to 6 inches from heat 1 to 2 minutes on each side or until toasted.

2 Mix spinach and dressing. Spoon spinach onto bread. Broil about 2 minutes or until hot.

3 Top with bacon and cheese. Broil about 1 minute or until cheese is melted.

1 SANDWICH: Calories 330 (Calories from Fat 145); Fat 16g (Saturated 7g); Cholesterol 55mg; Sodium 1010mg; Carbohydrate 15g (Dietary Fiber 1g); Protein 22g • **% DAILY VALUE:** Vitamin A 18%; Vitamin C 2%; Calcium 30%; Iron 8% • **DIET EXCHANGES:** 1 Starch, 2 1/2 High-Fat Meat

4 SERVINGS

Super Grilled Cheese Sandwiches

4 slices (1 ounce each) Cheddar, mozzarella, Colby or Monterey Jack cheese

8 slices Italian, sourdough, white or whole wheat bread

2 medium green onions, sliced (2 tablespoons)

1 medium tomato, seeded and chopped (3/4 cup)

8 teaspoons butter or margarine, softened

1 Place cheese slices on 4 slices bread. Top with onions, tomato and remaining bread. Spread 1 teaspoon of the butter over each top slice of bread.

2 Place sandwiches, butter sides down, in skillet. Spread remaining butter over top slices of bread. Cook uncovered over medium heat about 5 minutes or until bottoms are golden brown. Turn and cook 2 to 3 minutes or until bottoms are golden brown and cheese is melted. Cut sandwiches into wedges or sticks, using pizza cutter.

COME &eat!

For an all-time favorite family dinner, serve with tomato soup and a fresh salad.

1 SERVING: Calories 295 (Calories from Fat 170); Fat 19g (Saturated 11g); Cholesterol 50mg; Sodium 460mg; Carbohydrate 22g (Dietary Fiber 2g); Protein 18g • **% DAILY VALUE:** Vitamin A 16%; Vitamin C 6%; Calcium 20%; Iron 8% • **DIET EXCHANGES:** 1 1/2 Starch, 2 High-Fat Meat, 2 Fat

6 SERVINGS

Italian Vegetable Focaccia Sandwich

1 round focaccia bread (10 to 12 inches in diameter)

2 cups shredded mozzarella cheese (8 ounces)

2 cups deli marinated Italian vegetable salad, drained and coarsely chopped

1 Cut focaccia vertically in half, then horizontally in half. Sprinkle bottom halves of focaccia with 1 cup of the cheese. Spread vegetables over cheese. Sprinkle with remaining cheese.

2 Top with tops of bread. Cut each half into 3 wedges.

IT'S **a**
snap!

This easy sandwich filling is great in crusty Italian or French rolls as well—and makes the sandwiches more portable. Slice off the top of each roll, and remove half of the soft bread from inside. Layer the cheese and vegetable salad inside the rolls.

1 SERVING: Calories 340 (Calories from Fat 145); Fat 16g (Saturated 6g); Cholesterol 55mg; Sodium 960mg; Carbohydrate 33g (Dietary Fiber 2g); Protein 18g • **% DAILY VALUE:** Vitamin A 20%; Vitamin C 2%; Calcium 32%; Iron 14% • **DIET EXCHANGES:** 2 Starch, 1 1/2 High-Fat Meat, 1 Vegetable

Italian Vegetable Focaccia Sandwich

prep: **15 min**

You can make this
sturdy sandwich
ahead of time.
Before cutting into
wedges, wrap it
securely with plastic
wrap and refrigerate
up to 6 hours.

6 SERVINGS

Stromboli Hero

1 round focaccia bread
(8 or 9 inches in diameter)

1/4 cup Italian dressing

4 or 5 leaves leaf lettuce

1/4 pound sliced provolone
cheese

1/4 pound sliced fully cooked
ham

1/4 pound sliced salami

8 pepperoncini peppers
(bottled Italian peppers),
cut lengthwise in half

1 Cut focaccia horizontally in half. Drizzle dressing evenly
over cut sides of focaccia.

2 Layer lettuce, cheese, ham, salami and peppers on bottom
half of focaccia. Top with top half. Secure loaf with toothpicks or small skewers. Cut into 6 wedges.

1 SERVING: Calories 320 (Calories from Fat 170); Fat 19g (Saturated 7g); Cholesterol 40mg;
Sodium 1170mg; Carbohydrate 24g (Dietary Fiber 2g); Protein 16g • **% DAILY VALUE:**
Vitamin A 20%; Vitamin C 48%; Calcium 16%; Iron 12% • **DIET EXCHANGES:** 1 1/2 Starch,
2 Medium-Fat Meat

3 Pressed for Time Pasta and Pizza

◔ = *super express* ready in 20 minutes or less

1-Step Recipes

Pasta and Pizza Toppings
Pasta and pizza are weeknight favorites. Try these easy ways to toss together great flavors in a flash.

1 Tomato-Cream Pasta
Heat 1/2 jar (26-ounce size) tomato pasta sauce and 1/4 cup half-and-half; toss with cooked penne or other desired pasta and sprinkle with grated Parmesan cheese.

2 Pesto and Red Pepper Cream Sauce
Mix heated whipping cream, pesto and chopped roasted red bell peppers (from 7-ounce jar); toss with cooked fusilli and sprinkle with grated Parmesan cheese.

3 Pasta-Bean Salad
Mix Italian dressing, sliced olives, drained canned kidney beans, cooked broccoli or corn and chopped cooked ham with cooked rotini and cool slightly.

4 Southwest Pasta-Chicken Salad
Stir cooked chicken, canned whole kernel corn with red and green peppers (drained), southwestern ranch dressing and chopped green chilies into deli pasta salad.

5 Cheesy Broccoli Pasta
Cook penne pasta, adding broccoli flowerets in last 5 minutes of cooking. Toss drained pasta and vegetables with cheese spread and add enough milk to make a sauce.

6 Cheese and Veggie Pita Pizzas
Top pita bread rounds with pizza sauce, sliced mushrooms and red bell peppers and shredded mozzarella cheese; melt cheese in microwave.

7 California Pizza
Top baked cheese pizza with sliced avocado, tomato and ripe olives.

8 Fresh Vegetable Pizza
Spread flatbread or pita breads with garlic-and-herb spreadable cheese; top with assorted fresh vegetables and shredded sharp Cheddar cheese. If desired, microwave 10 to 20 seconds or broil tops 1 to 2 minutes, or until cheese is melted.

9 Tostada-Bean Pizzas
Drizzle tostada shells with pizza sauce and salsa; top with black beans, chopped tomato, shredded lettuce and cheese.

10 Design-Your-Own Pizza
Top pizza crust with pizza sauce, sliced mushrooms, chopped green onions or peppers, cooked ground beef, chicken or turkey and mozzarella, Cheddar or Monterey Jack cheese; bake.

Pasta with Turkey and Asian Vegetables

super
express

prep: **10 min**
cook: **10 min**

8 ounces uncooked capellini (angel hair) pasta

1 package (10 ounces) frozen snap pea pods

12 ounces turkey breast tenderloins, cut into thin strips

1 large red bell pepper, cut into thin strips (1 1/2 cups)

2 cloves garlic, finely chopped

1 tablespoon grated gingerroot

4 medium green onions, sliced (1/4 cup)

1 tablespoon sesame seed, toasted*

1 Cook pasta as directed on package, adding frozen pea pods to the cooking water with the pasta. Drain well; transfer to large serving bowl.

2 While pasta is cooking, spray 12-inch skillet with cooking spray; heat over medium-high heat. Cook turkey, bell pepper, garlic and gingerroot in skillet 5 to 10 minutes, stirring constantly, until turkey is no longer pink and bell pepper is crisp-tender.

3 Toss turkey mixture, pasta and pea pods. Sprinkle with onions and sesame seed.

✳ HOW TO toast sesame seed: Bake sesame seed uncovered in ungreased shallow pan in 350° oven 8 to 10 minutes, stirring occasionally, until golden brown. Or cook in ungreased heavy skillet over medium heat about 2 minutes, stirring frequently until browning begins, then stirring constantly until golden brown.

IT'S **a**

snap!

Warm a large bowl with hot water and dry before tossing pasta. A large bowl is handy for tossing fine and delicate angel hair pasta with other ingredients and helps keep the pasta from clumping or breaking.

1 SERVING: Calories 355 (Calories from Fat 25); Fat 3g (Saturated 1g); Cholesterol 55mg; Sodium 45mg; Carbohydrate 54g (Dietary Fiber 5g); Protein 31g • % DAILY VALUE: Vitamin A 24%; Vitamin C 92%; Calcium 6%; Iron 28% • DIET EXCHANGES: 3 Starch, 2 1/2 Very Lean Meat, 2 Vegetable

Fettuccine and Chicken in Orange-Cherry Sauce

IT'S **a**
snap!

Boneless chicken
breast for stir-fry
is available in most
larger grocery
stores, but if you
can't find it, cut
boneless, skinless
chicken breast halves
into thin strips.

6 ounces uncooked fettuccine	**I tablespoon cornstarch**
1/2 pound cut-up boneless chicken breast for stir-fry	**I tablespoon orange marmalade**
1/4 teaspoon salt	**1/4 cup dried cherries**
I 1/2 cups or I package (9 ounces) frozen whole green beans	**1/4 cup chopped walnuts, toasted* if desired**
I cup orange juice	

1 Cook and drain fettuccine as directed on package.

2 While fettuccine is cooking, spray 12-inch nonstick skillet with cooking spray; heat over medium heat. Cook chicken and salt in skillet 2 to 3 minutes, stirring occasionally, until chicken is brown. Stir in frozen green beans. Cover and cook over medium heat 3 to 4 minutes, stirring occasionally, until beans are crisp-tender.

3 Mix orange juice and cornstarch until smooth. Stir orange juice mixture, marmalade and cherries into chicken mixture. Heat to boiling, stirring constantly; reduce heat to medium. Cover and cook 2 to 3 minutes, stirring occasionally, until beans are tender and chicken is no longer pink in center. Add fettuccine to chicken mixture; toss. Sprinkle each serving with walnuts.

✳ **HOW TO toast nuts:** Bake nuts uncovered in ungreased shallow pan in a 350° oven about 10 minutes, stirring occasionally, until golden brown. Or cook in ungreased heavy skillet over medium-low heat 5 to 7 minutes, stirring frequently until browning begins, then stirring constantly until golden brown.

1 SERVING: Calories 325 (Calories from Fat 70); Fat 8g (Saturated 1g); Cholesterol 70mg; Sodium 190mg; Carbohydrate 49g (Dietary Fiber 6g); Protein 20g • **% DAILY VALUE:** Vitamin A 4%; Vitamin C 26%; Calcium 6%; Iron 18% • **DIET EXCHANGES:** 3 Starch, 1 Lean Meat, 1 Vegetable, 1/2 Fat

Fettuccine and Chicken in Orange-Cherry Sauce

Pantry Recipes

If you have a well-stocked pantry (see pages 6–7), you'll be able to make this recipe anytime, even when there's no time to shop.

Ravioli Rescue

1 package (9 ounces) refrigerated Italian sausage- or cheese-filled ravioli

1 can (15 ounces) chunky tomato sauce with garlic and herbs or plain tomato sauce

1 can (8 ounces) sliced mushrooms, drained

4 green onions, sliced

Cook and drain **ravioli** as directed on package in 3-quart saucepan. While ravioli is cooking, heat **tomato sauce** and **mushrooms** in 2- or 3-quart saucepan over medium heat 3 to 4 minutes, stirring occasionally, until hot. Stir in **onions** and the ravioli. Cook 2 to 4 minutes or until hot. MAKES 4 SERVINGS IN 15 MINUTES

serve it 3 ways!

1 Cheesy
Sprinkle with shredded Parmesan, mozzarella, or Italian-blend cheese; let stand 1 to 2 minutes.

2 Add Meat
Stir in pieces of cooked chicken, turkey, ham or sausage with the onions.

3 Very Veggie
Heat a 1-pound bag of frozen mixed vegetables with the tomato sauce and mushrooms.

super
express

prep: **10 min**
cook: **10 min**

4 SERVINGS

Chili Beef 'n Noodles

**4 cups uncooked wide
egg noodles (8 ounces)**

1 pound ground beef

**1 medium onion, chopped
(1/2 cup)**

**1 can (11 1/4 ounces)
condensed fiesta chili beef
with beans soup**

**1 jar (8 ounces) salsa
(1 cup)**

1/2 cup water

**1 cup shredded Cheddar
cheese (4 ounces)**

1 Cook and drain noodles as directed on package.

2 While noodles are cooking, cook beef and onion in 12-inch
skillet over medium-high heat, stirring occasionally, until
beef is brown; drain. Reduce heat to medium. Stir soup,
salsa and water into beef. Cook until thoroughly heated.

3 Serve beef mixture over noodles. Sprinkle with cheese.

COME
&eat!

Here's the perfect
choice for a hearty
dinner for a crowd.
If you want to jazz
it up a bit, stir in
1/4 cup each whole
pimiento-stuffed
green olives and
pitted ripe olives with
the soup in step 2.

1 SERVING: Calories 400 (Calories from Fat 180); Fat 20g (Saturated 9g); Cholesterol 95mg;
Sodium 650mg; Carbohydrate 32g (Dietary Fiber 3g); Protein 26g • **% DAILY VALUE:**
Vitamin A 10%; Vitamin C 10%; Calcium 14%; Iron 20% • **DIET EXCHANGES:** 2 Starch,
3 Medium-Fat Meat

4 SERVINGS

Orange Teriyaki Beef with Noodles

**1 pound beef boneless sirloin,
cut into thin strips**

**1 can (14 1/2 ounces)
beef broth**

1/4 cup teriyaki stir-fry sauce

**2 tablespoons orange
marmalade**

**Dash of ground red pepper
(cayenne)**

1 1/2 cups snap pea pods

**1 1/2 cups uncooked fine
egg noodles (3 ounces)**

1 Spray 12-inch skillet with cooking spray; heat over
medium-high heat. Cook beef in skillet 2 to 4 minutes,
stirring occasionally, until brown. Remove beef from
skillet; keep warm.

2 Add broth, stir-fry sauce, marmalade and red pepper to
skillet. Heat to boiling. Stir in pea pods and noodles;
reduce heat to medium. Cover and cook about 5 minutes
or until noodles are tender.

3 Stir in beef. Cook uncovered 2 to 3 minutes or until sauce
is slightly thickened.

1 SERVING: Calories 230 (Calories from Fat 35); Fat 4g (Saturated 1g); Cholesterol 65mg;
Sodium 1210mg; Carbohydrate 22g (Dietary Fiber 2g); Protein 28g • **% DAILY VALUE:**
Vitamin A 4%; Vitamin C 14%; Calcium 4%; Iron 22% • **DIET EXCHANGES:** 1 Starch,
3 Very Lean Meat, 2 Vegetable

Orange Teriyaki Beef with Noodles

IT'S **a**
snap!

Crumble, cook
and drain sausage
ahead to save time.
Cooked and drained
ground beef is a
quick substitution
for the sausage in
this easy lasagna.

6 SERVINGS

Stove-Top Lasagna

I pound bulk Italian sausage

I green pepper, sliced

I package (8 ounces) sliced mushrooms (3 cups)

I medium onion, chopped (1/2 cup)

3 cups uncooked mafalda (mini-lasagna noodle) pasta (6 ounces)

2 1/2 cups water

1/2 teaspoon Italian seasoning

I jar (26 to 30 ounces) chunky tomato pasta sauce (any variety)

I cup 4-blend Italian shredded or shredded mozzarella cheese (4 ounces)

1 Cook sausage, pepper, mushrooms and onion in 12-inch skillet or 4-quart Dutch oven over medium-high heat, stirring occasionally, until sausage is no longer pink; drain.

2 Stir in remaining ingredients except cheese. Heat to boiling, stirring occasionally; reduce heat. Simmer uncovered about 10 minutes or until pasta is tender. Sprinkle with cheese.

1 SERVING: Calories 495 (Calories from Fat 205); Fat 23g (Saturated 8g); Cholesterol 55mg; Sodium 1280 mg; Carbohydrate 53 (Dietary Fiber 4g); Protein 23g • **% DAILY VALUE:** Vitamin A 22%; Vitamin C 34%; Calcium 20%; Iron 20% • **DIET EXCHANGES:** 3 Starch, 1 1/2 High-Fat Meat, 1 Vegetable, 2 Fat

Stove-Top Lasagna

4 SERVINGS

Ravioli in Tomato-Cream Sauce

IT'S **a**
snap!
Here's a great way
to keep leftover
tomato paste: divide
it among small
containers and
freeze for later use.
Ice-cube trays are
perfect for freezing
1 to 2 tablespoons
of tomato paste.
When ready to use,
thaw slightly and add
to sauces, casseroles
and soups.

12 ounces frozen cheese-filled ravioli

1 pound bulk Italian sausage

1 large onion, chopped (1 cup)

1 medium green bell pepper, chopped (1 cup)

1 can (14 1/2 ounces) beef broth

1/4 cup tomato paste

1/2 teaspoon crushed fennel seed

1/4 cup half-and-half

1 Cook and drain ravioli as directed on package.

2 While ravioli is cooking, cook sausage, onion and bell pepper in 10-inch nonstick skillet over medium-high heat, stirring occasionally, until sausage is no longer pink; drain.

3 Stir broth, tomato paste and fennel seed into sausage mixture. Heat to boiling; reduce heat to medium. Cook 5 minutes, stirring occasionally. Stir in half-and-half. Cook 5 to 6 minutes, stirring occasionally, until sauce is desired consistency. Serve sauce over ravioli.

1 SERVING: Calories 480 (Calories from Fat 270); Fat 30g (Saturated 12g); Cholesterol 155mg; Sodium 1860mg; Carbohydrate 25g (Dietary Fiber 2g); Protein 30g • **% DAILY VALUE:** Vitamin A 12%; Vitamin C 32%; Calcium 20%; Iron 16% • **DIET EXCHANGES:** 1 1/2 Starch, 4 Medium-Fat Meat, 1 Vegetable, 1 Fat

Ravioli in Tomato-Cream Sauce

prep: **10 min**
cook: **10 min**

4 SERVINGS

Countryside Pasta Toss

IT'S **a**
snap!

Frozen baby carrots
and snap pea pods
can be used if you
don't have fresh.
Prepare following the
package directions
before tossing with
the other vegetables.

1 cup uncooked rotini pasta (3 ounces)	**1 tablespoon butter or margarine**
3/4 pound new potatoes, cut into 1/2-inch wedges	**2 tablespoons chopped fresh parsley**
1 cup baby-cut carrots	**1 teaspoon dried dill weed**
1 cup broccoli flowerets	**1/2 teaspoon salt**
1/2 cup snap pea pods	**2 ounces fully cooked ham, cut into thin strips**

1 Cook and drain pasta as directed on package.

2 While pasta is cooking, place steamer basket in 1/2 inch water in 3-quart saucepan (water should not touch bottom of basket). Place potatoes and carrots in basket. Cover tightly and heat to boiling; reduce heat to medium-low. Steam 5 minutes. Add broccoli and pea pods. Cover and steam about 2 minutes longer or until potatoes are tender.

3 Place vegetables in medium bowl. Add butter, parsley, dill weed and salt; toss. Add ham and pasta; toss.

1 SERVING: Calories 245 (Calories from Fat 45); Fat 5g (Saturated 2g); Cholesterol 15mg; Sodium 550mg; Carbohydrate 45g (Dietary Fiber 5g); Protein 10g • **% DAILY VALUE:** Vitamin A 100%; Vitamin C 32%; Calcium 4%; Iron 16% • **DIET EXCHANGES:** 2 Starch, 3 Vegetable

Countryside Pasta Toss

COME
&eat!

Need a little
crunch without a
lot of work? Baby-
cut carrots, apple
wedges, bell pepper
strips, celery sticks
and crisp dill pickles
are good choices
to serve with this
quick pasta and
pork dinner.

4 SERVINGS

Couscous and Sweet Potatoes with Pork

1 1/2 cups uncooked couscous

1 pound pork tenderloin, thinly sliced

1 medium sweet potato, peeled and sliced into thin strips

1 cup thick-and-chunky salsa

1/2 cup water

2 tablespoons honey

1/4 cup chopped fresh cilantro

1 Cook couscous as directed on package.

2 While couscous is cooking, spray 12-inch skillet with cooking spray. Cook pork in skillet over medium heat 2 to 3 minutes, stirring occasionally, until brown.

3 Stir sweet potato, salsa, water and honey into pork. Heat to boiling; reduce heat to medium. Cover and cook 5 to 6 minutes, stirring occasionally, until potato is tender. Sprinkle with cilantro. Serve pork mixture over couscous.

1 SERVING: Calories 440 (Calories from Fat 45); Fat 5g (Saturated 2g); Cholesterol 70mg; Sodium 230mg; Carbohydrate 70g (Dietary Fiber 6g); Protein 35g • **% DAILY VALUE:** Vitamin A 86%; Vitamin C 18%; Calcium 6%; Iron 14% • **DIET EXCHANGES:** 4 Starch, 3 Very Lean Meat, 2 Vegetable

Pasta with Prosciutto and Asiago Cheese

2 cups uncooked fusilli (corkscrew) pasta (6 ounces)

2 tablespoons olive or vegetable oil

1 package (8 ounces) sliced mushrooms (3 cups)

6 medium green onions, cut into 1/2-inch pieces

1 medium red bell pepper, coarsely chopped (1 cup)

1 clove garlic, finely chopped

1 package (3 ounces) sliced prosciutto ham or fully cooked ham, cut into thin strips

1 tablespoon chopped fresh or 1/2 teaspoon dried basil leaves

2 teaspoons chopped fresh or 1/4 teaspoon dried oregano leaves

1/4 teaspoon salt

1/4 cup shredded Asiago cheese

IT'S **a**
snap!

Love the ham and cheese idea, but not familiar with prosciutto and Asiago? Use deli ham and shredded Cheddar cheese as quick substitutes.

1 Cook and drain pasta as directed on package.

2 While pasta is cooking, heat 1 tablespoon of the oil in 10-inch nonstick skillet over medium-high heat. Cook mushrooms, onions, bell pepper and garlic in oil 2 to 3 minutes, stirring occasionally, until vegetables are tender.

3 Stir in prosciutto, basil, oregano and salt. Stir in pasta and remaining 1 tablespoon oil; toss. Sprinkle each serving with cheese.

1 SERVING: Calories 335 (Calories from Fat 115); Fat 13g (Saturated 3g); Cholesterol 70mg; Sodium 440mg; Carbohydrate 43g (Dietary Fiber 3g); Protein 15g • % DAILY VALUE: Vitamin A 20%; Vitamin C 52%; Calcium 8%; Iron 20% • DIET EXCHANGES: 2 Starch, 1 Lean Meat, 2 Vegetable, 2 Fat

IT'S **a** snap!

Try shopping instead of chopping time— look for the small jars of chopped gar- lic and red jalapeño chilies in the pro- duce section of your supermarket.

4 SERVINGS

Spaghetti with Shrimp

8 ounces uncooked spaghetti pasta

1/4 cup olive or vegetable oil

2 tablespoons chopped fresh parsley

2 cloves garlic, finely chopped

I small red jalapeño chili, seeded and finely chopped

1/3 cup dry white wine or vegetable broth

1/8 teaspoon ground nutmeg

3/4 pound uncooked peeled deveined small shrimp, thawed if frozen

1 Cook and drain pasta as directed on package.

2 While pasta is cooking, heat oil in 4-quart Dutch oven or 12-inch skillet over medium-high heat. Cook parsley, garlic and chili in oil 1 minute, stirring occasionally. Stir in wine, nutmeg and shrimp; reduce heat. Cover and simmer about 5 minutes or until shrimp are pink and firm.

3 Mix pasta and shrimp mixture in Dutch oven. Cook over medium heat 2 minutes, stirring occasionally.

1 SERVING: Calories 385 (Calories from Fat 135); Fat 15g (Saturated 2g); Cholesterol 80mg; Sodium 95mg; Carbohydrate 47g (Dietary Fiber 2g); Protein 7g • **% DAILY VALUE:** Vitamin A 14%; Vitamin C 20%; Calcium 4%; Iron 22% • **DIET EXCHANGES:** 3 Starch, I Very Lean Meat, 2 1/2 Fat

6 SERVINGS

Angel Hair Pasta with Fresh Basil, Avocado and Tomatoes

super express

prep: 15 min
cook: 5 min

8 ounces uncooked angel hair pasta

2 tablespoons olive or vegetable oil

2 cloves garlic, finely chopped

3/4 cup chopped fresh basil leaves

1/2 to 3/4 large avocado, peeled and cut into small cubes

4 medium tomatoes, cut into small cubes

1/2 teaspoon salt

1/4 teaspoon pepper

1 Cook and drain pasta as directed on package.

2 While pasta is cooking, heat oil in 3-quart saucepan over medium heat. Cook garlic in oil about 5 minutes, stirring occasionally, until garlic is tender but not brown; remove from heat.

3 Stir basil, avocado and tomatoes into garlic in saucepan. Toss vegetable mixture and pasta. Sprinkle with salt and pepper.

IT'S **a** snap!

This comforting recipe goes together in just minutes, thanks to angel hair, a thin pasta that cooks quickly. Vermicelli and couscous are other quick-cooking pastas. To avoid overcooking delicate pastas, always check the package to determine accurate cook times.

1 SERVING: Calories 220 (Calories from Fat 90); Fat 10g (Saturated 1g); Cholesterol 30mg; Sodium 210mg; Carbohydrate 30g (Dietary Fiber 3g); Protein 6g • **% DAILY VALUE:** Vitamin A 22%; Vitamin C 14%; Calcium 2%; Iron 12% • **DIET EXCHANGES:** 1 1/2 Starch, 2 Vegetable, 1 Fat

prep: **5 min**
cook: **15 min**

6 SERVINGS

Southwest Cheese 'n Pasta

COME
&eat!

Add ham to part of this skillet dish for the meat lovers in your family. Remove half of the macaroni and cheese from the skillet; keep warm. Stir 1 cup of cubed fully cooked ham into the remaining macaroni in the skillet, and heat through.

2 2/3 cups uncooked cavatappi pasta

1 cup green salsa (salsa verde)

1 1/2 cups milk

1 can (15 ounces) cream-style corn

1 can (11 ounces) whole kernel corn with red and green peppers, drained

8 ounces process cheese product loaf, cubed

1 Mix all ingredients except cheese in 12-inch nonstick skillet. Heat to boiling, stirring occasionally; reduce heat to low. Cover and cook 10 to 14 minutes, stirring frequently, until pasta is tender.

2 Stir in cheese until melted.

1 SERVING: Calories 405 (Calories from Fat 135); Fat 15g (Saturated 8g); Cholesterol 40mg; Sodium 960mg; Carbohydrate 54g (Dietary Fiber 5g); Protein 18g • % DAILY VALUE: Vitamin A 18%; Vitamin C 16%; Calcium 30%; Iron 14% • DIET EXCHANGES: 3 Starch, 2 Fat, 1 Skim Milk

Southwest Cheese 'n Pasta

prep: **5 min**
cook: **15 min**

COME

&eat!

For a hearty
Southern-style
meal, serve the
mac 'n cheese with
warm pork and
beans and corn
bread or muffins
on the side.

4 SERVINGS

Easy Macaroni and Cheese

2 cups uncooked small shell pasta or elbow macaroni (8 ounces)

1 1/2 cups shredded Cheddar cheese (6 ounces) or 8 ounces process cheese spread loaf, cut into cubes

1 cup milk

1 tablespoon butter or margarine, if desired

1/2 teaspoon salt

1/2 teaspoon ground mustard

1/4 teaspoon pepper

1 Cook and drain pasta as directed on package.

2 In 2-quart saucepan, stir remaining ingredients into pasta. Cook over low heat about 5 minutes, stirring occasionally, until cheese is melted and sauce is desired consistency.

1 SERVING: Calories 435 (Calories from Fat 145); Fat 16g (Saturated 10g); Cholesterol 50mg; Sodium 590 mg; Carbohydrate 54g (Dietary Fiber 2g); Protein 21g • **% DAILY VALUE:** Vitamin A 12%; Vitamin C 0%; Calcium 30%; Iron 16% • **DIET EXCHANGES:** 3 Starch, 2 1/2 Very Lean Meat, 2 Vegetable

Minestrone Pasta Salad

prep: **10 min**
cook: **10 min**

3 cups uncooked medium pasta shells (7 1/2 ounces)

2 medium carrots, sliced (1 cup)

1 medium green bell pepper, chopped (1 cup)

1 can (15 to 16 ounces) kidney beans, rinsed and drained

1 can (15 to 16 ounces) garbanzo beans, rinsed and drained

1 can (14 1/2 ounces) Italian-style stewed or diced tomatoes, drained

2/3 cup Italian dressing

1/2 cup shredded Parmesan cheese

1 Cook and drain pasta as directed on package.

2 Toss pasta and remaining ingredients. Serve warm or cold.

IT'S **a**
snap!
Dinner prep time is slashed when you use bottled salad dressing. Besides using your favorite dressing in salads, try it as a sauce for hot pasta or as a brush-on sauce when cooking chicken.

1 SERVING: Calories 550 (Calories from Fat 145); Fat 16g (Saturated 3g); Cholesterol 10mg; Sodium 800mg; Carbohydrate 91g (Dietary Fiber 14g); Protein 24g • **% DAILY VALUE:** Vitamin A 36%; Vitamin C 24%; Calcium 18%; Iron 38% • **DIET EXCHANGES:** 5 Starch, 3 Vegetable, 2 Fat

prep: **10 min**
cook: **10 min**

IT'S **a**
snap!

Fresh can be fast!
In this recipe you
can speed prepara-
tion time by leaving
the carrot and
zucchini unpeeled.
Just scrub them well
before chopping.

4 SERVINGS

Penne with Vegetables in Tomato-Basil Sauce

2 cups uncooked penne pasta (6 ounces)

1 tablespoon olive or vegetable oil

1 medium onion, chopped (1/2 cup)

1 medium carrot, chopped (1/2 cup)

1 can (14 1/2 ounces) diced tomatoes with basil, garlic and oregano, undrained

1 can (8 ounces) tomato sauce

1 small unpeeled zucchini, chopped (1 cup)

1 tablespoon chopped fresh or 1/2 teaspoon dried basil leaves

2 tablespoons chopped fresh parsley

1/4 cup shredded Parmesan cheese

1 Cook and drain pasta as directed on package.

2 While pasta is cooking, heat oil in 10-inch nonstick skillet over medium-high heat. Cook onion and carrot in oil 2 to 3 minutes, stirring occasionally, until crisp-tender. Stir in tomatoes and tomato sauce. Cook 5 minutes.

3 Stir in zucchini and basil; reduce heat to medium. Cook about 5 minutes, stirring occasionally, until sauce is desired consistency. Stir in parsley. Serve over pasta. Sprinkle with cheese.

1 SERVING: Calories 330 (Calories from Fat 55); Fat 6g (Saturated 2g); Cholesterol 5mg; Sodium 760mg; Carbohydrate 62g (Dietary Fiber 5g); Protein 12g • **% DAILY VALUE:** Vitamin A 40%; Vitamin C 24%; Calcium 14%; Iron 20% • **DIET EXCHANGES:** 3 Starch, 3 Vegetable, 1/2 Fat

Penne with Vegetables in Tomato-Basil Sauce

6 SERVINGS

Fajita Pizza

2 tablespoons vegetable oil

1/2 pound boneless, skinless chicken breasts, cut into 1/8- to 1/4-inch strips

1/2 medium bell pepper, cut into thin strips

1 small onion, sliced

1/2 cup salsa or picante sauce

1 1/2 cups Original Bisquick

1/3 cup very hot water

1 1/2 cups shredded mozzarella cheese (6 ounces)

1 Move oven rack to lowest position. Heat oven to 450°. Grease 12-inch pizza pan with shortening or butter. Heat 10-inch skillet over medium-high heat. Add oil; rotate skillet to coat bottom and side. Cook chicken in oil 3 minutes, stirring frequently. Stir in bell pepper and onion. Cook 3 to 4 minutes, stirring frequently, until vegetables are crisp and chicken is no longer pink in center; remove from heat. Stir in salsa; set aside.

2 In another bowl stir together Bisquick and very hot water until soft dough forms; beat vigorously with spoon 20 strokes. Press dough in pizza pan, using fingers dipped in Bisquick; pinch edge to form 1/2-inch rim. Sprinkle 3/4 cup of the cheese over crust. Top with chicken mixture. Sprinkle with remaining 3/4 cup cheese.

3 Bake about 12 minutes or until crust is brown and cheese is melted and bubbly.

1 SERVING: Calories 295 (Calories from Fat 135); Fat 15g (Saturated 5g); Cholesterol 40mg; Sodium 690mg; Carbohydrate 22g (Dietary Fiber 1g); Protein 19g • **% DAILY VALUE:** Vitamin A 8%; Vitamin C 10%; Calcium 26%; Iron 8% • **DIET EXCHANGES:** 1 Starch, 2 Medium Fat Meat, 1 Vegetable, 1 Fat

Fajita Pizza

prep: **5 min**
bake: **15 min**

IT'S **a**
snap!
Why not buy bags of fresh spinach and shredded cheese? All the hard work of washing and shredding is already done.

6 SERVINGS

Double-Cheese, Spinach and Chicken Pizza

1 ready-to-serve pizza crust (12 to 14 inches in diameter)

1 cup shredded Havarti cheese (4 ounces)

2 cups bagged washed fresh baby spinach leaves

1 cup diced cooked chicken

1/4 cup chopped drained roasted red bell peppers (from 7-ounce jar)

1/2 teaspoon garlic salt

1 cup shredded Cheddar cheese (4 ounces)

1 Heat oven to 425°. Place pizza crust on ungreased pizza pan.

2 Top with Havarti cheese, spinach, chicken, bell peppers, garlic salt and Cheddar cheese.

3 Bake 8 to 10 minutes or until crust is golden brown.

1 SERVING: Calories 450 (Calories from Fat 160); Fat 18g (Saturated 9g); Cholesterol 60mg; Sodium 750mg; Carbohydrate 51g (Dietary Fiber 2g); Protein 23g • **% DAILY VALUE:** Vitamin A 34%; Vitamin C 12%; Calcium 22%; Iron 22% • **DIET EXCHANGES:** 3 Starch, 2 Medium-Fat Meat, 1 Vegetable, 1 Fat

Double-Cheese, Spinach and Chicken Pizza

6 SERVINGS

Thai Chicken Pizzas

6 flour tortillas (8 to 10 inches in diameter)

1/2 cup peanut butter

1/4 cup soy sauce

2 tablespoons seasoned rice vinegar

2 teaspoons sugar

2 cups shredded mozzarella cheese (8 ounces)

2 cups chopped cooked chicken breast

1 bag (1 pound) frozen stir-fry vegetables, thawed and drained

1 Heat oven to 400°. Place tortillas on ungreased cookie sheet. Bake about 5 minutes or until crisp.

2 Mix peanut butter, soy sauce, vinegar and sugar; spread over tortillas. Top each with 1/4 cup of the cheese. Spread chicken and vegetables evenly over tortillas. Sprinkle with remaining 1/2 cup cheese.

3 Bake 10 to 15 minutes or until pizzas are hot and cheese is melted.

IT'S **a**
snap!
For added speed, you can use slightly less than 1 cup of purchased peanut sauce, found in the Asian foods section of your grocery store, in place of the peanut butter, soy sauce, vinegar and sugar.

1 SERVING: Calories 490 (Calories from Fat 215); Fat 24g (Saturated 10g); Cholesterol 60mg; Sodium 1430mg; Carbohydrate 37g (Dietary Fiber 5g); Protein 36g • **% DAILY VALUE:** Vitamin A 16%; Vitamin C 20%; Calcium 50%; Iron 20% • **DIET EXCHANGES:** 2 Starch, 4 Lean Meat, 1 Vegetable, 2 Fat

Chicken Enchilada Pizzas

super express

prep: **5 min**
cook: **8 min**
bake: **6 min**

4 flour tortillas (8 to 10 inches in diameter)

1 tablespoon vegetable oil

1 medium onion, thinly sliced

2 cups chopped cooked chicken breast

1/2 cup green salsa (salsa verde)

1 can (2 1/4 ounces) sliced ripe olives, drained

1/3 cup sour cream

1 cup shredded Monterey Jack cheese (4 ounces)

1 Heat oven to 400°. Place tortillas on ungreased cookie sheet. Bake about 5 minutes or until crisp.

2 While tortillas are baking, heat oil in 10-inch nonstick skillet over medium heat. Cook onion in oil, stirring frequently, until tender; remove from heat. Stir in chicken, salsa and olives.

3 Spread sour cream on tortillas. Top with chicken mixture and cheese. Bake 5 to 6 minutes, or until cheese is melted.

COME
&eat!

As a quick addition, chop a large tomato and toss on this flavorful pizza between the chicken mixture and the cheese to add color and a fresh-from-the-garden flavor. Or sprinkle the top with chopped fresh cilantro.

1 SERVING: Calories 445 (Calories from Fat 205); Fat 23g (Saturated 10g); Cholesterol 95mg; Sodium 650mg; Carbohydrate 30g (Dietary Fiber 3g); Protein 33g • % DAILY VALUE: Vitamin A 24%; Vitamin C 6%; Calcium 52%; Iron 16% • DIET EXCHANGES: 2 Starch, 4 Lean Meat, 1 1/2 Fat

IT'S **a**
snap!

Look to your deli
for jump starts to
dinner. Cooked
turkey, chicken
or roast beef—
whatever you have
on hand—works
great in this recipe.

4 SERVINGS

Turkey Gyros Pizzas

4 pita breads (6 inches in diameter)

1/2 cup sour cream

1 1/2 teaspoons chopped fresh or 1/2 teaspoon dried mint leaves

1 1/2 cups shredded mozzarella cheese (6 ounces)

1/2 pound sliced cooked deli turkey breast, cut into strips

1/2 cup chopped cucumber

1 small tomato, chopped (1/2 cup)

1 cup crumbled feta cheese (4 ounces)

1 Heat oven to 400°.

2 Place pita breads on ungreased cookie sheet. Mix sour cream and mint; spread evenly over pitas. Sprinkle each pita with 1/4 cup of the mozzarella cheese. Top with turkey, cucumber, tomato and feta cheese. Sprinkle with remaining 1/2 cup mozzarella cheese.

3 Bake about 10 minutes or until pizzas are hot and cheese is melted.

1 SERVING: Calories 475 (Calories from Fat 205); Fat 23g (Saturated 14g); Cholesterol 100mg; Sodium 1600mg; Carbohydrate 35g (Dietary Fiber 1g); Protein 33g • **% DAILY VALUE:** Vitamin A 16%; Vitamin C 4%; Calcium 58%; Iron 12% • **DIET EXCHANGES:** 2 Starch, 3 Lean Meat, 1 Vegetable, 3 Fat

6 SERVINGS

Sloppy Joe Pizza

prep: **10 min**
bake: **10 min**

1 pound ground beef	1/3 cup purchased black bean dip
3 tablespoons taco seasoning mix	1 cup shredded Monterey Jack cheese with jalapeño peppers (4 ounces)
1 ready-to-serve pizza crust (12 to 14 inches in diameter)	Salsa and guacamole, if desired

1 Heat oven to 425°. Cook beef in 10-inch nonstick skillet over medium heat 8 to 10 minutes, stirring occasionally, until brown; drain. Stir in taco seasoning mix.

2 Place pizza crust on ungreased cookie sheet. Spread evenly with bean dip. Spoon beef over bean layer. Sprinkle with cheese.

3 Bake 8 to 10 minutes or until cheese is melted. Cut into wedges. Serve with salsa and guacamole.

IT'S **a**
snap!

Cook up a storm! To save time during the week, cook on the weekends for the week ahead. Choose a combination of oven, range-top and microwave recipes to ensure sufficient cooking space. After preparing the recipes, label and refrigerate or freeze immediately.

1 SERVING: Calories 565 (Calories from Fat 205); Fat 23g (Saturated 9g); Cholesterol 65mg; Sodium 1030mg; Carbohydrate 73g (Dietary Fiber 3g); Protein 29g • % DAILY VALUE: Vitamin A 12%; Vitamin C 0%; Calcium 18%; Iron 32% • DIET EXCHANGES: 5 Starch, 2 High-Fat Meat

prep: **10 min**
bake: **10 min**

6 SERVINGS

Easy Philly Cheesesteak Pizza

1 can (10 ounces) refrigerated pizza crust dough

2 cups frozen stir-fry bell peppers and onions (from 1-pound bag)

2 tablespoons Dijon-mayonnaise blend

8 ounces thinly sliced cooked deli roast beef

2 cups shredded process American cheese (8 ounces)

1 Heat oven to 425°. Grease 12-inch pizza pan with shortening or butter. Press pizza crust dough in pan. Bake 8 minutes.

2 While crust is baking, spray 10-inch nonstick skillet with cooking spray; heat over medium-high heat. Cook frozen bell pepper mixture in skillet 4 to 5 minutes, stirring frequently, until crisp-tender.

3 Spread Dijon-mayonnaise blend over partially baked crust. Top with roast beef, bell pepper mixture and cheese. Bake 8 to 10 minutes or until crust is golden brown.

IT'S **a**
snap!
Here's a quick take on the cheese-steak sandwich made famous in Philadelphia in the 1930s. Turning it into a hearty pizza means it can serve the whole family super-fast.

1 SERVING: Calories 330 (Calories from Fat160); Fat 18g (Saturated 9g); Cholesterol 50mg; Sodium 490mg; Carbohydrate 28g (Dietary Fiber 2g); Protein 16g • **% DAILY VALUE:** Vitamin A 8%; Vitamin C 14%; Calcium 20%; Iron 12% • **DIET EXCHANGES:** 2 Starch, 1 1/2 High-Fat Meat, 1 Fat

Easy Philly Cheesesteak Pizza

Ranchero Beef Pizza

**1 ready-to-serve pizza crust
(12 to 14 inches in diameter)**

**2 cups shredded smoked or
regular Cheddar cheese
(8 ounces)**

**2 cups shredded or sliced
cooked barbecued beef**

**4 slices red onion,
separated into rings**

1 Heat oven to 400°.

2 Place pizza crust on ungreased cookie sheet. Sprinkle with 1 cup of the cheese. Top with beef and onion. Sprinkle with remaining cup of cheese.

3 Bake 15 minutes, or until hot.

**COME
&eat!**
**Serve this pizza
with a refreshing
cucumber and
tomato salad, and
for a quick dessert,
orange or lemon
sherbet.**

1 SERVING: Calories 535 (Calories from Fat 235); Fat 26g (Saturated 12g); Cholesterol 70mg; Sodium 710mg; Carbohydrate 52g (Dietary Fiber 2g); Protein 25g • **% DAILY VALUE:** Vitamin A 10%; Vitamin C 0%; Calcium 22%; Iron 24% • **DIET EXCHANGES:** 3 Starch, 2 High-Fat Meat, 1 Vegetable, 2 1/2 Fat

8 SERVINGS

Tex-Mex Pizza

prep: **10 min**
bake: **10 min**

1/4 pound bulk chorizo sausage

**1 ready-to-serve pizza crust
(12 to 14 inches in diameter)**

**1 1/2 cups shredded Monterey
Jack cheese (6 ounces)**

1 jar (8 ounces) salsa (1 cup)

**1 small bell pepper, chopped
(1/2 cup)**

**1/2 cup canned black beans,
rinsed and drained, or
1 can (2 1/4 ounces) sliced
ripe olives, drained**

IT'S **a**
snap!
**If you prefer a
milder version of
this spicy pizza,
use sweet Italian
sausage instead.**

1 Heat oven to 450°. Cook sausage in 8-inch skillet over medium-high heat, stirring occasionally, until no longer pink; drain.

2 Place pizza crust on ungreased cookie sheet. Sprinkle with 1 cup of the cheese. Top with salsa, sausage, bell pepper and beans. Sprinkle with remaining 1/2 cup cheese.

3 Bake 8 to 10 minutes or until pizza is hot and cheese is melted.

1 SERVING: Calories 425 (Calories from Fat 145); Fat 16g (Saturated 7g); Cholesterol 30mg; Sodium 850mg; Carbohydrate 56g (Dietary Fiber 3g); Protein 17g • **% DAILY VALUE:** Vitamin A 8%; Vitamin C 12%; Calcium 18%; Iron 22% • **DIET EXCHANGES:** 3 Starch, 1/2 High-Fat Meat, 2 Vegetable, 2 Fat

prep: **8 min**
cook: **5 min**
broil: **2 min**

IT'S **a**
snap!
To make the most of
your preparation
time, organize your
recipes in advance,
reading through
them and setting out
everything you'll
need. As you use
each ingredient, set
it aside. Then put
everything away
after you're done.

6 SERVINGS

Pizza Alfredo

1/2 pound bulk Italian sausage

1 large onion, chopped (1 cup)

1 package (8 ounces) sliced mushrooms (3 cups)

1 container (10 ounces) refrigerated Alfredo sauce

1 loaf French bread (12 inches long), cut horizontally in half

1 cup shredded mozzarella cheese (4 ounces)

1 Cook sausage, onion and mushrooms in 10-inch skillet over medium-high heat, stirring occasionally, until sausage is no longer pink; drain. Stir in Alfredo sauce.

2 Place bread halves, cut sides up, on ungreased cookie sheet. Spread with sausage mixture. Sprinkle with cheese.

3 Set oven control to broil. Broil with tops 5 inches from heat 1 to 2 minutes or until pizzas are hot and cheese begins to brown.

1 SERVING: Calories 385 (Calories from Fat 245); Fat 27g (Saturated 15g); Cholesterol 80mg; Sodium 690mg; Carbohydrate 19g (Dietary Fiber 2g); Protein 18g • **% DAILY VALUE:** Vitamin A 14%; Vitamin C 2%; Calcium 30%; Iron 8% • **DIET EXCHANGES:** 1 Starch, 2 High-Fat Meat, 1 Vegetable, 2 Fat

prep: **10 min**
bake: **10 min**

6 SERVINGS

Kielbasa and Sauerkraut Pizza

1 package (16 ounces) ready-to-serve original Italian pizza crust (12 inches in diameter)

2 tablespoons Dijon-mayonnaise blend

1 can (8 ounces) sauerkraut, drained

1/4 pound fully cooked kielbasa sausage, cut lengthwise in half, then cut crosswise into slices

4 medium green onions, sliced (1/4 cup)

1 cup shredded Swiss cheese (4 ounces)

1 Heat oven to 425°.

2 Place pizza crust on ungreased cookie sheet. Spread with Dijon-mayonnaise blend. Top with sauerkraut, sausage, onions and cheese.

3 Bake about 10 minutes or until thoroughly heated and cheese is melted.

COME
&eat!

Take me out to the ballgame! Make sure to have some ballpark mustard on hand to serve with this flavorful, fun pizza.

1 SERVING: Calories 400 (Calories from Fat 135); Fat 15g (Saturated 6g); Cholesterol 30mg; Sodium 940mg; Carbohydrate 54g (Dietary Fiber 3g); Protein 15g • % DAILY VALUE: Vitamin A 2%; Vitamin C 6%; Calcium 20%; Iron 22% • DIET EXCHANGES: 3 Starch, 1/2 High-Fat Meat, 1 Vegetable, 2 Fat

prep: **10 min**
bake: **10 min**

6 SERVINGS

Antipasto French Bread Pizzas

I loaf French bread (12 inches long), cut horizontally in half

1/4 cup basil pesto

10 slices salami (3 1/2 inches in diameter)

2 or 3 roma (plum) tomatoes, thinly sliced

I small green bell pepper, cut into thin rings

2 medium green onions, chopped (2 tablespoons)

1/4 cup sliced ripe olives

6 slices (I 1/2 ounces each) provolone cheese

1 Heat oven to 425°.

2 Place bread halves, cut sides up, on ungreased cookie sheet. Spread with pesto. Top with salami, tomatoes, bell pepper, onions, olives and cheese.

3 Bake 8 to 10 minutes or until cheese is melted.

IT'S **a**
snap!

For some quick substitutions, use pepperoni slices in place of the salami and sliced or shredded mozzarella cheese for the provolone. If you don't have roma tomatoes, thinly slice regular tomatoes.

1 SERVING: Calories 415 (Calories from Fat 225); Fat 25g (Saturated 11g); Cholesterol 50mg; Sodium 1120mg; Carbohydrate 29g (Dietary Fiber 2g); Protein 20g • **% DAILY VALUE:** Vitamin A 14%; Vitamin C 12%; Calcium 38%; Iron 14% • **DIET EXCHANGES:** 2 Starch, 2 High-Fat Meat, 1 Fat

Antipasto French Bread Pizzas

IT'S **a**
snap!

No time to make
the Basil-Spinach
Pesto? No problem.
Just substitute
1/2 cup basil pesto
available in the
refrigerated section
of the supermarket.

6 SERVINGS

Focaccia Pesto Pizza

**I plain round focaccia bread
or ready-to-serve pizza crust
(12 to 14 inches in diameter)**

Basil-Spinach Pesto (below)

2 cups spaghetti sauce

**I medium green bell pepper,
cut into rings**

**I medium red bell pepper,
cut into rings**

**I cup shredded mozzarella
cheese (4 ounces)**

1 Heat oven to 500°. Place focaccia on ungreased cookie sheet.

2 Make Basil-Spinach Pesto; spread over focaccia. Spread spaghetti sauce over pesto. Top with bell peppers. Sprinkle with cheese.

3 Bake about 10 minutes or until cheese is melted and bubbly.

Basil-Spinach Pesto

1/3 cup plain yogurt

1/3 cup soft bread crumbs

**3 tablespoons grated Parmesan
cheese**

I tablespoon olive or vegetable oil

2 cloves garlic, finely chopped

**2 cups lightly packed fresh
basil leaves**

**I cup lightly packed chopped
spinach leaves**

Place all ingredients in food processor in order listed. Cover and process about 2 minutes, stopping occasionally to scrape side of bowl, until mixture is a thick paste.

1 SERVING: Calories 490 (Calories from Fat 170); Fat 19g (Saturated 5g); Cholesterol 15mg; Sodium 1410mg; Carbohydrate 69g (Dietary Fiber 5g); Protein 16g • **% DAILY VALUE:** Vitamin A 32%; Vitamin C 60%; Calcium 26%; Iron 26% • **DIET EXCHANGES:** 4 Starch, 2 Vegetable, 3 Fat

4 Breakfast for Dinner

◐ = *super express* ready in 20 minutes or less

1-Step Recipes

Easy Breakfasts for Dinner "Breakfasts for dinner" can be simple and hearty, all at the same time. Check out these easy and fun ideas!

1 Muffin Meal

Top toasted English muffin halves with cooked sausage patties and scrambled eggs.

2 Egg in a Frame

Cut circle out of center of bread slice and place bread "frame" in heated skillet; break egg into cutout and cook over low heat 5 to 7 minutes.

3 Peanut Butter–Banana Pancakes

Stir mashed banana into pancake batter; serve pancakes with peanut butter, honey or your favorite jelly.

4 Italian Pancake Dunkers

Stir chopped pepperoni, chopped green bell pepper and Italian seasoning into pancake batter; dip cooked pancakes into warmed pasta sauce.

5 Ham and Swiss Waffles

Stir chopped cooked ham, and shredded Swiss cheese into waffle batter; serve cooked waffles with Alfredo sauce.

6 Egg Tacos

Fill taco shells with cooked scrambled eggs, Cheddar cheese, shredded lettuce, sliced avocado and salsa.

7 Mexican Pancake Roll-Ups

Roll a pancake around a cooked sausage link; serve with warmed salsa.

8 Egg Salad Pockets

Fill pita breads with chopped, hard-boiled eggs, a spoonful of mayonnaise, and sprinkle with shredded cheese.

9 Top-Your-Own Eggs

Sprinkle scrambled eggs with chopped green onions, green chilies and tomatoes and shredded cheese.

10 "Waffle-icious"

Spread waffles or pancakes with American cheese spread and top with crumbled cooked bacon or bacon flavor bits.

4 SERVINGS

Home-Style Scrambled Eggs

6 eggs

3/4 teaspoon salt

3 tablespoons water

1/4 cup butter or margarine

1 cup refrigerated diced
potatoes with onions or
frozen hash brown potatoes

1 small zucchini, chopped
(1 cup)

1 medium tomato, seeded and
chopped (3/4 cup)

1 Beat eggs, salt and water with fork or wire whisk until
well mixed.

2 Melt butter in 10-inch skillet over medium heat. Cook
potatoes, zucchini and tomato in butter, stirring occasionally,
until hot.

3 Pour egg mixture over vegetable mixture. As mixture begins
to set at bottom and side, gently lift cooked portions with
spatula so that thin, uncooked portion can flow to bottom.
Avoid constant stirring. Cook 3 to 5 minutes or until eggs
are thickened throughout but still moist.

C O M E
&eat!

Potatoes and eggs
are natural partners
for quick and easy
cooking. Starting
with refrigerated or
frozen potatoes
gives you a head
start on dinner.
Add a garden salad,
toast and milk for a
quick yet substantial
"breakfast for dinner."

1 SERVING: Calories 235 (Calories from Fat 150); Fat 17g (Saturated 8g); Cholesterol 340mg;
Sodium 600mg; Carbohydrate 11g (Dietary Fiber 1g); Protein 11g • % DAILY VALUE:
Vitamin A 24%; Vitamin C 8%; Calcium 4%; Iron 6% • **DIET EXCHANGES:** 1/2 Starch,
1 Medium-Fat Meat, 1 Vegetable, 2 Fat

prep: **10 min**
cook: **10 min**

5 SERVINGS

Potato, Bacon and Egg Scramble

1 pound small red potatoes (6 or 7), cubed

6 eggs

1/3 cup milk

1/4 teaspoon salt

1/8 teaspoon pepper

2 tablespoons butter or margarine

4 medium green onions, sliced (1/4 cup)

5 slices bacon, crisply cooked and crumbled

IT'S **a**
snap!
If you don't have time to cube potatoes, use purchased refrigerated cubed potatoes instead.

1 Heat 1 inch water to boiling in 2-quart saucepan. Add potatoes. Cover and heat to boiling; reduce heat to medium-low. Cover and cook 6 to 8 minutes or until potatoes are tender; drain. Beat eggs, milk, salt and pepper with fork or wire whisk until well mixed; set aside.

2 Melt butter in 10-inch skillet over medium-high heat. Cook potatoes in butter 3 to 5 minutes, turning potatoes occasionally, until light brown. Stir in onions. Cook 1 minute, stirring constantly.

3 Pour egg mixture into skillet. As mixture begins to set at bottom and side, gently lift cooked portions with spatula so that thin, uncooked portion can flow to bottom. Avoid constant stirring. Cook 3 to 4 minutes or until eggs are thickened throughout but still moist. Sprinkle with bacon.

1 SERVING: Calories 255 (Calories from Fat 135); Fat 15g (Saturated 6g); Cholesterol 275mg; Sodium 340mg; Carbohydrate 20g (Dietary Fiber 2g); Protein 12g • **% DAILY VALUE:** Vitamin A 12%; Vitamin C 10%; Calcium 6%; Iron 10% • **DIET EXCHANGES:** 1 Starch, 1 High-Fat Meat, 1 Vegetable, 1 Fat

Potato, Bacon and Egg Scramble

Pantry Recipes

If you have a well-stocked pantry (see pages 6–7), you'll be able to make this recipe anytime, even when there's no time to shop.

Suppertime Scrambled Eggs

8 eggs

Salsa, sour cream and green onions

Spray 10-inch skillet with cooking spray; heat skillet over medium heat. Beat **eggs** and pour into skillet. As eggs begin to set at bottom and side, gently lift cooked portions with spatula so that thin, uncooked portion can flow to bottom. Cook 3 to 4 minutes or until eggs are thickened throughout but still moist. Top with **salsa, sour cream** and **green onions.** MAKES 4 SERVINGS IN 10 MINUTES

serve it 3 ways!

1 Sandwich
Fill pita breads or tortillas with egg mixture and wrap.

2 Light Meal
Heat oven to 350°. Cut flour tortillas into thin strips; place on ungreased cookie sheet. Bake about 8 minutes or until lightly browned. Serve eggs over tortilla strips.

3 Main Course
Cook refrigerated diced potatoes with onions or frozen hash brown potatoes, 1 small zucchini, chopped, and 1 small tomato, seeded and chopped, with the eggs.

Smoked Salmon and Egg Wraps

prep: **10 min**
cook: **5 min**
bake: **10 min**

6 eggs

1 tablespoon milk or water

1/4 teaspoon seasoned salt

2 tablespoons chopped fresh or 1 teaspoon dried dill weed

6 flour tortillas (8 inches in diameter)

1 package (4 1/2 ounces) smoked salmon, broken into pieces

1/2 cup finely chopped red onion

3/4 cup shredded Havarti cheese (3 ounces)

Dill weed sprigs, if desired

1 Heat oven to 350°. Line jelly roll pan, 15 1/2 × 10 1/2 × 1 inch, with aluminum foil. Beat eggs, milk and seasoned salt with fork or wire whisk until well mixed.

2 Spray 12-inch nonstick skillet with cooking spray; heat over medium heat. Pour egg mixture into skillet. As eggs begin to set at bottom and side, gently lift cooked portions with spatula so that thin, uncooked portion can flow to bottom. Avoid constant stirring. Cook 3 to 4 minutes or until eggs are thickened throughout but still moist. Stir in chopped dill weed.

3 Spoon 2 to 3 tablespoons eggs down center of each tortilla. Top with salmon, onion and cheese. Fold opposite sides of each tortilla over filling (sides will not meet in center). Roll up tortilla, beginning at one of the open ends. Place wraps, seam sides down, in pan. Cover with foil. Bake about 10 minutes or until cheese is melted. Garnish with dill weed sprigs.

IT'S **a**
snap!

Use flavored tortillas to add extra color and flavor. Then, to make egg wraps extra special for friends or family, wrap each one in a pretty napkin or piece of brightly colored food-safe paper.

1 SERVING: Calories 290 (Calories from Fat 125); Fat 14g (Saturated 6g); Cholesterol 230mg; Sodium 620mg; Carbohydrate 26g (Dietary Fiber 2g); Protein 17g • **% DAILY VALUE:** Vitamin A 8%; Vitamin C 0%; Calcium 16%; Iron 12% • **DIET EXCHANGES:** 2 Starch, 2 Medium-Fat Meat

4 SERVINGS

Country Eggs in Tortilla Cups

4 flour tortillas (6 inches in diameter)

2 cups frozen Southern-style hash brown potatoes

1/4 cup chopped green bell pepper

3 eggs

1/4 cup milk

1/4 teaspoon salt

3/4 cup shredded Cheddar cheese (3 ounces)

1/4 cup sour cream

Salsa, if desired

1 Heat oven to 400°. Turn four 6-ounce custard cups upside down onto cookie sheet. Spray both sides of each tortilla lightly with cooking spray. Place tortilla over each cup, gently pressing edges toward cup. Bake 8 to 10 minutes or until light golden brown. Remove tortillas from cups; place upright on serving plates.

2 Spray 8- or 10-inch nonstick skillet with cooking spray; heat over medium heat. Cook potatoes and bell pepper in skillet about 5 minutes, stirring occasionally, until potatoes are light brown. Beat eggs, milk and salt with fork or wire whisk until well mixed; stir into potatoes. Cook about 3 minutes, stirring occasionally, until eggs are almost set.

3 Spoon one-fourth of the egg mixture into each tortilla cup. Top with cheese and sour cream. Serve immediately with salsa.

1 SERVING: Calories 255 (Calories from Fat 70); Fat 8g (Saturated 4g); Cholesterol 20mg; Sodium 720mg; Carbohydrate 36g (Dietary Fiber 3g); Protein 13g • **% DAILY VALUE:** Vitamin A 10%; Vitamin C 12%; Calcium 14%; Iron 12% • **DIET EXCHANGES:** 2 Starch, 1 Medium-Fat Meat, 1 Vegetable

Country Eggs in Tortilla Cups

prep: **10 min**
cook: **8 min**

4 SERVINGS

Pepper and Egg Fajitas

6 eggs

1/3 cup milk

1 tablespoon butter or
margarine

1 medium bell pepper,
cut into 1/4-inch strips

1 medium onion, thinly sliced

1 tablespoon fajita seasoning
mix (from 1.27-ounce envelope)

4 flour tortillas (8 to 10 inches
in diameter)

1/2 cup salsa

1 Beat eggs and milk with fork or wire whisk until well mixed;
set aside. Melt butter in 12-inch skillet over medium-high
heat. Cook bell pepper, onion and seasoning mix in butter
about 4 minutes, stirring occasionally, until vegetables are
tender. Remove vegetables from skillet; keep warm.

2 Reduce heat to medium; pour egg mixture into skillet. As
mixture begins to set at bottom and side, gently lift cooked
portions with spatula so that thin, uncooked portion can
flow to bottom. Avoid constant stirring. Cook 3 to 4 minutes or until eggs are thickened throughout but still moist.

3 While eggs are cooking, microwave 1 tortilla shell on
microwavable plate on High 20 to 30 seconds. Repeat
with remaining tortillas. Spoon one-fourth of the egg mixture onto center of each tortilla; top with vegetables. Fold
right and left sides of tortilla over mixture, overlapping.
Top each fajita with 2 tablespoons salsa.

1 SERVING: Calories 310 (Calories from Fat 125); Fat 14g (Saturated 5g); Cholesterol 320mg;
Sodium 580mg; Carbohydrate 34g (Dietary Fiber 3g); Protein 15g • **% DAILY VALUE:**
Vitamin A 22%; Vitamin C 28%; Calcium 14%; Iron 16% • **DIET EXCHANGES:** 2 Starch,
1 High-Fat Meat, 1 Vegetable, 1/2 Fat

4 SERVINGS

Salmon and Cream Cheese Omelet

4 teaspoons butter or margarine

8 eggs, beaten

1/2 cup soft cream cheese with chives and onion

1 cup flaked smoked salmon

Chopped fresh chives, if desired

COME

&eat!

Omelets make great dinner entrées, accompanied by biscuits and a salad or fresh fruit

1 Heat 2 teaspoons of the butter in 8-inch omelet pan or skillet over medium-high heat until butter is hot and sizzling.

2 Pour half of the beaten eggs (about 1 cup) into pan. As eggs begin to set at bottom and side, gently lift cooked portions with spatula so that thin, uncooked portion can flow to bottom. Avoid constant stirring. Cook 3 to 4 minutes or until eggs are thickened throughout but still moist.

3 Spoon 1/4 cup of the cream cheese in dollops evenly over omelet; sprinkle with 1/2 cup of the salmon. Tilt skillet and slip pancake turner under omelet to loosen. Remove from heat. Fold omelet in half; let stand 2 minutes. Repeat with remaining ingredients to make second omelet. Cut each omelet crosswise in half to serve; sprinkle with chives.

1 SERVING: Calories 290 (Calories from Fat 200); Fat 22g (Saturated 10g); Cholesterol 460mg; Sodium 470mg; Carbohydrate 2g (Dietary Fiber 0g); Protein 20g • **% DAILY VALUE:** Vitamin A 20%; Vitamin C 0%; Calcium 6%; Iron 10% • **DIET EXCHANGES:** 3 High-Fat Meat

IT'S **a**
snap!
Purchase prewashed
and bagged spinach
to speed prepara-
tion for this tasty
breakfast, lunch or
dinner dish.

4 SERVINGS

Fresh Spinach and New Potato Frittata

6 eggs

2 tablespoons milk

1/4 teaspoon dried marjoram leaves

1/4 teaspoon salt

2 tablespoons butter or margarine

1 pound small red potatoes (6 or 7), thinly sliced (2 cups)

1/4 teaspoon salt

1 cup firmly packed bite-size pieces spinach

1/4 cup oil-packed sun-dried tomatoes, drained and sliced

3 medium green onions, cut into 1/4-inch pieces

1/2 cup shredded Swiss cheese (2 ounces)

1 Beat eggs, milk, marjoram and 1/4 teaspoon salt with fork or wire whisk until well mixed; set aside. Melt butter in 10-inch nonstick skillet over medium heat. Cover and cook potatoes and 1/4 teaspoon salt in butter about 8 minutes, stirring occasionally, until potatoes are tender.

2 Stir in spinach, tomatoes and onions. Cook, stirring occasionally, just until spinach is wilted; reduce heat to low.

3 Carefully pour egg mixture over potato mixture. Cover and cook about 6 minutes or just until top is set. Sprinkle with cheese. Cover and cook about 1 minute or until cheese is melted.

1 SERVING: Calories 330 (Calories from Fat 170); Fat 19g (Saturated 9g); Cholesterol 345mg; Sodium 500mg; Carbohydrate 27g (Dietary Fiber 3g); Protein 14g • **% DAILY VALUE:** Vitamin A 32%; Vitamin C 18%; Calcium 20%; Iron 14% • **DIET EXCHANGES:** 1 1/2 Starch, 1 1/2 High-Fat Meat, 1 Vegetable, 1 Fat

Fresh Spinach and New Potato Frittata

6 SERVINGS

Vegetables and Cheese Frittata

8 eggs

1/2 teaspoon salt

1/8 teaspoon pepper

1/2 cup shredded Swiss cheese (2 ounces)

2 tablespoons butter or margarine

2 medium bell peppers, chopped (2 cups)

1 medium onion, chopped (1/2 cup)

1 Beat eggs, salt and pepper in medium bowl with fork or wire whisk until well mixed. Stir in cheese; set aside.

2 Melt butter in ovenproof 10-inch nonstick skillet over medium heat. Cook bell peppers and onion in butter, stirring occasionally, until onion is tender. Pour egg mixture over pepper mixture. Cover and cook over medium-low heat 8 to 10 minutes or until eggs are set and light brown on bottom.

3 Set oven control to broil. Broil frittata with top 4 to 6 inches from heat about 2 minutes or until golden brown. Cut into wedges.

IT'S **a** snap!

Make this a very veggie dinner by tossing in any fresh or frozen (thawed) vegetables you have on hand. Just chop and cook with the peppers in step 2.

1 SERVING: Calories 190 (Calories from Fat 125); Fat 14g (Saturated 6g); Cholesterol 300mg; Sodium 330mg; Carbohydrate 3g (Dietary Fiber 1g); Protein 12g • **% DAILY VALUE:** Vitamin A 14%; Vitamin C 30%; Calcium 12%; Iron 6% • **DIET EXCHANGES:** 1 1/2 High-Fat Meat, 1 Vegetable

10 SERVINGS (3 FRENCH TOAST STICKS EACH)

prep: **10 min**
cook: **10 min**

Cinnamon French Toast Sticks with Spicy Cider Syrup

Spicy Cider Syrup (below)

1/2 cup all-purpose flour

1 1/4 cups milk

2 teaspoons ground cinnamon

1 teaspoon vanilla

2 eggs

10 slices sandwich bread, cut into thirds

1 Make Spicy Cider Syrup; keep warm. Spray griddle or skillet with cooking spray; heat griddle to 375° or heat skillet over medium-high heat.

2 Beat remaining ingredients except bread with fork until smooth. Dip breadsticks into batter; drain excess batter back into bowl.

3 Place breadsticks on griddle. Cook about 4 minutes on each side or until golden brown. Serve with syrup.

Spicy Cider Syrup

1 cup sugar

3 tablespoons all-purpose flour

1/4 teaspoon ground cinnamon

1/4 teaspoon ground nutmeg

2 cups apple cider

2 tablespoons lemon juice

1/4 cup butter or margarine

Mix sugar, flour, cinnamon and nutmeg in 2-quart saucepan. Stir in cider and lemon juice. Cook over medium heat, stirring constantly, until mixture thickens and boils. Boil and stir 1 minute; remove from heat. Stir in butter.

1 SERVING: Calories 265 (Calories from Fat 65); Fat 7g (Saturated 4g); Cholesterol 60mg; Sodium 200mg; Carbohydrate 46g (Dietary Fiber 1g); Protein 5g • **% DAILY VALUE:** Vitamin A 6%; Vitamin C 0%; Calcium 8%; Iron 8% • **DIET EXCHANGES:** 2 Starch, 1 Fruit, 1 Fat

COME **&eat!**

The kids will love these! For a completely easy kid-friendly dinner, serve with grapes, watermelon or cantaloupe, baby carrots and broccoli tops. For dessert, serve Licorice Wands (page 412).

prep: **12 min**
cook: **6 min**

COME
&eat!

Serve with green
beans, peas or a
green salad and, for
dessert, fresh fruit.

6 SERVINGS

Stuffed French Toast

12 slices French bread,
1/2 inch thick

6 tablespoons reduced-fat
cream cheese (Neufchâtel)

1/4 cup preserves or jam
(any flavor)

3 eggs

1/2 cup fat-free (skim) milk

2 tablespoons granulated sugar

Powdered sugar, if desired

Maple-flavored syrup, if desired

1 Spread one side of 6 bread slices with 1 tablespoon of the cream cheese. Spread one side of remaining bread slices with 2 teaspoons of the preserves. Make 6 cream-cheese-and-preserve sandwiches.

2 Beat eggs, milk and granulated sugar with fork or wire whisk until well mixed; pour into shallow bowl.

3 Spray griddle or skillet with cooking spray; heat griddle to 325° or heat skillet over medium-low heat. Dip each side of sandwich into egg mixture. Cook sandwiches 2 to 3 minutes on each side or until golden brown. Transfer to plate; dust with powdered sugar. Serve with syrup.

1 SERVING: Calories 270 (Calories from Fat 70); Fat 8g (Saturated 3g); Cholesterol 120mg; Sodium 400mg; Carbohydrate 40g (Dietary Fiber 1g); Protein 10g • % DAILY VALUE: Vitamin A 6%; Vitamin C 0%; Calcium 8%; Iron 10% • **DIET EXCHANGES:** 2 Starch, 1/2 Medium-Fat Meat, 1/2 Fruit, 1 Fat

Stuffed French Toast

IT'S **a**
snap!

**Make yours
eggs-actly right!
Use a wire whisk or
a fork to beat the
eggs, and always
remove scrambled
eggs from the heat a
minute before you
think they're done
because they'll
continue to cook.**

6 SERVINGS

Ham and Swiss Pizza

6 large eggs, beaten

1 package (10 ounces) ready-to-serve thin Italian pizza crust (10 inches in diameter)

1/4 cup mayonnaise or salad dressing

2 tablespoons Dijon mustard

1/2 cup diced fully cooked ham

4 medium green onions, sliced (1/4 cup)

1/4 cup chopped red bell pepper

1 cup shredded Swiss cheese (4 ounces)

1 Heat oven to 400°. Spray 10-inch nonstick skillet with cooking spray; heat over medium heat.

2 Pour eggs into skillet. As eggs begin to set at bottom and side, gently lift cooked portions with spatula so that thin, uncooked portion can flow to bottom. Avoid constant stirring. Cook 4 to 5 minutes or until eggs are thickened throughout but still moist.

3 Place pizza crust on ungreased cookie sheet. Mix mayonnaise and mustard; spread evenly over crust. Top with eggs, ham, onions, bell pepper and cheese. Bake about 10 minutes, or until cheese is melted.

1 SERVING: Calories 370 (Calories from Fat 200); Fat 22g (Saturated 7g); Cholesterol 240mg; Sodium 680mg; Carbohydrate 26g (Dietary Fiber 1g); Protein 18g • **% DAILY VALUE:** Vitamin A 10%; Vitamin C 6%; Calcium 22%; Iron 14% • **DIET EXCHANGES:** 1 1/2 Starch, 2 High-Fat Meat, 1 Fat

Ham and Swiss Pizza

Mom's Best Waffles

prep: **5 min**
bake: **20 min**

2 eggs

2 cups all-purpose or
whole wheat flour

1 3/4 cups milk

1/2 cup vegetable oil

1 tablespoon granulated or
packed brown sugar

4 teaspoons baking powder

1/4 teaspoon salt

COME
&eat!

The wonderful
thing about this
easy recipe is that
you can make it as
simple or as elabo-
rate as you want.
Drizzle waffles with
plain maple syrup, or
serve with fresh fruit
and another topping
such as Spicy Cider
Syrup (page 139)
or Lemon–Cream
Cheese Topping
(page 148).

1 Heat waffle iron; grease with shortening if necessary. Beat
eggs in large bowl with hand beater until fluffy. Beat in
remaining ingredients just until smooth.

2 Pour about 1/2 cup batter from cup or pitcher onto center
of hot waffle iron. (Waffle irons vary in size; check manufacturer's directions for recommended amount of batter.)
Close lid of waffle iron.

3 Bake about 5 minutes or until steaming stops. Carefully
remove waffle. Repeat with remaining batter.

1 SERVING: Calories 385 (Calories from Fat 200); Fat 22g (Saturated 4g); Cholesterol 75mg; Sodium 480mg; Carbohydrate 38g (Dietary Fiber 1g); Protein 9g • **% DAILY VALUE:** Vitamin A 4%; Vitamin C 0%; Calcium 28%; Iron 14% • **DIET EXCHANGES:** 2 Starch, 1/2 Milk, 4 Fat

Cheesy Veggie Waffles

prep: **8 min**
cook: **12 min**

1 envelope (1.8 ounces) white sauce mix

2 cups milk

1 1/2 cups shredded sharp Cheddar cheese (6 ounces)

1 bag (1 pound) frozen broccoli, green beans, pearl onions and red peppers (or other combination)

1/2 teaspoon garlic salt

12 frozen multigrain waffles

1/3 cup slivered almonds, toasted*

1 Make white sauce mix as directed on envelope, using 2 cups milk; remove from heat. Stir in cheese until melted; cover to keep warm.

2 While sauce is heating, cook frozen vegetables as directed on package; drain. Sprinkle with garlic salt.

3 Prepare waffles as directed on package. For each serving, place 2 waffles on each plate. Top with vegetables; spoon cheese sauce over vegetables. Sprinkle with almonds.

✳ **HOW TO toast nuts:** Cook nuts in ungreased heavy skillet over medium-low heat 5 to 7 minutes, stirring frequently until browning begins, then stirring constantly until golden brown. Or bake uncovered in ungreased shallow pan in 350° oven about 10 minutes, stirring occasionally, until golden brown.

IT'S **a**
snap!
It's easy to toast extra almonds. Keep them on hand in the freezer and use whenever you need them for salads, casseroles or other dishes.

1 SERVING: Calories 435 (Calories from Fat 205); Fat 23g (Saturated 9g); Cholesterol 60mg; Sodium 1190mg; Carbohydrate 42g (Dietary Fiber 4g); Protein 19g • **% DAILY VALUE:** Vitamin A 52%; Vitamin C 22%; Calcium 40%; Iron 16% • **DIET EXCHANGES:** 2 Starch, 1 High-Fat Meat, 2 Vegetable, 3 Fat

10 SERVINGS

Tostada Waffles

2 cups Original Bisquick

1 1/3 cups milk

2 tablespoons vegetable oil

1 egg

1 can (4 ounces) diced green chilies, drained

1 teaspoon chili powder

1 pound ground beef

1 envelope (1 1/4 ounces) taco seasoning mix

6 cups shredded lettuce

1 cup shredded Cheddar cheese (4 ounces)

2 medium tomatoes, chopped (1 1/2 cups)

1 1/2 cups sour cream

2 medium green onions, sliced (2 tablespoons)

IT'S **a**
snap!
For an easy do-ahead, prepare waffles, wrap and refrigerate. When ready to serve, toast the waffles and serve with beef mixture.

1 Heat waffle iron; grease with shortening if necessary. Stir Bisquick, milk, oil and egg in large bowl until blended. Stir in chilies and chili powder.

2 Pour batter from cup or pitcher onto center of hot waffle iron. (Waffle irons vary in size; check manufacturer's directions for recommended amount of batter.) Close lid of waffle iron. Bake until steaming stops and waffle is golden brown. Carefully remove waffle.

3 Cook beef as directed on envelope of taco seasoning mix. Top waffles with beef and remaining ingredients.

1 SERVING: Calories 370 (Calories from Fat 215); Fat 24g (Saturated 11g); Cholesterol 85mg; Sodium 660mg; Carbohydrate 23g (Dietary Fiber 1g); Protein 16g • **% DAILY VALUE:** Vitamin A 16%; Vitamin C 12%; Calcium 20%; Iron 12% • **DIET EXCHANGES:** 1 Starch, 1 High-Fat Meat, 2 Vegetable, 3 Fat

Tostada Waffles

COME
&eat!

To round out a quick
and easy dinner,
serve with blueberries
or other fresh fruit
and a green veg-
etable. For dessert,
Strawberry-Rhubarb
Frozen-Yogurt
Parfaits (page 397)
would be very
refreshing!

8 SERVINGS (2 PANCAKES AND 2 TEASPOONS
TOPPING EACH)

Ginger Pancakes with Lemon–Cream Cheese Topping

**Lemon–Cream Cheese Topping
(below)**

I egg

I 1/3 cups all-purpose flour

I 1/4 cups fat-free (skim) milk

1/4 cup molasses

2 tablespoons vegetable oil

I teaspoon baking powder

I teaspoon ground cinnamon

1/2 teaspoon ground ginger

1/4 teaspoon baking soda

1/4 teaspoon salt

1 Make Lemon–Cream Cheese Topping. Beat egg in medium
bowl with hand beater until fluffy. Beat in remaining ingredients just until smooth.

2 Spray griddle or skillet with cooking spray; heat griddle to
375° or heat skillet over medium heat. For each pancake,
pour slightly less than 1/4 cup batter from cup or pitcher
onto hot griddle.

3 Cook pancakes until puffed. Turn; cook other sides until
dry around edges. Serve with topping.

Lemon–Cream Cheese Topping

**3 ounces reduced-fat cream cheese
(Neufchâtel), softened**

I tablespoon powdered sugar

1/2 teaspoon grated lemon peel

I 1/2 teaspoons lemon juice

Beat all ingredients with electric mixer on medium speed
until fluffy.

1 SERVING: Calories 180 (Calories from Fat 55); Fat 6g (Saturated 2g); Cholesterol 30mg;
Sodium 250mg; Carbohydrate 27g (Dietary Fiber 1g); Protein 5g • **% DAILY VALUE:**
Vitamin A 4%; Vitamin C 0%; Calcium 12%; Iron 8% • **DIET EXCHANGES:** 2 Starch,
1/2 Fat

4 SERVINGS

Spicy Pumpkin Pancakes with Maple-Pecan Syrup

super express

prep: **10** min
cook: **10** min

Maple-Pecan Syrup (below)

2 1/3 cups Original Bisquick

1/3 cup canned pumpkin (not pumpkin pie mix)

1 1/4 cups milk

2 eggs

1/4 cup vegetable oil

2 tablespoons sugar

1/4 teaspoon ground cinnamon

1/4 teaspoon ground nutmeg

1/4 teaspoon ground ginger

1 Make Maple-Pecan Syrup; keep warm. Stir remaining ingredients until blended.

2 Heat griddle to 375° or heat skillet over medium heat; grease with butter if necessary. For each pancake, pour slightly less than 1/4 cup batter from cup or pitcher onto hot griddle.

3 Cook pancakes until edges are dry. Turn; cook other sides until golden brown. Serve with syrup.

Maple-Pecan Syrup

1 cup maple-flavored syrup

1 tablespoon butter or margarine

1/4 cup chopped pecans

Heat syrup and butter until butter is melted; remove from heat. Stir in pecans.

IT'S **a**
snap!

Add sausage to make Easy Maple-Sausage Syrup. Cut 7 to 8 ounces of frozen brown-and-serve sausage links into 1/2-inch pieces. Cook in 2-quart saucepan over medium heat, stirring frequently, until light brown; drain. Stir in 1 cup maple syrup. Heat to boiling, stirring occasionally.

1 SERVING: Calories 180 (Calories from Fat 70); Fat 8g (Saturated 2g); Cholesterol 25mg; Sodium 270mg; Carbohydrate 26g (Dietary Fiber 1g); Protein 2g • % DAILY VALUE: Vitamin A 12%; Vitamin C 0%; Calcium 4%; Iron 4% • DIET EXCHANGES: 1 Starch, 1 Fruit, 1 Fat

Potato Pancakes with Chunky Gingered Applesauce

COME
&eat!

A twist on home-made applesauce, these apples offer a big cinnamon taste. For variety, try adding 1/4 teaspoon ground nutmeg and 1/4 teaspoon ground cloves in addition to the cinnamon and enjoy this easy recipe also as a snack or dessert.

Chunky Gingered Applesauce (below)

1/2 cup Original Bisquick

1/2 cup milk

1 teaspoon salt

3 eggs

3 cups finely shredded uncooked potatoes

1 Make Chunky Gingered Applesauce. Stir Bisquick, milk, salt and eggs in large bowl until blended. Stir in potatoes.

2 Heat griddle to 375° or heat skillet over medium heat; grease with butter if necessary. For each pancake, pour slightly less than 1/4 cup batter from cup or pitcher onto hot griddle, spreading each slightly to make 4-inch pancake.

3 Cook pancakes until dry around edges. Turn; cook other sides until golden brown. Serve with applesauce.

Chunky Gingered Applesauce

4 medium tart cooking apples (Granny Smith, Greening, Rome), coarsely chopped (4 cups)

1/2 cup water

1/4 cup finely chopped crystallized ginger

1 tablespoon packed brown sugar

1/4 teaspoon ground cinnamon

Mix all ingredients except cinnamon in 1-quart saucepan. Cover and heat to boiling; reduce heat. Simmer covered 10 to 15 minutes, stirring occasionally, until apples are tender. Drain off excess liquid. Stir cinnamon into apple-sauce. Serve warm or cold.

1 SERVING: Calories 210 (Calories from Fat 45); Fat 5g (Saturated 1g); Cholesterol 105mg; Sodium 580mg; Carbohydrate 38g (Dietary Fiber 3g); Protein 6g • **% DAILY VALUE:** Vitamin A 4%; Vitamin C 8%; Calcium 6%; Iron 8% • **DIET EXCHANGES:** 1 1/2 Starch, 1 Fruit, 1 Fat

Potato Pancakes with Chunky Gingered Applesauce

4 SERVINGS

Cheesy Pear Oven Pancake

IT'S **a**
snap!
You can substitute
finely chopped
scallions, green
parts only, for the
chives. Rosemary is
also delicious with
pears; just use less
of it (about 2 tea-
spoons fresh or
1/2 teaspoon dried)
because it has a
stronger taste.

1 cup all-purpose flour

1 cup milk

1/4 teaspoon salt

4 eggs

1 tablespoon butter or margarine

2 medium unpeeled pears, thinly sliced (2 cups)

2 tablespoons chopped fresh or 2 teaspoons freeze-dried chives

2 tablespoons sugar

3/4 cup shredded Cheddar cheese (3 ounces)

1 Heat oven to 450°. Grease bottom and sides of rectangular baking dish, 13 × 9 × 2 inches, with shortening. Mix flour, milk, salt and eggs with wire whisk until smooth. Pour into baking dish. Bake 15 to 18 minutes or until puffy and golden brown.

2 While pancake is baking, melt butter in 10-inch nonstick skillet over medium-high heat. Cook pears and chives in butter about 5 minutes, stirring frequently, until pears are slightly softened. Stir in sugar.

3 Spoon pear mixture onto pancake. Sprinkle with cheese. Bake about 1 minute or until cheese is melted.

1 SERVING: Calories 325 (Calories from Fat 110); Fat 12g (Saturated 7g); Cholesterol 330mg; Sodium 330mg; Carbohydrate 46g (Dietary Fiber 3g); Protein 11g • **% DAILY VALUE:** Vitamin A 10%; Vitamin C 4%; Calcium 20%; Iron 10% • **DIET EXCHANGES:** 2 Starch, 1/2 High-Fat Meat, 1 Fruit, 1 Fat

Cheesy Pear Oven Pancake

prep: **15 min**
cook: **5 min**

6 SERVINGS

Oatmeal Pancakes with Strawberry Topping

IT'S **a**
snap!
A quick way to get this dinner on the table in 15 minutes is to start the topping first, heating and stirring it occasionally while measuring the ingredients for and cooking the pancakes.

Strawberry Topping (below)

1/2 cup quick-cooking or old-fashioned oats

1/4 cup all-purpose flour

1/4 cup whole wheat flour

3/4 cup buttermilk

1/4 cup fat-free (skim) milk

1 tablespoon sugar

2 tablespoons vegetable oil

1 teaspoon baking powder

1/2 teaspoon baking soda

1/2 teaspoon salt

1 egg

1 Make Strawberry Topping; keep warm. Beat remaining ingredients with hand beater or wire whisk just until smooth. (For thinner pancakes, stir in additional 2 to 4 tablespoons milk.)

2 Spray griddle or 10-inch nonstick skillet with cooking spray; heat griddle to 375° or heat skillet over medium heat. For each pancake, pour slightly less than 1/4 cup batter from cup or pitcher onto hot griddle.

3 Cook pancakes until puffed and dry around edges. Turn; cook other sides until golden brown. Serve with topping.

Strawberry Topping

1 jar (12 ounces) strawberry preserves

1 cup quartered fresh or frozen (thawed) strawberries

2 tablespoons butter or margarine

Heat all ingredients over low heat, stirring occasionally, until butter is melted and mixture is hot.

1 SERVING: Calories 325 (Calories from Fat 100); Fat 11g (Saturated 4g); Cholesterol 50mg; Sodium 400mg; Carbohydrate 55g (Dietary Fiber 3g); Protein 5g • % DAILY VALUE: Vitamin A 4%; Vitamin C 6%; Calcium 14%; Iron 8% • **DIET EXCHANGES:** 1 1/2 Starch, 2 Fruit, 2 Fat

5 Quick Delicious Chicken and Turkey

● = *super express* ready in 20 minutes or less

1-Step Recipes

All-in-One Seasonings
For easy chicken and turkey with just a quick shake, your chicken or turkey can have plenty of added zip. Stock your shelf with favorite seasoning blends to add great flavor quickly and easily.

1 Curry powder
Sprinkle on bone-in chicken breasts before grilling; serve with yogurt mixed with chopped green onions and cucumbers.

2 Italian seasoning
Sprinkle on boneless chicken breasts before sautéing, then top with pizza sauce and shredded cheese and heat through.

3 Cajun/Creole seasoning
Brush chicken pieces with melted butter then roll in breadcrumbs mixed with seasoning and bake.

4 Lemon pepper or garlic pepper
Sprinkle on boneless chicken breasts or strips and sauté in olive oil with white wine.

5 Herb blend
Rub chicken or turkey breasts with lemon juice and sprinkle with herbs before baking.

6 Mesquite
Sprinkle on poultry before grilling. Serve with baked beans and corn bread.

7 Fajita seasoning
Sprinkle on shredded cooked chicken; stuff tortilla with seasoned chicken, chopped lettuce, salsa and sour cream.

8 Barbecue seasoning
Mix with ground chicken or turkey and form into burgers for grilling.

9 Salt-free herb blends
Heat herb blend with chicken broth to boiling; stir in uncooked egg noodles, chunk chicken and cooked vegetables and simmer until noodles are tender. Serve with oyster crackers.

10 Caribbean jerk
Brush boneless chicken breasts with lime juice and sprinkle with seasoning. Serve chicken with salsa and fresh mango slices.

6 SERVINGS

Parmesan-Dijon Chicken

prep: **5 min**
bake: **25 min**

3/4 cup dry bread crumbs

1/4 cup grated Parmesan cheese

1/4 cup butter or margarine, melted

2 tablespoons Dijon mustard

6 boneless, skinless chicken breast halves (about 1 3/4 pounds)

1 Heat oven to 375°. Grease rectangular pan, 13 × 9 × 2 inches.

2 Mix bread crumbs and cheese in large resealable plastic food-storage bag. Mix butter and mustard in shallow dish. Dip chicken into butter mixture, then shake in bag to coat with crumb mixture. Place in pan.

3 Bake uncovered 20 to 25 minutes, turning once, until juice of chicken is no longer pink when centers of thickest pieces are cut.

IT'S **a**
snap!

Boneless, skinless chicken breasts will bake even faster, in 15 to 20 minutes, if you pound them between sheets of waxed paper with a meat mallet or the bottom of a heavy pan to about 1/4-inch thickness.

1 SERVING: Calories 285 (Calories from Fat 125); Fat 14g (Saturated 7g); Cholesterol 95mg; Sodium 440mg; Carbohydrate 10g (Dietary Fiber 0g); Protein 30g • **% DAILY VALUE:** Vitamin A 6%; Vitamin C 0%; Calcium 10%; Iron 10% • **DIET EXCHANGES:** 1/2 Starch, 4 Lean Meat

prep: **7 min**
cook: **13 min**

4 SERVINGS

Taco Chicken with Corn Salsa

1 envelope (1 1/4 ounces) taco seasoning mix	**1 medium avocado, pitted, peeled and chopped**
4 boneless, skinless chicken breast halves (1 1/4 pounds)	**2 tablespoons finely chopped red onion**
2 tablespoons vegetable oil	**2 tablespoons chopped fresh cilantro**
1 can (11 ounces) whole kernel corn with red and green peppers, drained	**1 tablespoon lime juice**
	1 teaspoon honey

1 Reserve 2 teaspoons of the taco seasoning mix in medium bowl. Coat chicken with remaining taco seasoning mix.

2 Heat oil in 12-inch skillet over medium heat. Cook chicken in oil 3 to 5 minutes, turning once, until brown. Reduce heat to medium-low. Cook about 8 minutes, turning once, until chicken is no longer pink when centers of thickest pieces are cut.

3 While chicken is cooking, add remaining ingredients to reserved taco seasoning mix; toss gently. Serve salsa with chicken.

1 SERVING: Calories 355 (Calories from Fat 155); Fat 17g (Saturated 3g); Cholesterol 75mg; Sodium 600mg; Carbohydrate 26g (Dietary Fiber 5g); Protein 30g • **% DAILY VALUE:** Vitamin A 12%; Vitamin C 12%; Calcium 4%; Iron 14% • **DIET EXCHANGES:** 1 1/2 Starch, 4 Lean Meat, 1/2 Fat

Taco Chicken with Corn Salsa

prep: **5 min**
cook: **20 min**

C O M E
&eat!

For an easy garnish
that adds dramatic
effect, sprinkle with
fresh dill sprigs or
basil leaves and curls
of lemon peel.

6 SERVINGS

Lemon-Dill Chicken

1/4 cup butter or margarine

6 boneless, skinless chicken breast halves (about 1 3/4 pounds)

1/2 cup dry white wine or chicken broth

1 tablespoon chopped fresh or 1/2 teaspoon dried dill weed

1 tablespoon lemon juice

1/4 teaspoon salt

2 medium green onions, sliced (2 tablespoons)

1 Melt butter in 10-inch skillet over medium-high heat. Cook chicken in butter about 6 minutes, turning once, until light brown.

2 Mix wine, dill weed, lemon juice and salt; pour over chicken. Heat to boiling; reduce heat. Cover and simmer 10 to 15 minutes or until juice of chicken is no longer pink when centers of thickest pieces are cut. Remove chicken from skillet; keep warm.

3 Heat wine mixture to boiling. Boil about 3 minutes or until reduced by about half; pour over chicken. Sprinkle with onions.

1 SERVING: Calories 220 (Calories from Fat 110); Fat 12g (Saturated 6g); Cholesterol 95mg; Sodium 220mg; Carbohydrate 1g (Dietary Fiber 0g); Protein 27g • **% DAILY VALUE:** Vitamin A 6%; Vitamin C 0%; Calcium 2%; Iron 6% • **DIET EXCHANGES:** 4 Lean Meat

Mediterranean Skillet Chicken

prep: **5 min**
cook: **20 min**

2 tablespoons olive or vegetable oil

4 boneless, skinless chicken breast halves (about 1 1/4 pounds)

1 can (14 1/2 ounces) Italian-style stewed tomatoes, undrained

1/2 cup sliced ripe olives

1 teaspoon grated lemon peel

1 Heat oil in 12-inch nonstick skillet over medium-high heat. Cook chicken in oil about 6 minutes, turning once, until brown.

2 Stir in remaining ingredients. Heat to boiling; reduce heat. Cover and simmer 15 to 20 minutes or until juice of chicken is no longer pink when centers of thickest pieces are cut.

C O M E
&eat!

Lemon, tomatoes, olives and garlic (in the tomatoes) combine with chicken to create a taste of the Mediterranean in this easy skillet dish. Serve this delicious chicken and sauce with couscous.

1 SERVING: Calories 260 (Calories from Fat 115); Fat 13g (Saturated 2g); Cholesterol 75mg; Sodium 500mg; Carbohydrate 8g (Dietary Fiber 1g); Protein 28g • % DAILY VALUE: Vitamin A 6%; Vitamin C 10%; Calcium 4%; Iron 10% • DIET EXCHANGES: 4 Lean Meat, 2 Vegetable

4 SERVINGS

Basil and Prosciutto Chicken

To make this dish special for friends, make a horizontal cut in each chicken breast half to within 1/2 inch of ends, forming a pocket. Brush inside of each pocket with 1 teaspoon mustard. Fill with prosciutto, cheese and basil. Secure pockets with toothpicks.

1 tablespoon vegetable oil

4 boneless, skinless chicken breast halves (about 1 1/4 pounds)

4 teaspoons Dijon mustard

4 thin slices prosciutto or fully cooked ham

1/4 cup shredded mozzarella cheese (1 ounce)

4 fresh basil leaves

1 Heat oil in 10-inch skillet over medium heat. Cook chicken in oil 6 minutes. Turn chicken; brush with mustard and top with prosciutto. Cook 6 to 8 minutes longer or until juice of chicken is no longer pink when centers of thickest pieces are cut.

2 Place cheese and basil on chicken. Cook about 2 minutes or until cheese is melted.

1 SERVING: Calories 215 (Calories from Fat 90); Fat 10g (Saturated 3g); Cholesterol 80mg; Sodium 380mg; Carbohydrate 1g (Dietary Fiber 0g); Protein 30g • **% DAILY VALUE:** Vitamin A 2%; Vitamin C 0%; Calcium 6%; Iron 6% • **DIET EXCHANGES:** 4 Lean Meat

Basil and Prosciutto Chicken

COME
&eat!

For easy, casual
entertaining, just
add some hot pasta
tossed with melted
butter or olive oil,
great crusty bread
and a salad of field
or baby greens
tossed ever so lightly
with your favorite
Italian dressing.

4 SERVINGS

Chicken Piccata

4 boneless, skinless chicken breast halves (about 1 1/4 pounds)	1 cup dry white wine or chicken broth
1/4 cup all-purpose flour	2 tablespoons lemon juice
1/4 cup butter or margarine	1/2 teaspoon pepper
2 cloves garlic, finely chopped	1 tablespoon capers, if desired

1 Coat chicken with flour, shaking off excess.

2 Melt butter in 12-inch skillet over medium-high heat. Cook chicken and garlic in butter 15 to 20 minutes, turning chicken once, until juice of chicken is no longer pink when centers of thickest pieces are cut.

3 Add wine and lemon juice; sprinkle with pepper. Heat until hot. Sprinkle with capers.

1 SERVING: Calories 300 (Calories from Fat 145); Fat 16g (Saturated 8g); Cholesterol 105mg; Sodium 280mg; Carbohydrate 7g (Dietary Fiber 0g); Protein 28g • **% DAILY VALUE:** Vitamin A 10%; Vitamin C 2%; Calcium 2%; Iron 8% • **DIET EXCHANGES:** 1/2 Starch, 4 Lean Meat, 1 Fat

prep: 5 min
cook: 15 min

4 SERVINGS

Spicy Mexican Skillet Chicken

1 to 2 teaspoons chili powder	1 can (15 ounces) black beans, rinsed and drained
1/4 teaspoon salt	1 cup frozen whole kernel corn
1/4 teaspoon pepper	1/3 cup thick-and-chunky salsa
4 boneless, skinless chicken breast halves (about 1 1/4 pounds)	Chopped fresh cilantro, if desired
1 tablespoon vegetable oil	

1 Mix chili powder, salt and pepper. Sprinkle evenly over both sides of chicken breast halves.

2 Heat oil in 10-inch skillet over medium heat. Cook chicken in oil 8 to 10 minutes, turning once, until juice is no longer pink when centers of thickest pieces are cut.

3 Stir in beans, corn and salsa. Heat to boiling; reduce heat. Cover and simmer 3 to 5 minutes or until vegetables are hot. Sprinkle with cilantro.

IT'S **a**
snap!

Black beans can be hard to find. Sometimes they're shelved with other canned beans, and they're often found with Mexican ingredients. If you can't find them in either location, use kidney or pinto beans instead.

1 SERVING: Calories 340 (Calories from Fat 70); Fat 8g (Saturated 2g); Cholesterol 75mg; Sodium 690mg; Carbohydrate 37g (Dietary Fiber 8g); Protein 37g • % DAILY VALUE: Vitamin A 4%; Vitamin C 6%; Calcium 10%; Iron 22% • DIET EXCHANGES: 2 Starch, 4 Very Lean Meat, 1 Vegetable

4 SERVINGS

Chicken Marsala

4 boneless, skinless chicken breast halves (about 1 1/4 pounds)

1/4 cup all-purpose flour

1/4 teaspoon salt

1/4 teaspoon pepper

2 tablespoons olive or vegetable oil

2 cloves garlic, finely chopped

1/4 cup chopped fresh parsley or 1 tablespoon parsley flakes

1 cup sliced mushrooms (3 ounces)

1/2 cup dry Marsala wine or chicken broth

Hot cooked pasta, if desired

1 Flatten each chicken breast half to 1/4-inch thickness by gently pounding between sheets of plastic wrap or waxed paper. Mix flour, salt and pepper. Coat chicken with flour mixture; shake off excess flour.

2 Heat oil in 10-inch skillet over medium-high heat. Cook garlic and parsley in oil 5 minutes, stirring frequently.

3 Add chicken to skillet. Cook, turning once, until brown. Add mushrooms and wine. Cook 8 to 10 minutes, turning chicken once, until chicken is no longer pink in center. Serve with pasta.

1 SERVING: Calories 255 (Calories from Fat 90); Fat 10g (Saturated 2g); Cholesterol 75mg; Sodium 220mg; Carbohydrate 9g (Dietary Fiber 1g); Protein 28g • **% DAILY VALUE:** Vitamin A 2%; Vitamin C 4%; Calcium 2%; Iron 10% • **DIET EXCHANGES:** 4 Lean Meat, 2 Vegetable

Chicken Marsala

prep: **10 min**
cook: **10 min**

COME
&eat!

Add basmati or
jasmine rice and
purchased egg rolls,
and you've got a
speedy dinner
in minutes.

4 SERVINGS

Thai Chicken with Basil

4 boneless, skinless chicken breast halves (about 1 1/4 pounds)

2 tablespoons vegetable oil

3 cloves garlic, finely chopped

2 red or green jalapeño chilies, seeded and finely chopped

1 tablespoon fish sauce

1 teaspoon sugar

1/4 cup chopped fresh basil leaves

1 tablespoon chopped fresh mint leaves

1 tablespoon chopped unsalted roasted peanuts

1 Cut each chicken breast half into 4 pieces.

2 Heat oil in wok or 12-inch skillet over medium-high heat. Cook garlic and chilies in oil, stirring constantly, until garlic is just golden.

3 Add chicken; stir-fry 8 to 10 minutes or until chicken is no longer pink in center. Stir in fish sauce and sugar. Sprinkle with basil, mint and peanuts.

1 SERVING: Calories 245 (Calories from Fat 110); Fat 12g (Saturated 2g); Cholesterol 75mg; Sodium 110mg; Carbohydrate 7g (Dietary Fiber 1g); Protein 28g • **% DAILY VALUE:** Vitamin A 24%; Vitamin C 38%; Calcium 2%; Iron 8% • **DIET EXCHANGES:** 4 Lean Meat, 1 Vegetable

prep: **10 min**
cook: **15 min**

Skillet Chicken Parmigiana

4 boneless, skinless chicken breast halves (about 1 1/4 pounds)

1/3 cup Italian-style dry bread crumbs

1/3 cup grated Parmesan cheese

1 egg, beaten

2 tablespoons olive or vegetable oil

2 cups spaghetti sauce

1/2 cup shredded mozzarella cheese (2 ounces)

1 Flatten each chicken breast half to 1/4-inch thickness between sheets of plastic wrap or waxed paper.

2 Mix bread crumbs and Parmesan cheese. Dip chicken into egg, then coat with bread crumb mixture.

3 Heat oil in 12-inch skillet over medium heat. Cook chicken in oil 10 to 15 minutes, turning once, until no longer pink in center. Pour spaghetti sauce around chicken in skillet; heat until hot. Sprinkle mozzarella cheese over chicken.

IT'S **a**
snap!

To make this meal even easier, start with purchased breaded chicken breast patties and cook according to package directions, adding the mozzarella cheese for the last minute of cooking just to melt it. Heat spaghetti sauce separately. Either way you choose to make this dish, serve it over hot cooked spaghetti—and enjoy.

1 SERVING: Calories 440 (Calories from Fat 190); Fat 21g (Saturated 6g); Cholesterol 140mg; Sodium 980mg; Carbohydrate 31g (Dietary Fiber 2g); Protein 38g • **% DAILY VALUE:** Vitamin A 14%; Vitamin C 14%; Calcium 26%; Iron 14% • **DIET EXCHANGES:** 2 Starch, 5 Lean Meat

Broiling or Grilling Poultry

Broiling and direct-heat grilling are quick, low-fat methods for cooking poultry. Follow the guidelines that came with your grill for more information.

1. Marinate poultry if desired.

2. **To Broil:** Set oven control to broil and position oven rack as shown in chart. Brush rack of broiler pan with vegetable oil or spray with cooking spray.

   To Grill: Brush grill rack with vegetable oil or spray with cooking spray. Place grill rack as shown in chart. Start grill. If using charcoal grill, wait until coals are covered with ash (medium heat).

3. **To Broil:** Place poultry on rack in broiler pan and place in oven. (For easy cleanup, line broiler pan with aluminum foil before placing poultry on rack.)

   To Grill: Place poultry on grill. For even cooking, place meatier poultry pieces in center of grill rack, smaller pieces on the edges.

4. Broil or grill, turning pieces frequently with tongs when grilling or turning once when broiling. If desired, brush with desired sauce during last few minutes of cooking. Cook until juices are no longer pink when centers of thickest pieces are cut.

Timetable for Broiling and Grilling Poultry

Poultry Cut	Weight (pounds)	Inches from Heat	Broiling Time (minutes)	Grilling Time (minutes)
Chicken Breast Halves (bone-in)	1	7 to 9	25 to 35	20 to 25
Chicken Breast Halves (boneless)	1	4 to 6	15 to 20	15 to 20
Chicken Wings	3 to 3 1/2	5 to 7	10	12 to 18
Turkey Breast Tenderloins	1 to 1 1/2	6	16 to 24	20 to 30
Turkey Breast Slices	1 to 1 1/2	4	7	8 to 10

Asian Tacos

super
express

prep: **12 min**
cook: **8 min**

1 tablespoon vegetable oil

1 1/4 pounds boneless, skinless chicken breasts, cut into thin strips

1 bag (1 pound) frozen broccoli, red peppers, onions and mushrooms (or other combination), thawed and drained

1/2 cup stir-fry sauce

8 flour tortillas (8 inches in diameter)

Additional stir-fry sauce, if desired

1 Wrap tortillas in foil and warm in oven at 300° while preparing chicken. Heat oil in 10-inch skillet or wok over high heat. Add chicken; stir-fry 3 to 4 minutes or until no longer pink in center. Remove from heat.

2 Cut vegetables into about 1/2-inch pieces; add to chicken in skillet. Stir-fry over medium-high heat about 2 minutes or until vegetables are crisp-tender; drain. Add stir-fry sauce. Cook and stir about 2 minutes or until hot.

3 Spread about 1/2 cup of the chicken mixture over half of each tortilla; fold tortillas in half. (Fold tortillas in half again if desired.) Serve with additional stir-fry sauce.

IT'S **a**

snap!

Heat-resistant, non-stick spoons and turners make it easy to toss food in a skillet or wok for quick-frying and to remove food from the skillet. Look for them wherever a large selection of kitchen tools is sold.

1 SERVING: Calories 505 (Calories from Fat 115); Fat 13g (Saturated 3g); Cholesterol 85mg; Sodium 1810mg; Carbohydrate 60g (Dietary Fiber 5g); Protein 42g • **% DAILY VALUE:** Vitamin A 42%; Vitamin C 54%; Calcium 14%; Iron 28% • **DIET EXCHANGES:** 3 Starch, 3 1/2 Lean Meat, 3 Vegetable

Cornmeal Chicken with Fresh Peach Salsa

Fresh Peach Salsa (below)

1/2 cup yellow cornmeal

1/2 teaspoon salt

1/4 teaspoon pepper

4 boneless, skinless chicken breast halves (about 1 1/4 pounds)

2 tablespoons vegetable oil

1 Make Peach Salsa.

2 Mix cornmeal, salt and pepper. Coat chicken with corn-meal mixture.

3 Heat oil in 10-inch skillet over medium-high heat. Cook chicken in oil 15 to 20 minutes, turning once, until juice is no longer pink when centers of thickest pieces are cut. Serve with salsa.

Fresh Peach Salsa

3 cups chopped peeled peaches

1 large tomato, chopped (1 cup)

1/4 cup chopped fresh cilantro

3 tablespoons vegetable oil

2 tablespoons white vinegar

1/4 teaspoon salt

Mix all ingredients.

1 SERVING: Calories 400 (Calories from Fat 180); Fat 20g (Saturated 3g); Cholesterol 75mg; Sodium 510mg; Carbohydrate 31g (Dietary Fiber 5g); Protein 29g • **% DAILY VALUE:** Vitamin A 12%; Vitamin C 14%; Calcium 2%; Iron 10% • **DIET EXCHANGES:** 1 Starch, 4 Lean Meat, 1 Fruit, 1 Fat

Cornmeal Chicken with Fresh Peach Salsa

prep: **10 min**
cook: **10 min**

C O M E
&eat!

With crisp vegetables
and gooey cheese,
this recipe is a sure
kid-pleaser.

6 SERVINGS

Cheesy Chicken Skillet Dinner

1 teaspoon vegetable oil

1 1/4 pounds boneless, skinless chicken breasts, cut into 3/4-inch pieces

2 large carrots, cut into 1/8-inch slices (2 cups)

1 medium zucchini, cut into 1/8-inch slices (2 cups)

2 tablespoons soy sauce

8 medium green onions, sliced (1/2 cup)

2 cups shredded sharp Cheddar cheese (8 ounces)

1 Heat 12-inch nonstick skillet over medium-high heat. Add oil; rotate skillet to coat bottom. Add chicken; stir-fry 4 to 5 minutes or until no longer pink in center. Remove from skillet.

2 Add carrots and zucchini to skillet; stir-fry 4 to 5 minutes or until crisp-tender. Add chicken and soy sauce; toss until chicken and vegetables are coated with soy sauce.

3 Sprinkle with onions and cheese. Cover skillet until cheese is melted.

1 SERVING: Calories 310 (Calories from Fat 145); Fat 16g (Saturated 8g); Cholesterol 105mg; Sodium 660mg; Carbohydrate 9g (Dietary Fiber 3g); Protein 35g • **% DAILY VALUE:** Vitamin A 100%; Vitamin C 12%; Calcium 24%; Iron 12% • **DIET EXCHANGES:** 5 Lean Meat, 2 Vegetable

Quick 'n Crunchy Potato Chip Chicken

prep: 5 min
cook: 12 min

super express

4 cups sour cream and onion-flavored potato chips, crushed (1 cup)

1 tablespoon parsley flakes

1 egg

2 teaspoons Worcestershire sauce

2 tablespoons vegetable oil

4 boneless, skinless chicken breast halves (about 1 1/4 pounds)

1 Mix crushed potato chips and parsley in shallow bowl. Beat egg and Worcestershire sauce in another shallow bowl.

2 Heat oil in 10-inch nonstick skillet over medium-low heat. Dip chicken into egg mixture, then coat with potato chip mixture.

3 Cook chicken in oil 10 to 12 minutes, turning once, until deep golden brown and juice of chicken is no longer pink when centers of thickest pieces are cut.

IT'S a snap!

Use your favorite flavor of potato chips, such as Cheddar cheese or barbecue, to coat the chicken in this recipe. In fact, why not use the crumbs in the bottom of the bag? A quick-crushing tip: Place potato chips in a tightly sealed plastic bag, and crush with rolling pin.

1 SERVING: Calories 280 (Calories from Fat 135); Fat 15g (Saturated 3g); Cholesterol 125mg; Sodium 510mg; Carbohydrate 8g (Dietary Fiber 1g); Protein 29g • % DAILY VALUE: Vitamin A 2%; Vitamin C 2%; Calcium 2%; Iron 8% • DIET EXCHANGES: 1/2 Starch, 4 Lean Meat, 1/2 Fat

4 SERVINGS

Lemon-Basil Chicken and Vegetables

1 cup uncooked brown rice

1 pound boneless, skinless chicken breasts

1/4 teaspoon coarsely ground pepper

1/4 teaspoon garlic powder

1 medium onion, cut into thin wedges

1 bag (1 pound) frozen baby bean and carrot blend (or other combination)

3/4 cup water

1/2 cup lemon-basil stir-fry sauce

1 teaspoon cornstarch

1 Cook rice as directed on package. While rice is cooking, cut chicken into 2 × 1/4-inch strips. Spray 12-inch nonstick skillet with cooking spray; heat over medium-high heat. Add chicken to skillet; sprinkle with pepper and garlic powder. Stir-fry 4 to 6 minutes or until brown. Add onion; stir-fry 2 minutes.

2 Stir in frozen vegetables and water. Heat to boiling; reduce heat to medium. Cover and cook 5 to 6 minutes, stirring occasionally, until vegetables are tender.

3 Mix stir-fry sauce and cornstarch until smooth; stir into mixture in skillet. Heat to boiling, stirring constantly. Boil and stir 1 minute. Divide rice among bowls. Top with chicken mixture.

1 SERVING: Calories 410 (Calories from Fat 65); Fat 7g (Saturated 2g); Cholesterol 70mg; Sodium 630mg; Carbohydrate 61g (Dietary Fiber 8g); Protein 33g • **% DAILY VALUE:** Vitamin A 100%; Vitamin C 6%; Calcium 10%; Iron 18% • **DIET EXCHANGES:** 3 Starch, 2 1/2 Very Lean Meat, 3 Vegetable

Lemon-Basil Chicken and Vegetables

6 SERVINGS

Alfredo Chicken and Mushrooms

1 tablespoon butter or margarine	1 1/2 cups sliced mushrooms (4 ounces)
1 cup soft whole wheat bread crumbs (about 1 1/2 slices bread)	4 medium green onions, sliced (1/4 cup)
6 boneless, skinless chicken breast halves (about 1 3/4 pounds)	2 tablespoons chopped fresh or 1/2 teaspoon dried basil leaves
1/4 teaspoon pepper	Additional chopped fresh basil, if desired
1 jar (17 ounces) Alfredo pasta sauce	

1   Melt butter in 12-inch nonstick skillet over medium heat. Cook bread crumbs in butter 2 to 3 minutes, stirring frequently, until golden brown. Remove bread crumbs from skillet.

2   Spray skillet with cooking spray; heat over medium heat. Sprinkle chicken with pepper. Cook chicken in skillet 3 to 4 minutes, turning once, until brown. Stir in pasta sauce, mushrooms, onions and 2 tablespoons basil. Cover and cook over medium-low heat about 10 minutes, turning once, until chicken is no longer pink when centers of thickest pieces are cut.

3   Arrange chicken on serving plate. Spoon sauce over top. Sprinkle with bread crumbs. Garnish with additional basil.

1 SERVING: Calories 470 (Calories from Fat 295); Fat 33g (Saturated 19g); Cholesterol 160mg; Sodium 480mg; Carbohydrate 10g (Dietary Fiber 1g); Protein 34g • **% DAILY VALUE:** Vitamin A 22%; Vitamin C 0%; Calcium 24%; Iron 8% • **DIET EXCHANGES:** 1/2 Starch, 5 Lean Meat, 3 1/2 Fat

prep: **10 min**
cook: **15 min**

Caramelized-Garlic Chicken

4 cloves garlic, finely chopped

1 tablespoon butter or margarine

2 teaspoons packed brown sugar

1/4 teaspoon salt

4 boneless, skinless chicken breast halves (about 1 1/4 pounds)

1/4 cup water

4 slices tomato

4 ounces Havarti or Swiss cheese, cut into 1/8-inch slices

1 tablespoon chopped fresh or 1/2 teaspoon dried basil leaves

1 Cook garlic in butter in 10-inch nonstick skillet over medium-low heat 1 to 2 minutes, stirring constantly, just until garlic begins to turn golden brown. Stir in brown sugar until melted.

2 Sprinkle salt over chicken. Add chicken to skillet. Cook 3 to 5 minutes, turning once, until brown. Add water. Cook over medium heat 8 to 10 minutes, turning once, until chicken is glazed and no longer pink when centers of thickest pieces are cut and liquid has evaporated. Chicken will be golden brown. Watch carefully to prevent scorching.

3 Top each chicken piece with tomato slice, cheese and basil. Cover and heat 1 to 2 minutes or until cheese is melted.

IT'S **a snap!**

Good things come in small packages—or jars! Save chopping time by purchasing a jar of chopped fresh garlic to keep in the fridge. One teaspoon of this handy product is equal to the 4 garlic cloves in this recipe.

1 SERVING: Calories 300 (Calories from Fat 145); Fat 16g (Saturated 9g); Cholesterol 110mg; Sodium 410mg; Carbohydrate 5g (Dietary Fiber 0g); Protein 34g • % DAILY VALUE: Vitamin A 10%; Vitamin C 4%; Calcium 16%; Iron 6% • DIET EXCHANGES: 5 Lean Meat, 1 Vegetable

4 SERVINGS

Citrus-Ginger Chicken

1/2 cup orange juice

1/4 cup lime juice

2 tablespoons honey

1 teaspoon finely chopped gingerroot

1 teaspoon chopped fresh or 1/4 teaspoon dried thyme leaves

1/4 teaspoon salt

1/4 teaspoon black and red pepper blend

4 boneless, skinless chicken breast halves (about 1 1/4 pounds)

1 tablespoon butter or margarine

1 medium seedless orange, peeled and cut into slices

Additional fresh thyme leaves, if desired

COME
&eat!

Serve this citrus-flavored chicken dish with rice or couscous and cooked beets tossed with butter.

1 Mix orange juice, lime juice, honey, gingerroot and 1 teaspoon thyme in medium bowl.

2 Spray 10-inch nonstick skillet with cooking spray; heat over medium-high heat. Sprinkle salt and pepper blend over chicken. Cook chicken in skillet 3 to 4 minutes, turning once, until brown. Stir in orange juice mixture. Heat to boiling; reduce heat to medium-low. Cover and cook 8 to 10 minutes or until chicken is no longer pink when centers of thickest pieces are cut. Remove chicken from skillet.

3 Heat sauce in skillet to boiling. Add butter. Cook, stirring constantly, until butter is melted and sauce is slightly thickened. Serve sauce over chicken and orange slices. Sprinkle with additional thyme.

1 SERVING: Calories 235 (Calories from Fat 65); Fat 7g (Saturated 3g); Cholesterol 80mg; Sodium 240mg; Carbohydrate 17g (Dietary Fiber 1g); Protein 27g • **% DAILY VALUE:** Vitamin A 4%; Vitamin C 26%; Calcium 2%; Iron 6% • **DIET EXCHANGES:** 4 Very Lean Meat, 1 Fruit, 1 Fat

Citrus-Ginger Chicken

Pantry Recipes

If you have a well-stocked pantry (see pages 6–7), you'll be able to make this recipe anytime, even when there's no time to shop.

Ranch Fried Chicken

4 boneless, skinless chicken breast halves (about 1 1/4 pounds)

Ranch dressing

Italian-style dry bread crumbs

Olive or vegetable oil

Dip **chicken breasts** into **dressing**, then coat with **crumbs**. Heat **oil** in 12-inch nonstick skillet over medium-high heat. Cook chicken in oil 12 to 15 minutes, turning once, until outside is golden brown and juice is no longer pink when centers of thickest pieces are cut.
MAKES 4 SERVINGS IN 20 MINUTES

serve it 3 ways!

1 Sandwich

Thinly slice chicken, and fill pita bread halves with chicken, cut-up cucumbers and shredded mozzarella cheese.

2 Light Salad

Cut chicken into pieces, and mix with green or red grapes, cantaloupe chunks and equal parts of mayonnaise and yogurt.

3 Main Course Salad

Stir together cut-up chicken and salsa. Toss with salad greens, shredded cheese, canned corn with red peppers and sliced ripe olives.

One-Pan Potatoes and Chicken

2 tablespoons vegetable oil

8 medium red potatoes, thinly sliced

1 pound boneless, skinless chicken breasts, cut into thin strips

1 medium red or green bell pepper, cut into thin strips

1 teaspoon garlic salt

1 Heat oil in 12-inch nonstick skillet over medium heat. Add potatoes, chicken and bell pepper to skillet. Sprinkle with garlic salt.

2 Cook about 15 minutes, stirring frequently, until potatoes are tender and chicken is no longer pink in center.

IT'S **a**
snap!

For a super-speedy garnish, sprinkle sliced green onions or chopped fresh basil or parsley over this all-in-one-pan dinner.

1 SERVING: Calories 385 (Calories from Fat 100); Fat 11g (Saturated 2g); Cholesterol 75mg; Sodium 320mg; Carbohydrate 46g (Dietary Fiber 5g); Protein 31g • % DAILY VALUE: Vitamin A 18%; Vitamin C 66%; Calcium 4%; Iron 18% • DIET EXCHANGES: 3 Starch, 3 Lean Meat

4 SERVINGS

Caesar Chicken with Orzo

C O M E

& eat!

Complete this quick
meal with warmed
purchased garlic
bread and fresh
pears or clusters of
red grapes.

I tablespoon vegetable oil

**4 boneless, skinless chicken
breast halves (1 1/4 pounds)**

**I can (14 1/2 ounces)
chicken broth**

I cup water

**I cup uncooked rosamarina
(orzo) pasta (6 ounces)**

**I bag (1 pound) frozen
baby whole carrots, green
beans and yellow beans
(or other combination)**

3 tablespoons Caesar dressing

**1/8 teaspoon coarsely ground
pepper**

1 Heat oil in 10-inch skillet over medium-high heat. Cook
chicken in oil about 10 minutes, turning once, until brown.
Remove chicken from skillet; keep warm.

2 Add broth and water to skillet; heat to boiling. Stir in
pasta; heat to boiling. Cook uncovered 8 to 10 minutes,
stirring occasionally, until pasta is tender. Stir in frozen vegetables and dressing. Add chicken. Sprinkle with pepper.

3 Heat to boiling; reduce heat. Simmer uncovered about
5 minutes or until vegetables are crisp-tender and juice of
chicken is no longer pink when centers of thickest pieces
are cut.

1 SERVING: Calories 405 (Calories from Fat 115); Fat 13g (Saturated 3g); Cholesterol 75mg;
Sodium 670mg; Carbohydrate 43g (Dietary Fiber 6g); Protein 38g • **% DAILY VALUE:**
Vitamin A 100%; Vitamin C 42%; Calcium 10%; Iron 24% • **DIET EXCHANGES:** 2 Starch,
4 Lean Meat, 1 Vegetable

Caesar Chicken with Orzo

prep: **5 min**
cook: **11 min**

IT'S **a**
snap!
Couscous, the
tiniest of all the
pastas, will come to
your rescue in the
timesaving depart-
ment. It's ready to
eat in just 5 minutes!
Be sure to check
out all the new
varieties available.

4 SERVINGS

Teriyaki Chicken Stir-Fry

1 tablespoon vegetable oil

1 pound cut-up boneless chicken breast for stir-fry

1/2 cup teriyaki baste and glaze

3 tablespoons lemon juice

1 bag (1 pound) frozen broccoli, carrots, onions, red peppers, celery, water chestnuts and mushrooms (or other combination)

Hot cooked couscous, rice or noodles, if desired

1 Heat wok or 12-inch skillet over high heat. Add oil; rotate wok to coat side. Add chicken; stir-fry 3 to 4 minutes or until chicken is no longer pink in center.

2 Stir in remaining ingredients except couscous. Heat to boiling, stirring constantly; reduce heat. Cover and simmer about 6 minutes or until vegetables are crisp-tender.

3 Serve with couscous.

1 SERVING: Calories 230 (Calories from Fat 65); Fat 7g (Saturated 2g); Cholesterol 70mg; Sodium 1480mg; Carbohydrate 15g (Dietary Fiber 2g); Protein 29g • % DAILY VALUE: Vitamin A 60%; Vitamin C 30%; Calcium 4%; Iron 12% • DIET EXCHANGES: 4 Very Lean Meat, 3 Vegetable

Sichuan Cashew Chicken

1 tablespoon chili oil or
vegetable oil

1 pound boneless, skinless
chicken breasts, cut into
1-inch pieces

1 bag (1 pound) frozen
cauliflower, carrots and
snow pea pods (or other
combination)

1/3 cup stir-fry sauce

Hot cooked rice or noodles,
if desired

1/4 cup cashew halves

C O M E
& eat!

**Fortune cookies
with vanilla ice
cream or orange
sherbet make a
refreshing, easy
dessert to top off
this meal.**

1 Heat wok or 12-inch skillet over high heat. Add oil; rotate
wok to coat side. Add chicken; stir-fry 1 minute.

2 Add frozen vegetables; stir-fry about 4 minutes or until
vegetables are crisp-tender and chicken is no longer pink in
center. Stir in stir-fry sauce; cook and stir about 30 seconds
or until hot.

3 Serve over rice. Sprinkle with cashews.

1 SERVING: Calories 265 (Calories from Fat 100); Fat 11g (Saturated 2g); Cholesterol 70mg;
Sodium 1070mg; Carbohydrate 14g (Dietary Fiber 3g); Protein 30g • **% DAILY VALUE:**
Vitamin A 94%; Vitamin C 22%; Calcium 4%; Iron 14% • **DIET EXCHANGES:** 4 Lean
Meat, 2 Vegetable

4 SERVINGS

Stir-Fry Chicken and Vegetables

IT'S **a**
snap!
If your super-
market doesn't
have packaged fresh
stir-fry vegetables,
make your own!
Mix 1 1/2 cups sliced
celery, 1 1/4 cups
sliced carrots,
3/4 cup snow
(Chinese) pea pods
and 1/2 cup coarsely
chopped onion.
Broccoli slaw
is another easy
addition.

1 cup uncooked regular long-grain rice

1 pound boneless, skinless chicken breasts

1/2 teaspoon peppered seasoned salt

1 bag (1 pound) fresh stir-fry vegetables (4 cups)

1/2 cup water

1/2 cup classic-style stir-fry sauce

1 tablespoon honey

2 cups chow mein noodles

1/4 cup cashew pieces

1 Cook rice as directed on package. While rice is cooking, cut chicken into 1/2-inch pieces. Spray 12-inch nonstick skillet with cooking spray; heat over medium-high heat. Add chicken; sprinkle with peppered seasoned salt. Stir-fry 4 to 6 minutes or until brown.

2 Add vegetables and water to skillet. Heat to boiling; reduce heat to medium. Cover and cook 5 to 7 minutes, stirring occasionally, until vegetables are crisp-tender.

3 Stir in stir-fry sauce and honey; heat through. Divide rice and noodles among bowls. Top with chicken mixture. Sprinkle with cashews.

1 SERVING: Calories 570 (Calories from Fat 135); Fat 15g (Saturated 3g); Cholesterol 70mg; Sodium 1800mg; Carbohydrate 73g (Dietary Fiber 4g); Protein 36g • **% DAILY VALUE:** Vitamin A 100%; Vitamin C 52%; Calcium 8%; Iron 30% • **DIET EXCHANGES:** 4 Starch, 2 1/2 Lean Meat, 3 Vegetable, 1 Fat

Orange- and Ginger-Glazed Turkey Tenderloins

prep: **3 min**
cook: **25 min**

1 tablespoon vegetable oil	1 teaspoon finely chopped gingerroot or 1/2 teaspoon ground ginger
1 1/4 pounds turkey breast tenderloins	
1/3 cup orange marmalade	1 teaspoon white or regular Worcestershire sauce

1 Heat oil in 10-inch skillet over medium heat. Cook turkey in oil about 5 minutes or until brown on one side; turn turkey.

2 Stir in remaining ingredients; reduce heat to low.

3 Cover and simmer 15 to 20 minutes, stirring occasionally, until sauce is thickened and juice of turkey is no longer pink when center of thickest piece is cut. Cut turkey into thin slices. Spoon sauce over turkey.

COME &eat!

This turkey is perfect served with rice, which cooks in about the same amount of time. Follow package directions for cooking the rice. By starting the turkey and rice at the same time, you'll be ready to eat in just 30 minutes, from beginning to end!

1 SERVING: Calories 365 (Calories from Fat 35); Fat 4g (Saturated 1g); Cholesterol 95mg; Sodium 85mg; Carbohydrate 17g (Dietary Fiber 0g); Protein 33g • % DAILY VALUE: Vitamin A 0%; Vitamin C 2%; Calcium 2%; Iron 10% • DIET EXCHANGES: 5 Very Lean Meat, 1 Fruit

IT'S a

snap!

Use chicken breast slices rather than turkey if that's what you have on hand. Any of the turkey recipes in this book will work equally well with chicken.

4 SERVINGS

Honey-Mustard Turkey with Snap Peas

1 pound uncooked turkey breast slices, about 1/4 inch thick

1/2 cup Dijon and honey poultry and meat marinade

1 cup baby-cut carrots, cut lengthwise in half

2 cups frozen snap pea pods (from 1-pound bag)

1 Place turkey in shallow glass or plastic dish. Pour marinade over turkey; turn slices to coat evenly. Cover dish and let stand 10 minutes at room temperature.

2 Spray 10-inch skillet with cooking spray; heat over medium heat. Drain most of marinade from turkey. Cook turkey in skillet about 5 minutes, turning once, until brown.

3 Add carrots, lifting turkey to place carrots on bottom of skillet. Top turkey with pea pods. Cover and simmer about 7 minutes or until carrots are tender and turkey is no longer pink in center.

1 SERVING: Calories 150 (Calories from Fat 10); Fat 1g (Saturated 0g); Cholesterol 75mg; Sodium 65mg; Carbohydrate 9g (Dietary Fiber 3g); Protein 29g • **% DAILY VALUE:** Vitamin A 60%; Vitamin C 28%; Calcium 4%; Iron 16% • **DIET EXCHANGES:** 3 Very Lean Meat, 2 Vegetable

Honey-Mustard Turkey with Snap Peas

prep: **15 min**
cook: **5 min**

COME
&eat!

Make an everyday meal extraordinary with a build-your-own-fajita buffet. Set out colorful bowls filled with the tomato, cheese, lettuce, sour cream and salsa. Add guacamole, sliced ripe olives and chopped fresh cilantro as well.

4 SERVINGS

Easy Turkey Fajitas

1 1/2 grilled turkey breast tenderloins (refer to chart on page 168)

1 medium onion, sliced

2 tablespoons Mexican seasoning

2 tablespoons vegetable oil

8 flour tortillas (6 inches in diameter)

1 medium tomato, chopped (3/4 cup)

1 cup shredded Cheddar cheese (4 ounces)

1 cup shredded lettuce

1/2 cup sour cream

1/2 cup salsa

1 Cut turkey into 1/4-inch slices; cut slices crosswise in half. Place onion, Mexican seasoning and oil in large bowl; toss.

2 Heat 12-inch skillet over medium-high heat; add onion mixture. Cook about 4 minutes, stirring frequently, until onion is crisp-tender. Stir in turkey. Cook about 1 minute or until heated through.

3 Divide turkey mixture among tortillas. Sprinkle with tomato and cheese. Add lettuce, sour cream and salsa. Roll up tortillas.

1 SERVING: Calories 520 (Calories from Fat 225); Fat 25g (Saturated 11g); Cholesterol 135mg; Sodium 560mg; Carbohydrate 35g (Dietary Fiber 4g); Protein 43g • **% DAILY VALUE:** Vitamin A 16%; Vitamin C 26%; Calcium 32%; Iron 28% • **DIET EXCHANGES:** 2 Starch, 5 Lean Meat, 1 Vegetable, 1 1/2 Fat

Easy Turkey Fajitas

6 SERVINGS

Turkey Club Squares

2 cups Original Bisquick

1/3 cup mayonnaise or salad dressing

1/3 cup milk

2 cups cubed cooked turkey

2 medium green onions, sliced (2 tablespoons)

4 slices bacon, crisply cooked and crumbled

1/4 cup mayonnaise or salad dressing

1 large tomato, chopped (1 cup)

1 cup shredded reduced-fat mozzarella cheese (4 ounces)

1 Heat oven to 450°. Grease cookie sheet with shortening or butter. Stir Bisquick, 1/3 cup mayonnaise and the milk until soft dough forms. Roll or pat dough into 12 × 8-inch rectangle on cookie sheet. Bake 8 to 10 minutes or until golden brown.

2 Mix turkey, onions, bacon and 1/4 cup mayonnaise. Spread over crust to within 1/4 inch of edge. Sprinkle with tomato and cheese.

3 Bake 5 to 6 minutes or until turkey mixture is hot and cheese is melted. Cut into squares.

COME
&eat!

Love the flavor of BLTs? While this "sandwich" bakes, shred 1 1/2 cups of iceberg or romaine lettuce; toss a couple handfuls over each serving immediately after cutting into squares.

1 SERVING: Calories 490 (Calories from Fat 290); Fat 32g (Saturated 8g); Cholesterol 65mg; Sodium 910mg; Carbohydrate 28g (Dietary Fiber 1g); Protein 23g • **% DAILY VALUE:** Vitamin A 8%; Vitamin C 4%; Calcium 24%; Iron 12% • **DIET EXCHANGES:** 2 Starch, 2 1/2 High-Fat Meat, 2 Fat

Turkey Club Squares

4 OPEN-FACE SANDWICHES

Turkey Patty Melts

1 medium onion, thinly sliced

1 medium bell pepper,
thinly sliced

1 pound lean ground turkey

1/4 cup chili sauce

1/2 teaspoon garlic powder

1/2 cup shredded Cheddar
cheese (2 ounces)

4 teaspoons mayonnaise or
salad dressing

4 slices whole-grain bread,
toasted

1 Spray 12-inch nonstick skillet with cooking spray; heat over medium heat. Cook onion and bell pepper in skillet 6 to 8 minutes, stirring frequently, until tender. Remove vegetables from skillet; keep warm.

2 Mix turkey, chili sauce and garlic powder. Shape mixture into 4 patties, each 5 inches in diameter. Cook patties in skillet over medium heat 4 to 5 minutes on each side or until turkey is no longer pink in center.

3 Top each patty with about 1/4 cup of the vegetables; sprinkle with 2 tablespoons of the cheese. Cover and cook 1 to 2 minutes or until cheese is melted. Spread 1 teaspoon mayonnaise on each slice toast. Top each with patty.

IT'S **a**
snap!
Don't waste time searching in the supermarket. Lean ground beef or ground chicken breast make delicious substitutes for the turkey.

1 SANDWICH: Calories 345 (Calories from Fat 145); Fat 16g (Saturated 5g); Cholesterol 95mg; Sodium 520mg; Carbohydrate 21g (Dietary Fiber 2g); Protein 31g • % DAILY VALUE: Vitamin A 10%; Vitamin C 24%; Calcium 12%; Iron 12% • DIET EXCHANGES: 1 Starch, 4 Lean Meat, 1 Vegetable, 1/2 Fat

6 Marvelous Meats in Minutes

◔ = *super express* ready in 20 minutes or less

1-Step Recipes

Easy Saucy Secrets for Main Dishes

The secret for creating easy sauces for meats? Start with a pantry staple and add pizzazz! With these tasty suggestions, you can turn simple meats into sensational meals.

1 Alfredo sauce
Heat and stir in cooked bacon and cooked peas and carrots. Serve over pork chops or pork cutlets.

2 Gravy
Heat and stir in sour cream and sliced mushrooms. Serve with roast beef or cooked meatballs.

3 Marinara sauce or seasoned diced tomatoes
Heat and stir in whipping (heavy) cream or Alfredo sauce; serve over meatballs.

4 Golden mushroom soup
Stir in mushrooms, fresh or dried thyme leaves and parsley; heat. Serve with pan-seared pork chops or beef steaks.

5 Apricot preserves
Stir in lime juice and ground mustard; use as a sandwich spread for cold roasted meat; or heat to use as a sauce with sautéed pork chops or ham steak.

6 Sour cream
Stir in prepared horseradish, Dijon mustard and pepper; use as a sandwich spread for cold roast beef, or heat to use as a sauce for cooked beef.

7 Yogurt
Stir in picante sauce and red or green salsa; add chopped green onions or sliced ripe olives. Serve with sliced broiled flank steak and tortillas.

8 Barbecue sauce
Stir in orange marmalade, cranberry sauce or Dijon mustard. Serve with burgers or meatloaf.

9 Dijon mustard
Mix with equal amounts of honey, olive oil and lemon juice. Serve over sliced roast beef.

10 Pesto
Stir into mayonnaise or salad dressing; use as a sandwich spread for cold roasted meat.

Savory Beef Tenderloin

3/4 pound beef tenderloin

2 teaspoons chopped fresh or 1/2 teaspoon dried marjoram leaves

2 teaspoons sugar

1 teaspoon coarsely ground pepper

1 tablespoon butter or margarine

1 cup sliced mushrooms (3 ounces)

1 small onion, thinly sliced

3/4 cup beef broth

1/4 cup dry red wine or nonalcoholic wine

1 tablespoon cornstarch

1 Cut beef into four 3/4-inch-thick slices. Mix marjoram, sugar and pepper; rub on both sides of beef slices. Melt butter in 10-inch skillet over medium heat. Cook beef in butter 3 to 5 minutes, turning once, until brown. Remove beef to serving platter; keep warm.

2 Cook mushrooms and onion in drippings in skillet over medium heat about 2 minutes, stirring occasionally, until onion is crisp-tender.

3 Mix broth, wine and cornstarch; stir into mushroom mixture. Cook over medium heat, stirring constantly, until mixture thickens and boils. Boil and stir 1 minute. Pour over beef.

COME
&eat!

Beef tenderloin can be more expensive than regular steak, but it's worth it for the time you'll save cooking. In just a few minutes of sautéing, this beef becomes melt-in-your-mouth tender. For a special occasion dinner, serve with mashed potatoes and steamed green beans.

1 SERVING: Calories 175 (Calories from Fat 70); Fat 8g (Saturated 2g); Cholesterol 40mg; Sodium 200mg; Carbohydrate 7g (Dietary Fiber 1g); Protein 17g • **% DAILY VALUE:** Vitamin A 4%; Vitamin C 0%; Calcium 0%; Iron 10% • **DIET EXCHANGES:** 2 Medium-Fat Meat, 1 Vegetable

prep: **10 min**
broil: **10 min**

4 SERVINGS

Strip Steaks with Mango-Peach Salsa

1/4 cup finely chopped red bell pepper

2 teaspoons finely chopped seeded jalapeño chilies

1 teaspoon finely chopped or grated gingerroot or 1/4 teaspoon ground ginger

1/4 cup peach preserves

1 tablespoon lime juice

1 small mango, chopped (1 cup)

4 beef boneless New York strip steaks (about 1 1/2 pounds)

1 to 2 teaspoons Caribbean jerk seasoning

1 Mix bell pepper, chilies and gingerroot in medium bowl. Stir in preserves, lime juice and mango.

2 Set oven control to broil. Sprinkle both sides of beef with jerk seasoning. Place on rack in broiler pan. Broil with tops 4 to 6 inches from heat 6 to 10 minutes; turning once, until desired doneness. Serve with salsa mixture.

IT'S **a**

snap!

Purchase fresh mangoes that are turning yellow with red mottling and are slightly soft to the touch. Need help cutting a mango? Score the skin lengthwise into fourths with a knife, and peel like a banana. Cut the peeled mango lengthwise close to both sides of the large, flat seed, then dice. Canned or jarred mangoes also can be used for this recipe; be sure to drain well before using.

1 SERVING: Calories 345 (Calories from Fat 110); Fat 12g (Saturated 5g); Cholesterol 95mg; Sodium 95mg; Carbohydrate 23g (Dietary Fiber 1g); Protein 37g • **% DAILY VALUE:** Vitamin A 26%; Vitamin C 30%; Calcium 2%; Iron 18% • **DIET EXCHANGES:** 5 Lean Meat, 1 1/2 Fruit

Strip Steaks with Mango-Peach Salsa

4 SERVINGS

Sirloin with Bacon-Dijon Sauce

IT'S a
snap!

Mustard varieties
abound. You'll find
many in your gro-
cery store and even
more in gourmet
and kitchen specialty
shops. Choose your
favorite, or experi-
ment with different
kinds to vary the
flavor of this great-
tasting beef.

**4 slices bacon, cut into
1/2-inch pieces**

**1 pound beef boneless
sirloin steak, 3/4 inch thick**

**1/2 teaspoon peppered
seasoned salt**

1/2 cup beef broth

2 teaspoons Dijon mustard

**1/2 teaspoon chopped fresh or
1/8 teaspoon dried thyme
leaves**

**4 medium green onions, sliced
(1/4 cup)**

1 Cook bacon in 12-inch nonstick skillet over medium heat, stirring occasionally, until crisp. Remove bacon from skillet with slotted spoon; drain on paper towels. Reserve 1 table-spoon bacon fat in skillet.

2 Cut beef into 4 serving pieces. Sprinkle with seasoned salt. Cook beef in bacon fat in skillet over medium heat about 6 minutes, turning once, until desired doneness. Remove beef from skillet; cover to keep warm.

3 Mix broth, mustard, thyme and onions in skillet. Cook over medium heat, stirring occasionally, until slightly thickened. Serve sauce over beef. Sprinkle with bacon.

1 SERVING: Calories 155 (Calories from Fat 55); Fat 6g (Saturated 2g); Cholesterol 60mg; Sodium 430mg; Carbohydrate 2g (Dietary Fiber 0g); Protein 23g • **% DAILY VALUE:** Vitamin A 0%; Vitamin C 2%; Calcium 2%; Iron 12% • **DIET EXCHANGES:** 3 Very Lean Meat, 1 Fat

Broiled Santa Fe Steaks

prep: **5 min**
broil: **11 min**

1/2 cup thick-and-chunky salsa

1/2 cup canned black beans, rinsed and drained

2 tablespoons finely chopped red onion

2 tablespoons chopped fresh cilantro

1 tablespoon lime juice

1 1/2 teaspoons chili powder

2 teaspoons chopped fresh or 1/2 teaspoon dried oregano leaves

4 beef boneless New York strip steaks (about 1 1/2 pounds)

1 Mix salsa, beans, onion, cilantro, lime juice and 1/2 teaspoon of the chili powder. Cover and refrigerate while preparing beef steaks.

2 Set oven control to broil. Sprinkle remaining 1 teaspoon chili powder and the oregano over both sides of beef; gently press into beef. Place beef on rack in broiler pan.

3 Broil beef with tops 4 to 6 inches from heat 6 minutes; turn. Broil 2 to 5 minutes longer for medium doneness. Serve with salsa mixture.

IT'S **a**
snap!
Speed up dinner preparation by gathering all the ingredients you'll need for dinner and measuring them out, if possible, the morning or night before.

1 SERVING: Calories 260 (Calories from Fat 100); Fat 11g (Saturated 4g); Cholesterol 85mg; Sodium 240mg; Carbohydrate 8g (Dietary Fiber 2g); Protein 34g • **% DAILY VALUE:** Vitamin A 2%; Vitamin C 6%; Calcium 4%; Iron 18% • **DIET EXCHANGES:** 4 Lean Meat, 2 Vegetable

6 SERVINGS

Old-Time Beef and Vegetable Stew

C O M E
&eat!

Like many stews, this
one tastes even
better the next day
when the flavors
have had a chance to
meld. You'll save lots
of time by making
this homey stew the
day before, chilling it
overnight, then
reheating at dinner
the next day.

**I pound beef boneless sirloin
steak, cut into 1/2-inch cubes**

**I bag (I pound) frozen stew
vegetables, thawed and drained**

**I can (15 ounces) chunky
garlic-and-herb or plain tomato
sauce**

**I can (14 1/2 ounces)
beef broth**

**2 cans (5 1/2 ounces each)
spicy eight-vegetable juice**

1 Spray 10-inch nonstick skillet with cooking spray; heat over
medium-high heat. Cook beef in skillet about 10 minutes,
stirring occasionally, until brown.

2 Stir in remaining ingredients. Heat to boiling; reduce heat.
Cover and simmer 5 minutes, stirring occasionally.

1 SERVING: Calories 175 (Calories from Fat 45); Fat 5g (Saturated 1g); Cholesterol 40mg;
Sodium 690mg; Carbohydrate 17g (Dietary Fiber 3g); Protein 18g • **% DAILY VALUE:**
Vitamin A 62%; Vitamin C 32%; Calcium 4%; Iron 14% • **DIET EXCHANGES:** 2 Lean Meat,
3 Vegetable

Old-Time Beef and Vegetable Stew

Thawing Meats

Thaw meat in the refrigerator or in the microwave, not on the countertop. To thaw meat in the refrigerator, place wrapped meat in a dish or plastic bag to catch any drips. Even if you forget to remove meat from the freezer in time to thaw, you can still make dinner the quick and easy way—using this handy chart.

1. Place wrapped meat in a microwavable dish. Pierce packages of bacon, hot dogs and sausages with a fork.

2. Microwave on Defrost setting until few ice crystals remain in center. Halfway through defrosting, remove wrapper, separate pieces and place in dish to catch juice, arranging thickest parts to outside edges of dish.

3. Let stand 5 to 10 minutes to complete thawing.

Timetable for Thawing Meats

Meat Type	Amount	Defrosting Time (minutes) on Defrost Setting
Steak 1/2 inch thick	1 pound	7 to 9, turning over after 4 minutes
1 inch thick	1 pound	8 to 11, turning over after 4 minutes
Chops 1/2 inch thick	1 pound (about 4 chops)	6 to 9, rearranging after 4 minutes
Ribs, back	1 pound	7 to 9, rearranging after 4 minutes
Ground Meatballs,	1 pound cooked (24 balls)	7 to 9, separating after 3 minutes
Ground Patties, 3/4 inch thick	1 pound (4 patties)	8 to 10, turning over after 4 minutes
Bacon, sliced	1 pound	5 to 6
Hot Dogs	1 pound (about 10)	5 to 7, turning over after 3 minutes
	1/2 pound (about 5)	2 to 4, turning over after 3 minutes
Sausages, cooked or uncooked (bratwurst, Italian, Polish)	1 pound (about 6)	6 to 8, turning over after 3 minutes

Sloppy Joe Rotini

**2 cups uncooked rotini pasta
(6 ounces)**

1 pound ground beef

**2 cups frozen whole kernel
corn**

1/2 cup water

**1 small zucchini, cut lengthwise
in half, then cut crosswise into
slices (1 cup)**

**1 can (15 1/2 ounces) sloppy joe
sauce**

1 Cook and drain pasta as directed on package.

2 While pasta is cooking, cook beef in 10-inch nonstick skillet over medium heat 8 to 10 minutes, stirring occasionally, until brown; drain. Stir in pasta and remaining ingredients.

3 Heat to boiling; reduce heat to medium. Cover and simmer about 5 minutes, stirring occasionally, until zucchini is crisp-tender.

**COME
&eat!**

Speedy Pasta: For
a quick and tasty
kid-pleasing favorite,
use tricolored wagon
wheel or rotini pasta
that has been already
cooked and refrig-
erated or frozen.
Sprinkle Cheddar
cheese–flavored
crackers over the top
just before serving.

1 SERVING: Calories 575 (Calories from Fat 190); Fat 21g (Saturated 7g); Cholesterol 65mg; Sodium 1150mg; Carbohydrate 60g (Dietary Fiber 4g); Protein 40g • **% DAILY VALUE:** Vitamin A 4%; Vitamin C 10%; Calcium 6%; Iron 28% • **DIET EXCHANGES:** 3 Starch, 3 1/2 Medium-Fat Meat, 3 Vegetable

Broiling or Grilling Beef

Broiling and direct-heat grilling are quick, low-fat methods for cooking tender cuts, such as steaks, or ground beef patties. Refer to the instructions that came with your grill for more information.

1. Marinate beef if desired.

2. **To Broil:** Set oven control to broil and position oven rack so top of meat will be 2 to 4 inches from heat.

   To Grill: Brush grill rack with vegetable oil or spray with cooking spray. Place rack of outdoor grill 2 to 4 inches above heat. Start grill. If using charcoal grill, wait until coals are covered with ash (medium heat).

3. **To Broil:** Place beef on rack in broiler pan and place in oven. (For easy cleanup, first line broiler pan with aluminum foil.)

   To Grill: Place beef on grill.

4. Broil or grill for about half the time shown in chart for beef cut or until beef is brown on one side.

5. Turn beef and continue cooking until desired doneness. (To check doneness, cut a small slit in the center of boneless cuts or in the center near the bone of bone-in cuts. Medium-rare is very pink in center and slightly brown toward exterior. Medium is light pink in center and brown toward exterior.) In order to be food-safe, burgers must be cooked until beef is no longer pink in center and juice is clear. If you like, season the beef after cooking.

Timetable for Broiling and Grilling Beef

Beef Cut	Thickness or Weight	Broiling Time (minutes)		Grilling Time (minutes)	
		145° (medium-rare)	160° (medium)	145° (medium-rare)	160° (medium)
Rib and Rib Eye Steaks	3/4 to 1 inch	8	15	7	12
Top Loin Steak (boneless)	3/4 to 1 inch	8	17	7	12
Porterhouse and T-Bone Steaks	1 inch	10	15	10	14
Sirloin Steak (boneless)	3/4 to 1 inch	10	21	12	16
Sirloin Cubes (kabobs)	1 to 1 1/4 inches	9	12	8	11
Tenderloin Steak	1 inch	10	15	11	13
Chuck Shoulder Steak (boneless)	1 inch	14	18	14	20
Eye Round Steak	1 inch	9	11	9	12
Top Round Steak	1 inch	15	18	12	14
Flank Steak	1 to 1 1/2 pounds	12	14	12	15
Ground Beef Patties	1/2 inch 3/4 inch	*	10 13	*	7 to 9 10 to 11

USDA recommends cooking ground beef to 160°.

4 SERVINGS

Ramen Stir-Fry

1 pound beef boneless sirloin

2 cups water

1 package (3 ounces) Oriental-flavor ramen noodle soup mix

1 bag (16 ounces) fresh stir-fry vegetables

1/4 cup stir-fry sauce

1 Cut beef into thin strips. Spray 12-inch nonstick skillet with cooking spray; heat over medium-high heat. Cook beef in skillet 3 to 5 minutes, stirring occasionally, until brown. Remove beef from skillet.

2 Heat water to boiling in skillet. Break block of noodles from soup mix into water; stir until slightly softened. Stir in vegetables. Heat to boiling. Boil 5 to 7 minutes, stirring occasionally, until vegetables are crisp-tender.

3 Stir in contents of seasoning packet from soup mix, stir-fry sauce and beef. Cook 2 to 3 minutes, stirring frequently, until hot.

IT'S **a**
snap!

Beef is easier to cut if partially frozen, 30 to 60 minutes. Quick-cooking ramen noodles, containing the seasoning packet, are perfect for fast dishes, because you don't have to add a lot of ingredients.

1 SERVING: Calories 245 (Calories from Fat 65); Fat 7g (Saturated 3g); Cholesterol 55mg; Sodium 860mg; Carbohydrate 25g (Dietary Fiber 3g); Protein 24g • % DAILY VALUE: Vitamin A 38%; Vitamin C 14%; Calcium 5%; Iron 18% • **DIET EXCHANGES:** 1 Starch, 2 1/2 Very Lean Meat, 2 Vegetable, 1 Fat

Ramen Stir-Fry

4 SERVINGS

Beef and Cheese Enchiladas

I pound lean ground beef

1/2 teaspoon salt

1/4 teaspoon pepper

I medium onion, chopped (1/2 cup)

I container (16 ounces) reduced-fat sour cream (2 cups)

I can (15 ounces) yellow and white corn, drained

2 cups shredded Mexican 4-cheese blend (8 ounces)

8 flour tortillas (8 inches in diameter)

I can (10 ounces) hot enchilada sauce

I can (10 ounces) mild enchilada sauce

1 Heat oven to 350°. Sprinkle beef with salt and pepper. Cook beef and onion in 10-inch skillet over medium heat 8 to 10 minutes, stirring occasionally, until beef is brown; drain. Stir in sour cream and corn.

2 Sprinkle 1 cup of the cheese in bottom of ungreased rectangular baking dish, 13 × 9 × 2 inches. Spoon about 1/2 cup beef mixture onto each tortilla; top with a few drops hot enchilada sauce. Roll tortilla around filling; place seam side down on cheese in baking dish. Pour remaining hot and mild sauces over enchiladas. Sprinkle with remaining 1 cup cheese.

3 Bake uncovered about 15 minutes or until cheese is bubbly.

1 SERVING: Calories 510 (Calories from Fat 215); Fat 24g (Saturated 12g); Cholesterol 80mg; Sodium 1080mg; Carbohydrate 50g (Dietary Fiber 4g); Protein 27g • **% DAILY VALUE:** Vitamin A 22%; Vitamin C 14%; Calcium 34%; Iron 20% • **DIET EXCHANGES:** 3 Starch, 2 High-Fat Meat, I Vegetable, I Fat

Mini Meat Loaves

prep: **5 min**
cook: **25 min**

I pound ground beef

1/2 cup dry bread crumbs

1/4 cup milk

1/2 teaspoon salt

1/2 teaspoon Worcestershire sauce, if desired

1/4 teaspoon pepper

I small onion, finely chopped (1/4 cup)

I egg

1 Heat oven to 400°. Mix all ingredients.

2 Pat mixture into a 9 × 3-inch rectangle in an ungreased rectangular baking dish. Cut into 1 1/2-inch squares; separate squares slightly.

3 Bake uncovered about 25 minutes or until no longer pink in center and juice is clear.

COME
&eat!

To make this into an all-American meal, bake frozen shoe-string potatoes while the meat loaf bakes. Serve with frozen or canned corn.

1 SERVING: Calories 315 (Calories from Fat 190); Fat 19g (Saturated 7g); Cholesterol 120mg; Sodium 490mg; Carbohydrate 12g (Dietary Fiber 1g); Protein 25g • % DAILY VALUE: Vitamin A 2%; Vitamin C 0%; Calcium 6%; Iron 16% • DIET EXCHANGES: 1 Starch, 3 Medium-Fat Meat, 0 Vegetable

IT'S **a**
snap!
This all-in-one bowl meal topped with crunchy tortilla strips is a fun twist on fajitas. To save even more time, top with packaged tortilla chips instead. Then reduce the amount of oil for sautéing the beef to 1 tablespoon.

4 SERVINGS

Beef Fajita Bowls

1 cup uncooked regular long-grain rice

1 pound beef boneless sirloin steak

2 tablespoons vegetable oil

1 flour tortilla (8 inches in diameter), cut into 4 × 1/2-inch strips

1 bag (1 pound) frozen stir-fry bell peppers and onions

1/2 cup frozen whole kernel corn

1 cup thick-and-chunky salsa

2 tablespoons lime juice

2 tablespoons chili sauce

1/2 teaspoon ground cumin

2 tablespoons chopped fresh cilantro

1 Cook rice as directed on package. While rice is cooking, cut beef with grain into 2-inch strips; cut strips across grain into 1/8-inch slices. (Beef is easier to cut if partially frozen, 30 to 60 minutes.)

2 Heat 12-inch nonstick skillet over medium-high heat. Add oil; rotate skillet to coat bottom. Cook tortilla strips in oil 1 to 2 minutes on each side, adding additional oil if necessary, until golden brown and crisp. Drain on paper towel.

3 Add beef to skillet; stir-fry over medium-high heat 4 to 5 minutes or until beef is brown; remove beef from skillet. Add frozen bell pepper mixture and corn to skillet; stir-fry 1 minute. Cover and cook 2 to 3 minutes, stirring twice, until crisp-tender. Stir in beef, salsa, lime juice, chili sauce and cumin. Cook 2 to 3 minutes, stirring occasionally, until hot. Stir in cilantro. Divide rice among 4 bowls. Top with beef mixture and tortilla strips.

1 SERVING: Calories 440 (Calories from Fat 80); Fat 9g (Saturated 2g); Cholesterol 60mg; Sodium 480mg; Carbohydrate 65g (Dietary Fiber 5g); Protein 30g • **% DAILY VALUE:** Vitamin A 20%; Vitamin C 66%; Calcium 6%; Iron 30% • **DIET EXCHANGES:** 4 Starch, 2 Lean Meat, 1 Vegetable

Beef Fajita Bowls

prep: **5 min**
cook: **15 min**

IT'S **a**
snap!

Forgot to thaw
the ground beef?
Here's an easy way
around it. Remove all
wrapping material,
then cook as you
would thawed beef,
except flip the
frozen block occa-
sionally and scrape
off the browned
areas as it cooks.

4 SERVINGS

Mexican Beef and Black Beans

1 pound ground beef	1/4 teaspoon red pepper sauce
1 tablespoon chopped fresh parsley or 1 teaspoon parsley flakes	1 medium red or green bell pepper, chopped (1 cup)
1 tablespoon white wine vinegar	4 medium green onions, thinly sliced (1/4 cup)
1 teaspoon grated lime or lemon peel	2 cans (15 ounces each) black beans, rinsed and drained

1 Cook beef in 10-inch skillet over medium heat 8 to 10 minutes, stirring occasionally, until brown; drain.

2 Stir in remaining ingredients. Cook about 5 minutes, stirring frequently, until hot.

1 SERVING: Calories 495 (Calories from Fat 155); Fat 17g (Saturated 7g); Cholesterol 65mg; Sodium 870mg; Carbohydrate 60g (Dietary Fiber 15g); Protein 40g • **% DAILY VALUE:** Vitamin A 2%; Vitamin C 30%; Calcium 16%; Iron 40% • **DIET EXCHANGES:** 3 Starch, 3 1/2 Lean Meat, 3 Vegetable

Spaghetti and Meat Squares

prep: **5 min**
bake: **15 min**
cook: **10 min**

I pound lean ground beef or ground turkey

1/2 cup dry bread crumbs

1/2 cup applesauce

I tablespoon instant minced onion

3/4 teaspoon garlic salt

1/4 teaspoon pepper

I jar (26 to 28 ounces) tomato pasta sauce (any variety)

3 cups hot cooked spaghetti

IT'S **a**
snap!
This recipe is a great timesaver— no need to form and fry individual meat- balls. Don't forget to heat the water for the spaghetti while the meat and sauce simmer.

1 Heat oven to 400°. Mix all ingredients except pasta sauce and spaghetti. Press mixture evenly in ungreased rectangu- lar pan, 11 × 7 × 1 1/2 inches. Cut into 1 1/4-inch squares.

2 Bake uncovered about 15 minutes or until no longer pink in center and juice is clear; drain. Separate meat squares.

3 Mix meat squares and pasta sauce in 3-quart saucepan. Heat to boiling; reduce heat. Simmer uncovered about 10 minutes, stirring occasionally, until hot. Serve over spaghetti.

1 SERVING: Calories 435 (Calories from Fat 145); Fat 16g (Saturated 5g); Cholesterol 45mg; Sodium 900mg; Carbohydrate 56g (Dietary Fiber 3g); Protein 20g • % DAILY VALUE: Vitamin A 18%; Vitamin C 16%; Calcium 6%; Iron 20% • DIET EXCHANGES: 3 Starch, 1 High-Fat Meat, 2 Vegetable, 1 Fat

prep: **5 min**
cook: **15 min**

4 SERVINGS

Monterey Skillet Hamburgers

I pound ground beef

I can (4 ounces) chopped green chilies, drained

2 tablespoons chopped fresh cilantro

I teaspoon chili powder

1/2 teaspoon salt

1/8 teaspoon ground red pepper (cayenne)

I medium red onion, thinly sliced

I medium avocado, sliced

4 slices (I ounce each) Monterey Jack cheese

1 Mix beef, chilies, cilantro, chili powder, salt and red pepper. Shape mixture into 4 patties, about 1/2 inch thick.

2 Spray 10-inch nonstick skillet with cooking spray; heat over medium-high heat. Cook onion in skillet 1 to 2 minutes, stirring occasionally, just until tender. Remove from skillet.

3 Add beef patties to skillet. Cook 10 to 12 minutes, turning once, until no longer pink in center and juice is clear. Top patties with onions, avocado and cheese. Cover and heat until cheese is melted.

IT'S **a** snap!

Want the secret to peeling and slicing avocados quickly? Cut ripe avocado lengthwise in half around the pit. Hit the pit with the blade of a sharp knife so it sticks; twist the knife to easily remove the pit. Peel off the leathery skin with your fingers, and slice the avocado.

1 SERVING: Calories 415 (Calories from Fat 280); Fat 31g (Saturated 13g); Cholesterol 90mg; Sodium 590mg; Carbohydrate 8g (Dietary Fiber 3g); Protein 29g • % DAILY VALUE: Vitamin A 14%; Vitamin C 20%; Calcium 22%; Iron 14% • DIET EXCHANGES: 4 High-Fat Meat, 1 Vegetable

Monterey Skillet Hamburgers

Pantry Recipes

If you have a well-stocked pantry (see pages 6–7), you'll
be able to make this recipe anytime, even when there's
no time to shop.

Sizzling Beef Stir-Fry

I pound ground beef

**I bag (I pound) frozen mixed vegetables
with snap pea pods**

1/4 cup stir-fry sauce

Brown **ground beef** in 12-inch skillet; drain. Stir in **vegetables**
and 1 tablespoon water; stir-fry 2 minutes. Stir in **sauce** until well
mixed; reduce heat to medium. Cover and cook 5 to 7 minutes,
stirring frequently, until vegetables are crisp-tender. MAKES 5 SERVINGS
IN 15 MINUTES

serve it 3 ways!

1 Sandwich
Fill individual hard rolls or hoagie or sandwich buns with
beef and vegetables.

2 Pasta
Serve over hot cooked rice, pasta or couscous.

3 Potatoes
Serve over baked potatoes.

Cheesy Hamburger Hash

super
express

prep: **5 min**
cook: **15 min**

1 pound ground beef

1 tablespoon butter or margarine

1 bag (1 pound 4 ounces) refrigerated diced potatoes with onions

1 can (14 1/2 ounces) diced tomatoes with Italian herbs, undrained

1 tablespoon pizza seasoning or Italian seasoning

1 1/2 cups shredded pizza cheese blend (mozzarella and Cheddar cheeses) (6 ounces)

2 tablespoons chopped fresh parsley

1 Cook beef in 12-inch nonstick skillet over medium-high heat about 5 minutes, stirring occasionally, until brown; drain. Remove beef and drippings from skillet.

2 Melt butter in same skillet. Add potatoes. Cover and cook over medium heat 8 to 10 minutes, stirring occasionally, until tender. Stir in beef, tomatoes and pizza seasoning. Cook, stirring occasionally, until thoroughly heated.

3 Sprinkle with cheese and parsley. Cover and heat until cheese is melted.

COME
&eat!

Corn on the cob and baking powder biscuits are great choices for sides with this quick everyone-likes-it dinner.

1 SERVING: Calories 520 (Calories from Fat 270); Fat 30g (Saturated 15g); Cholesterol 105mg; Sodium 470mg; Carbohydrate 31g (Dietary Fiber 3g); Protein 35g • **% DAILY VALUE:** Vitamin A 16%; Vitamin C 26%; Calcium 32%; Iron 20% • **DIET EXCHANGES:** 2 Starch, 4 Medium-Fat Meat, 1 1/2 Fat

Pork Chop Dinner with Rice and Veggies

C O M E
&eat!

Finish off this quick
meal with a colorful
coleslaw made by
stirring cubed
unpeeled red apple
into purchased
coleslaw. Add crusty
hard rolls for hearty
appetites.

**6 pork boneless loin chops,
1/2 inch thick (about 1 1/4 pounds)**

**2 cans (10 3/4 ounces each)
condensed reduced-fat cream
of mushroom soup**

**1 bag (1 pound) frozen baby
peas, carrots, pea pods and corn
(or other combination), thawed
and drained**

**1 can (14 1/2 ounces)
chicken broth**

**2 cups uncooked instant
brown rice**

1 Spray 12-inch nonstick skillet with cooking spray; heat
over medium heat. Cook pork in skillet about 5 minutes,
turning once, until brown. Remove pork from skillet;
keep warm.

2 Heat soup, vegetables and broth to boiling in same skillet,
stirring occasionally. Stir in rice; reduce heat. Cover and
simmer 5 minutes.

3 Top with pork. Cover and simmer about 5 minutes longer
or until pork is slightly pink in center and rice is tender.

1 SERVING: Calories 495 (Calories from Fat 115); Fat 13g (Saturated 4g); Cholesterol 75mg;
Sodium 1170mg; Carbohydrate 66g (Dietary Fiber 6g); Protein 33g • **% DAILY VALUE:**
Vitamin A 80%; Vitamin C 8%; Calcium 6%; Iron 14% • **DIET EXCHANGES:** 3 Starch,
2 Lean Meat, 4 Vegetable, 1 Fat

Pork Chop Dinner with Rice and Veggies

prep: **5 min**
cook: **10 min**

IT'S **a**
snap!
Dinner in a Flash:
Freeze leftovers of
main dishes in
microwavable serving-
size containers. For
one of those evenings
when there's no time
to cook, pull them
from the freezer and
zap them in your
microwave! Just add
a salad and bread
for a no-fuss meal
in minutes.

4 SERVINGS

Pork with Sweet Mustard Sauce

1 pound pork tenderloin, cut into 1/4-inch slices

1/4 teaspoon peppered seasoned salt

1 jar (12 ounces) pork gravy

2 tablespoons red currant jelly

1 teaspoon ground mustard

2 medium green onions, sliced (2 tablespoons)

1 Spray 12-inch nonstick skillet with cooking spray; heat over medium heat. Sprinkle both sides of pork with seasoned salt. Cook pork in skillet about 5 minutes, turning once, until brown.

2 Stir in remaining ingredients. Heat to boiling; reduce heat to medium. Cook 3 to 4 minutes, stirring occasionally, until sauce is desired consistency and pork is slightly pink in center.

1 SERVING: Calories 205 (Calories from Fat 55); Fat 6g (Saturated 2g); Cholesterol 70mg; Sodium 630mg; Carbohydrate 11g (Dietary Fiber 1g); Protein 28g • % DAILY VALUE: Vitamin A 0%; Vitamin C 2%; Calcium 2%; Iron 10% • **DIET EXCHANGES:** 1 Starch, 4 Very Lean Meat

Chicken-Fried Pork

prep: **10 min**
cook: **10 min**

I 1/2 pounds pork cutlets

I tablespoon water

I egg

28 saltine cracker squares, crushed (I cup)

1/4 teaspoon pepper

1/4 cup vegetable oil

Milk Gravy (below)

1 If pork cutlets are large, cut into 6 serving pieces. Beat water and egg with wire whisk or hand beater in a shallow bowl. Mix cracker crumbs and pepper in another shallow bowl. Dip pork into egg, then coat with cracker crumbs.

2 Heat oil in 12-inch skillet over medium-high heat. Cook pork in oil 3 to 4 minutes, turning once, until brown on outside and slightly pink in center. Remove pork from skillet; keep warm.

3 Make Milk Gravy. Serve with pork.

Milk Gravy

Drippings from pork and vegetable oil

1/4 cup all-purpose flour

1/2 teaspoon salt

2 cups milk

Measure pork drippings; add enough oil to drippings, if necessary, to measure 1/4 cup. Return drippings to skillet. Stir in flour and salt. Cook over low heat, stirring constantly to loosen brown particles from skillet, until smooth and bubbly; remove from heat. Slowly pour milk into skillet, stirring constantly. Heat to boiling over low heat, stirring constantly. Boil and stir 1 minute.

IT'S **a**
snap!

If you don't have saltines, use cheese-flavored or buttery crackers or whatever kind you have on hand. Crush crackers quickly and easily into crumbs with a rolling pin.

1 SERVING: Calories 400 (Calories from Fat 205); Fat 23g (Saturated 6g); Cholesterol 115mg; Sodium 430mg; Carbohydrate 17g (Dietary Fiber 1g), Protein 32g • % DAILY VALUE: Vitamin A 6%; Vitamin C 0%; Calcium 10%; Iron 10% • DIET EXCHANGES: I Starch, 4 Medium-Fat Meat, 1/2 Vegetable

prep: **10 min**
cook: **10 min**

C O M E
&eat!

**These pork chops
make a tasty dinner
served with green
beans and steamed
red potatoes.**

4 SERVINGS

Breaded Pork Chops

1/4 cup Original Bisquick

**7 saltine cracker squares,
crushed (1/2 cup)**

1/2 teaspoon seasoned salt

1/8 teaspoon pepper

1 egg

1 tablespoon water

**4 pork boneless loin chops,
1/2 inch thick (about 1 pound)**

1 Mix Bisquick, cracker crumbs, seasoned salt and pepper
in a plate or shallow bowl. Mix egg and water in another
shallow bowl.

2 Dip pork into egg mixture, then coat with Bisquick mixture.

3 Spray 12-inch nonstick skillet with cooking spray; heat over
medium-high heat. Cook pork in skillet 8 to 10 minutes,
turning once, until slightly pink in center.

1 SERVING: Calories 215 (Calories from Fat 90); Fat 10g (Saturated 3g); Cholesterol 90mg;
Sodium 580mg; Carbohydrate 8g (Dietary Fiber 0g); Protein 24g • **% DAILY VALUE:**
Vitamin A 0%; Vitamin C 0%; Calcium 2%; Iron 6% • **DIET EXCHANGES:** 1/2 Starch,
3 Lean Meat

Breaded Pork Chops

IT'S **a**
snap!

Keep 'em small:
Whenever possible,
use smaller, thinner
pieces or cuts of
meat in recipes.
They're a time-saver
because they cook
more quickly than
larger pieces.

4 SERVINGS

Apricot-Glazed Pork

1 tablespoon chili oil or vegetable oil

1 pound pork tenderloin, cut into 1/2-inch slices

1 bag (1 pound) frozen broccoli, cauliflower and carrots (or other combination)

3 tablespoons apricot preserves

1 tablespoon oyster sauce or hoisin sauce

Hot cooked rice or noodles, if desired

1 Heat wok or 12-inch skillet over high heat. Add oil; rotate wok to coat side. Add pork; stir-fry 4 to 5 minutes or until no longer pink.

2 Add frozen vegetables; stir-fry 2 minutes. Stir in preserves and oyster sauce; cook and stir about 30 seconds or until hot. Serve with rice.

1 SERVING: Calories 230 (Calories from Fat 70); Fat 8g (Saturated 2g); Cholesterol 65mg; Sodium 110mg; Carbohydrate 16g (Dietary Fiber 3g); Protein 27g • **% DAILY VALUE:** Vitamin A 36%; Vitamin C 32%; Calcium 4%; Iron 10% • **DIET EXCHANGES:** 1 Starch, 3 Lean Meat

Skillet Barbecue Pork Chops

prep: **5 min**
cook: **20 min**

4 pork loin or rib chops, 1/2 inch thick (about 1 1/4 pounds)

1/4 teaspoon salt

1/8 teaspoon pepper

1 can (15 ounces) chunky tomato sauce with onions, celery and green bell peppers

2 tablespoons packed brown sugar

2 tablespoons white vinegar

2 tablespoons Worcestershire sauce

1 teaspoon ground mustard

1 Spray 12-inch nonstick skillet with cooking spray; heat over medium heat. Sprinkle both sides of pork with salt and pepper. Cook pork in skillet about 5 minutes, turning once, until brown.

2 Stir remaining ingredients into skillet. Heat to boiling; reduce heat. Cover and simmer 10 to 15 minutes, stirring occasionally, until pork is slightly pink when cut near bone.

COME &eat!

Old-fashioned favorites just seem to hit the spot. Why not serve these yummy pork chops with potato salad, green beans or peas and, for dessert, brownies or ginger cookies? It's a quick and easy dinner that everyone will love!

1 SERVING: Calories 230 (Calories from Fat 70); Fat 8g (Saturated 3g); Cholesterol 65mg; Sodium 560mg; Carbohydrate 16g (Dietary Fiber 1g); Protein 24g • **% DAILY VALUE:** Vitamin A 4%; Vitamin C 10%; Calcium 4%; Iron 10% • **DIET EXCHANGES:** 1 Starch, 3 Lean Meat

Broiling or Grilling Pork

Broiling and direct-heat grilling are quick, low-fat methods for cooking chops and other small pieces. Refer to the instructions that came with your grill for more information.

1. Marinate pork if desired.

2. **To Broil:** Set oven control to broil and position oven rack so top of meat will be 3 to 4 inches from heat.

   To Grill: Brush grill rack with vegetable oil or spray with cooking spray. Place rack of outdoor grill 3 to 4 inches above heat. Start grill. If using charcoal grill, wait until coals are covered with ash (medium heat).

3. **To Broil:** Place pork on rack in broiler pan and place in oven. (For easy cleanup, first line broiler pan with aluminum foil.)

   To Grill: Place pork on grill.

4. Broil or grill for about half the time shown in chart for pork cut or until pork is brown on one side.

   Turn pork and continue cooking until done. (To check doneness, cut a small slit in the center of boneless cuts or in the center near the bone of bone-in cuts. Medium pork is slightly pink in center. Well-done pork is creamy-tan all the way through.) Well-done pork, although a little less juicy, is recommended for some cuts for food-safety purposes. Season each side after cooking if desired.

Timetable for Broiling and Grilling Pork

Pork Cut	Thickness	Meat Doneness	Broiling Time (minutes)	Grilling Time (minutes)
Loin or Rib Chops (bone-in)	3/4 inch	160° (medium)	8 to 11	6 to 8
	1 1/2 inches	160° (medium)	19 to 22	12 to 16
Loin Chop (boneless)	1 inch	160° (medium)	11 to 13	8 to 10
Blade Chop (bone-in)	3/4 inch	170° (well)	13 to 15	11 to 13
	1 1/2 inches	170° (well)	26 to 29	19 to 22
Arm Chop (bone-in)	3/4 inch	170° (well)	16 to 18	13 to 15
	1 inch	170° (well)	18 to 20	15 to 18
Cubes for Kabobs Loin or Leg	1-inch pieces	160° (medium)	9 to 11	10 to 20
Tenderloin	1-inch pieces	160° (medium)	12 to 14	13 to 21
Ground Pork Patties	1/2 inch thick	170° (well)	7 to 9	7 to 9

4 SERVINGS

Polynesian Pork Stir-Fry

1/4 cup shredded coconut

I pound pork tenderloin, cut into 1/8-inch slices

I small onion, cut into thin wedges

I teaspoon finely chopped gingerroot

1/4 teaspoon salt

I medium sweet potato, peeled and cut into 1 1/2 × 1/4-inch strips (1 1/2 cups)

I 1/2 cups frozen snap pea pods (from 1-pound bag)

1/4 cup stir-fry sauce

I can (8 ounces) pineapple tidbits or chunks in juice, drained and juice reserved

I tablespoon honey

1 Cook coconut in 10-inch nonstick skillet over medium heat 2 to 3 minutes, stirring constantly, just until golden brown. Remove from skillet.

2 Spray same skillet with cooking spray. Cook pork, onion, gingerroot and salt in skillet over medium-high heat, stirring occasionally, until pork is brown. Stir in sweet potato and frozen pea pods. Cover and cook over medium heat 4 to 6 minutes, stirring occasionally, until potato is tender.

3 Stir in stir-fry sauce, pineapple juice and honey until pork mixture is coated. Stir in pineapple; cook until heated through. Sprinkle each serving with coconut.

1 SERVING: Calories 330 (Calories from Fat 65); Fat 7g (Saturated 3g); Cholesterol 70mg; Sodium 770mg; Carbohydrate 40g (Dietary Fiber 4g); Protein 30g • **% DAILY VALUE:** Vitamin A 100%; Vitamin C 38%; Calcium 6%; Iron 18% • **DIET EXCHANGES:** 1 Starch, 4 Very Lean Meat, 1 Fruit, 1 Fat

Polynesian Pork Stir-Fry

prep: **5 min**
cook: **15 min**

COME
&eat!

This recipe is a
good choice for
family or company.
To quickly dress it
up for serving,
garnish with fresh
marjoram sprigs and
serve with steamed
white rice. A few
slices of red or green
apple on the platter
will add color
and crunch.

4 SERVINGS

Pork Chops with Apple-Cranberry Sauce

4 pork boneless loin chops (3/4 to 1 pound)

1/2 teaspoon salt

1/4 teaspoon coarsely ground pepper

3/4 cup apple juice

1/4 cup dry sherry or cranberry juice

1 tablespoon chopped fresh or 1/2 teaspoon dried marjoram leaves

1/4 cup sweetened dried cranberries

4 medium green onions, sliced (1/4 cup)

2 teaspoons cornstarch

1 Spray 10-inch nonstick skillet with cooking spray; heat over medium-high heat. Sprinkle pork chops with salt and pepper. Cook in skillet, turning once, until brown.

2 Stir in 1/2 cup of the apple juice, the sherry and marjoram. Cover and cook over medium-low heat 5 minutes. Stir in cranberries and onions. Cook 3 to 5 minutes, turning pork once, until pork is slightly pink in center.

3 Mix cornstarch and remaining 1/4 cup apple juice until smooth. Remove pork from skillet; cover to keep warm. Stir cornstarch mixture into skillet; cook and stir until thickened. Serve sauce over pork.

1 SERVING: Calories 240 (Calories from Fat 70); Fat 8g (Saturated 3g); Cholesterol 65mg; Sodium 340mg; Carbohydrate 18g (Dietary Fiber 3g); Protein 23g • **% DAILY VALUE:** Vitamin A 0%; Vitamin C 10%; Calcium 2%; Iron 6% • **DIET EXCHANGES:** 3 Lean Meat, 1 Fruit

4 SERVINGS

Sichuan Pork Fried Rice

prep: **15 min**
cook: **15 min**

1 pound pork boneless loin

1 tablespoon vegetable oil

2 medium carrots, chopped (1 cup)

1 medium onion, chopped (1/2 cup)

1 small green or red bell pepper, chopped (1/2 cup)

3 cups cold cooked rice

1/4 cup Sichuan (Szechuan) stir-fry sauce

1 cup bean sprouts

1 Cut pork into thin strips. (Pork is easier to cut if partially frozen, 30 to 60 minutes.) Heat oil in 10-inch skillet over medium-high heat. Cook pork in oil 3 to 5 minutes, stirring occasionally, until brown.

2 Stir in carrots, onion and bell pepper. Cook about 5 minutes, stirring occasionally, until vegetables are crisp-tender.

3 Stir in rice and stir-fry sauce until well mixed. Stir in bean sprouts. Cook about 5 minutes, stirring occasionally, until hot.

IT'S **a**

snap!

Today's leaner pork is a time-saver in itself because it requires shorter cook times. Over-cooking pork will make it tough, so be sure to follow the recipe times carefully.

1 SERVING: Calories 430 (Calories from Fat 125); Fat 14g (Saturated 4g); Cholesterol 75mg; Sodium 750mg; Carbohydrate 45g (Dietary Fiber 3g); Protein 33g • % DAILY VALUE: Vitamin A 48%; Vitamin C 20%; Calcium 4%; Iron 18% • DIET EXCHANGES: 2 1/2 Starch, 3 Lean Meat, 1 Vegetable, 1 Fat

Zesty Autumn Pork Stew

1 pound lean pork tenderloin, cut into 1-inch cubes

2 medium sweet potatoes, peeled and cubed (2 cups)

1 medium green bell pepper, chopped (1 cup)

2 cloves garlic, finely chopped

1 cup coarsely chopped cabbage

1 teaspoon Cajun seasoning

1 can (14 1/2 ounces) chicken broth

1 Spray 4-quart Dutch oven with cooking spray; heat over medium-high heat. Cook pork in Dutch oven, stirring occasionally, until brown.

2 Stir in remaining ingredients. Heat to boiling; reduce heat. Cover and simmer about 15 minutes, stirring once, until sweet potatoes are tender.

1 SERVING: Calories 240 (Calories from Fat 45); Fat 5g (Saturated 2g); Cholesterol 70mg; Sodium 730mg; Carbohydrate 22g (Dietary Fiber 3g); Protein 29g • **% DAILY VALUE:** Vitamin A 100%; Vitamin C 44%; Calcium 4%; Iron 12% • **DIET EXCHANGES:** 1 Starch, 3 Very Lean Meat, 2 Vegetable

Zesty Autumn Pork Stew

4 SERVINGS

Pork and White Bean Cassoulet

IT'S **a**
snap!
For speedier preparation at dinner time, cut the meats and onion the evening before or in the morning; wrap tightly and refrigerate until needed.

1/2 pound pork boneless loin, cut into 1/2-inch pieces

1 medium onion, chopped (1/2 cup)

1/4 teaspoon garlic powder

1/2 pound fully cooked kielbasa sausage, cut into 1/4-inch slices

1 can (14 1/2 ounces) stewed tomatoes, undrained

1/4 cup chili sauce or ketchup

1 tablespoon chopped fresh or 1/4 teaspoon dried thyme leaves

1 cup frozen cut green beans

1 can (15 to 16 ounces) great northern beans, drained

2 tablespoons chopped fresh parsley

1 Spray 12-inch nonstick skillet with cooking spray; heat over medium heat. Cook pork, onion and garlic powder in skillet 3 to 4 minutes, stirring occasionally, until pork is brown.

2 Stir in kielbasa, tomatoes, chili sauce, thyme and frozen green beans. Heat to boiling over medium heat. Cover and boil 5 minutes, stirring occasionally.

3 Stir in great northern beans. Cover and cook 8 to 10 minutes, stirring occasionally, until green beans are tender. Sprinkle with parsley.

1 SERVING: Calories 460 (Calories from Fat 190); Fat 21g (Saturated 7g); Cholesterol 70mg; Sodium 1090mg; Carbohydrate 44g (Dietary Fiber 9g); Protein 32g • **% DAILY VALUE:** Vitamin A 8%; Vitamin C 16%; Calcium 16%; Iron 32% • **DIET EXCHANGES:** 2 Starch, 3 Medium-Fat Meat, 3 Vegetable

prep: **5 min**
cook: **15 min**

6 SERVINGS

Sausage Skillet Supper

3 tablespoons vegetable oil

1 bag (24 ounces) frozen diced potatoes with onions and peppers

1/2 teaspoon dried oregano or basil leaves

1/2 teaspoon pepper

2 cups broccoli flowerets

1 ring (about 3/4 pound) Polish or smoked sausage, cut into 6 pieces

3 slices process American cheese, cut diagonally in half

IT'S **a**

snap!

If you don't want to spend the time cutting broccoli, look for the bags of cut-up broccoli flowerets in the produce section.

1 Heat oil in 10-inch skillet over medium-high heat. Add potatoes, oregano and pepper. Cover and cook 6 to 8 minutes, stirring occasionally, until potatoes are light brown.

2 Stir in broccoli; add sausage. Cover and cook about 8 minutes or until sausage is hot.

3 Top with cheese. Cover and heat until cheese is melted.

1 SERVING: Calories 395 (Calories from Fat 245); Fat 27g (Saturated 9g); Cholesterol 40mg; Sodium 1080mg; Carbohydrate 30g (Dietary Fiber 4g); Protein 12g • **% DAILY VALUE:** Vitamin A 8%; Vitamin C 40%; Calcium 8%; Iron 6% • **DIET EXCHANGES:** 1 Starch, 1/2 High-Fat Meat, 3 Vegetable, 4 Fat

Cajun Pork Burgers

C O M E
&eat!

For a quick flavor-adder, spread the toasted buns with mayonnaise and sprinkle with a dash of ground red pepper.

1 tablespoon olive or vegetable oil

1 1/2 cups frozen stir-fry bell peppers and onions (from 1-pound bag)

1 medium stalk celery, sliced (1/2 cup)

2 tablespoons chopped fresh parsley

1 pound ground pork

2 tablespoons chili sauce

1/2 teaspoon garlic salt

1/4 teaspoon dried thyme leaves

1/8 teaspoon ground red pepper (cayenne)

4 sandwich buns

1 Heat oven to 375°. Heat oil in 10-inch nonstick skillet over medium-high heat. Cook frozen bell pepper mixture and celery in oil 3 to 4 minutes, stirring occasionally, until tender. Stir in parsley; remove from skillet. Cover to keep warm.

2 Mix pork, chili sauce, garlic salt, thyme and red pepper. Shape mixture into 4 oval patties, 1/2 inch thick. Cook patties in hot skillet over medium heat 8 to 10 minutes, turning once, until no longer pink in center.

3 Place buns, cut sides up, on ungreased cookie sheet. Bake 3 to 5 minutes or until toasted. Serve patties on buns topped with vegetables.

1 SANDWICH: Calories 370 (Calories from Fat 190); Fat 21g (Saturated 7g); Cholesterol 70mg; Sodium 470mg; Carbohydrate 24g (Dietary Fiber 2g); Protein 24g • % DAILY VALUE: Vitamin A 4%; Vitamin C 22%; Calcium 6%; Iron 12% • DIET EXCHANGES: 1 Starch, 2 1/2 High-Fat Meat, 2 Vegetable

Cajun Pork Burgers

prep: **5 min**
cook: **15 min**

4 SERVINGS

Ham with Cabbage and Apples

4 cups coleslaw mix or shredded cabbage

1 tablespoon packed brown sugar

1 tablespoon cider vinegar

1/8 teaspoon pepper

1 large onion, chopped (1 cup)

1 large green cooking apple, sliced

1 pound fully cooked ham slice, about 1/2 inch thick

1 Spray 10-inch nonstick skillet with cooking spray; heat over medium heat.

2 Cook all ingredients except ham in skillet about 5 minutes, stirring frequently, until apple is crisp-tender.

3 Place ham on cabbage mixture; reduce heat to low. Cover and cook 5 to 10 minutes or until ham is hot.

1 SERVING: Calories 240 (Calories from Fat 80); Fat 9g (Saturated 3g); Cholesterol 55mg; Sodium 1460mg; Carbohydrate 20g (Dietary Fiber 4g); Protein 24g • **% DAILY VALUE:** Vitamin A 0%; Vitamin C 28%; Calcium 6%; Iron 12% • **DIET EXCHANGES:** 2 Medium-Fat Meat, 4 Vegetable

7 Fast Flavorful Fish and Seafood

● = _super express_ ready in 20 minutes or less

1-Step Recipes

Quick Coatings for Fish and Seafood
Pick a super-easy coating for fish fillets or seafood; bake or cook in a skillet. To quickly crush chips, crackers and cereal, place in a resealable plastic bag and crush with a rolling pin.

1 Salsa-Corn
Dip in salsa and coat with crushed tortilla or corn chips.

2 Mustard-Pretzel
Dip in yellow or Dijon mustard and coat with crushed pretzels.

3 Pesto-Butter
Dip in pesto and coat with finely crushed butter crackers.

4 Honey-Nut
Dip in honey or honey mustard and coat with finely chopped almonds.

5 All-American
Dip in ketchup and coat with crushed potato chips.

6 Chili-Cornmeal
Dip in chili sauce and coat with cornmeal.

7 Ranch and Cheese
Dip in ranch dressing and coat with crushed cheese-flavored crackers.

8 Maple-Walnut
Dip in maple syrup and coat with chopped walnuts.

9 Butter-Herb
Dip in melted butter and coat with crushed herb croutons.

10 Parmesan-Creole
Dip in mayonnaise and coat with grated Parmesan cheese mixed with Creole or Cajun seasoning or chili powder.

Savory Tuna

prep: **5 min**
cook: **13 min**

1 pound tuna, halibut or other firm fish fillets, about 3/4 inch thick

1 teaspoon olive or vegetable oil

2 medium green onions, sliced (2 tablespoons)

1/2 cup basil pesto

2 tablespoons lemon juice

1 If fish fillets are large, cut into 4 serving pieces.

2 Heat oil in 10-inch nonstick skillet over medium heat. Cook onions in oil 2 to 3 minutes, stirring occasionally, until crisp-tender.

3 Stir in pesto and lemon juice. Top with fish. Heat to boiling; reduce heat to low. Cover and cook 5 to 10 minutes or until tuna is slightly pink in center.

COME
&eat!

Nestle this tuna on a bed of linguine, drizzle with the pan juices and add a dollop of extra pesto. Serve with green beans and red, green, yellow or orange bell pepper strips.

1 SERVING: Calories 325 (Calories from Fat 205); Fat 23g (Saturated 5g); Cholesterol 45mg; Sodium 300mg; Carbohydrate 2g (Dietary Fiber 1g); Protein 29g • % DAILY VALUE: Vitamin A 70%; Vitamin C 2%; Calcium 12%; Iron 10% • DIET EXCHANGES: 4 Lean Meat, 2 Fat

prep: **5 min**
cook: **15 min**

COME
&eat!

Fresh asparagus and
lightly buttered new
potatoes comple-
ment this citrus-
flavored fish. For
an easy yet elegant
garnish, use orange
slices and dill sprigs.

4 SERVINGS

Orange and Dill Pan-Seared Tuna

4 tuna, swordfish or other firm fish steaks, 3/4 inch thick (4 ounces each)

1/2 teaspoon peppered seasoned salt

1 small red onion, thinly sliced (1/2 cup)

3/4 cup orange juice

1 tablespoon chopped fresh or 1/4 teaspoon dried dill weed

1 tablespoon butter or margarine

1 teaspoon grated orange peel, if desired

1 Spray 10-inch nonstick skillet with cooking spray; heat over medium-high heat. Sprinkle both sides of fish with seasoned salt. Add fish to skillet; reduce heat to medium-low. Cover and cook 6 to 8 minutes, turning once, until tuna is slightly pink in center. Remove fish from skillet and keep warm.

2 Add onion to skillet. Cook over medium-high heat 2 minutes, stirring occasionally. Stir in orange juice; cook 2 minutes. Stir in dill weed, butter and orange peel. Cook 1 to 2 minutes or until slightly thickened. Serve sauce over fish.

1 SERVING: Calories 215 (Calories from Fat 80); Fat 9g (Saturated 3g); Cholesterol 50mg; Sodium 240mg; Carbohydrate 6g (Dietary Fiber 0g); Protein 27g • **% DAILY VALUE:** Vitamin A 72%; Vitamin C 14%; Calcium 2%; Iron 8% • **DIET EXCHANGES:** 4 Lean Meat

Orange and Dill Pan-Seared Tuna

prep: **10 min**
cook: **7 min**

4 SERVINGS

Red Snapper Teriyaki

I tablespoon vegetable oil

I pound red snapper, amberjack or other medium-firm fish fillets, cut into I-inch pieces

3 cups I-inch pieces asparagus

I medium red bell pepper, cut into thin strips

1/2 cup teriyaki baste and glaze

Hot cooked noodles or rice, if desired

1 Heat wok or 12-inch skillet over medium-high heat. Add oil; rotate wok to coat side.

2 Add fish; stir-fry 2 minutes. Add asparagus and bell pepper; stir-fry 2 to 3 minutes or until vegetables are crisp-tender. Stir in teriyaki baste and glaze; cook 30 seconds or until hot.

3 Serve over noodles.

IT'S **a**
snap!

Look for teriyaki baste and glaze in the Asian foods section in your supermarket. Don't confuse the baste and glaze, which is thick like molasses, with teriyaki marinade, which is watery.

1 SERVING (NOT INCLUDING NOODLES): Calories 180 (Calories from Fat 45); Fat 5g (Saturated Ig); Cholesterol 50mg; Sodium 1470mg; Carbohydrate 12g (Dietary Fiber 2g); Protein 24g • **% DAILY VALUE:** Vitamin A 24%; Vitamin C 66%; Calcium 4%; Iron 8% • **DIET EXCHANGES:** 3 Very Lean Meat, 2 Vegetable, 1/2 Fat

4 SERVINGS

Snapper with Sautéed Tomato-Pepper Sauce

prep: **10 min**
cook: **12 min**

1 pound red snapper, grouper or other medium-firm fish fillets

1 large tomato, chopped (1 cup)

1 small green bell pepper, chopped (1/2 cup)

1 small onion, sliced

2 tablespoons finely chopped fresh cilantro or parsley

1/4 teaspoon salt

1/4 cup dry white wine or chicken broth

COME
&eat!

Sautéed pea pods and seasoned rice from a mix fill the bill for a quick serve-along.

1 If fish fillets are large, cut into 4 serving pieces. Spray 10-inch nonstick skillet with cooking spray; heat over medium heat.

2 Arrange fish in single layer in skillet. Cook uncovered 4 to 6 minutes, turning once, until fish flakes easily with fork. Remove fish to warm platter; keep warm.

3 Cook remaining ingredients except wine in same skillet over medium heat 3 to 5 minutes, stirring frequently, until bell pepper and onion are crisp-tender. Stir in wine; cook until hot. Spoon tomato mixture over fish.

1 SERVING: Calories 115 (Calories from Fat 10); Fat 1g (Saturated 0g); Cholesterol 50mg; Sodium 230mg; Carbohydrate 5g (Dietary Fiber 1g); Protein 19g • % DAILY VALUE: Vitamin A 4%; Vitamin C 22%; Calcium 2%; Iron 4% • DIET EXCHANGES: 3 Very Lean Meat, 1 Vegetable

Baked Fish with Tropical Fruit Salsa

IT'S a
snap!

A couple of ways to slash time from this recipe: Purchase jarred cubed mango and papaya, and select precut pineapple from the salad bar or produce area of the store. Or simply purchase one of the fruit salsas available in most grocery stores.

Tropical Fruit Salsa (below)	**1 teaspoon chili powder**
3 tablespoons butter or margarine	**1 1/4 teaspoons salt**
2/3 cup Original Bisquick	**1 pound orange roughy or other mild-flavored fish fillets**
1/4 cup yellow cornmeal	**1 egg, beaten**

1 Make Tropical Fruit Salsa. Heat oven to 425°. Melt butter in rectangular pan, 13 × 9 × 2 inches, in oven.

2 Mix Bisquick, cornmeal, chili powder and salt. Dip fish into egg, then coat with Bisquick mixture. Place in pan.

3 Bake uncovered 10 minutes; turn fish. Bake about 10 minutes longer or until fish flakes easily with fork. Serve with salsa.

Tropical Fruit Salsa

1 cup pineapple chunks

1 tablespoon finely chopped red onion

1 tablespoon chopped fresh cilantro

2 tablespoons lime juice

2 kiwifruit, peeled and chopped

1 mango, cut lengthwise in half, pitted and chopped

1 papaya, peeled, seeded and chopped

1 jalapeño chili, seeded and finely chopped

Mix all ingredients in glass or plastic bowl. Cover and refrigerate while fish is baking to blend flavors.

1 SERVING: Calories 400 (Calories from Fat 110); Fat 12g (Saturated 2g); Cholesterol 100mg; Sodium 1070mg; Carbohydrate 51g (Dietary Fiber 5g); Protein 27g • **% DAILY VALUE:** Vitamin A 46%; Vitamin C 100%; Calcium 10%; Iron 10% • **DIET EXCHANGES:** 1 Starch, 3 1/2 Very Lean Meat, 2 Fruit, 2 Fat

Baked Fish with Tropical Fruit Salsa

IT'S **a**
snap!
In a time crunch?
Use 1/2 cup of a
purchased seasoned
fish coating mix
instead of preparing
the coating mixture
yourself.

4 SERVINGS

Crispy Baked Catfish

**1 pound catfish, flounder or
other delicate-texture fish fillets**

1/4 cup yellow cornmeal

1/4 cup dry bread crumbs

1 teaspoon chili powder

1/2 teaspoon paprika

1/2 teaspoon garlic salt

1/4 teaspoon pepper

**1/4 cup French or ranch
dressing**

1 Heat oven to 450°. Spray broiler pan rack with cooking spray. If fish fillets are large, cut into 4 serving pieces.

2 Mix cornmeal, bread crumbs, chili powder, paprika, garlic salt and pepper. Lightly brush dressing on all sides of fish. Coat fish with cornmeal mixture.

3 Place fish on rack in broiler pan. Bake uncovered 15 to 18 minutes or until fish flakes easily with fork.

1 SERVING: Calories 235 (Calories from Fat 70); Fat 8g (Saturated 1g); Cholesterol 75mg; Sodium 450mg; Carbohydrate 14g (Dietary Fiber 1g); Protein 28g • **% DAILY VALUE:** Vitamin A 4%; Vitamin C 0%; Calcium 6%; Iron 6% • **DIET EXCHANGES:** 1 Starch, 4 Very Lean Meat

prep: **10 min**
grill: **10 min**

Grilled Salmon with Hazelnut Butter

Hazelnut Butter (below)

1 pound salmon, trout or other medium-firm fish fillets

1/2 teaspoon salt

1/8 teaspoon pepper

1 Brush grill rack with vegetable oil. Heat coals or gas grill for direct heat. Make Hazelnut Butter.

2 If fish fillets are large, cut into 4 serving pieces. Sprinkle both sides of fish with salt and pepper.

3 Cover and grill fish 4 to 6 inches from medium heat 4 minutes. Turn; spread about 1 tablespoon Hazelnut Butter over each fillet. Cover and grill 4 to 6 minutes longer or until fish flakes easily with fork.

Hazelnut Butter

2 tablespoons finely chopped hazelnuts

3 tablespoons butter or margarine, softened

1 tablespoon chopped fresh parsley

1 teaspoon lemon juice

Spread nuts in shallow microwavable bowl or pie plate. Microwave uncovered on High 30 seconds to 1 minute, stirring once or twice, until light brown; cool. Mix hazelnuts and remaining ingredients.

IT'S **a**
snap!

Any type of nut—almond, pecan, walnut or cashew—can be substituted for the hazelnuts. Nuts can become rancid quickly, so it's best to store them in the freezer and to taste them before using in your recipes.

1 SERVING: Calories 215 (Calories from Fat 125); Fat 14g (Saturated 5g); Cholesterol 80mg; Sodium 390mg; Carbohydrate 1g (Dietary Fiber 0g); Protein 21g • **% DAILY VALUE:** Vitamin A 8%; Vitamin C 2%; Calcium 2%; Iron 4% • **DIET EXCHANGES:** 3 Lean Meat, 1 Fat

4 SERVINGS

Baked Salmon with Cilantro

COME
&eat!

For easy entertaining, just double this recipe. Serve the salmon on a bed of angel hair pasta or skin-on mashed potatoes on a pretty serving platter. Garnish the platter with cilantro sprigs and slices of lemon.

1/4 cup butter or margarine, slightly softened

1 tablespoon chopped fresh cilantro

1/2 teaspoon grated lemon peel

1 pound salmon, snapper or other medium-firm fish fillets, about 1 inch thick

1/4 teaspoon salt

1/4 teaspoon ground cumin

1 tablespoon lemon juice

1 Heat oven to 425°. Line rectangular pan, 13 × 9 × 2 inches, with aluminum foil; spray foil with cooking spray. Mix butter, cilantro and lemon peel. Cover and refrigerate butter while preparing fish.

2 Cut fish into 4 serving pieces. Place fish, skin side down, in pan. Sprinkle with salt and cumin. Drizzle with lemon juice.

3 Bake uncovered 15 to 20 minutes or until fish flakes easily with fork. Carefully lift fish from skin with pancake turner. Top each serving of fish with some cilantro butter mixture.

1 SERVING: Calories 260 (Calories from Fat 160); Fat 18g (Saturated 9g); Cholesterol 105mg; Sodium 290mg; Carbohydrate 0g (Dietary Fiber 0g); Protein 24g • **% DAILY VALUE:** Vitamin A 12%; Vitamin C 2%; Calcium 2%; Iron 4% • **DIET EXCHANGES:** 3 1/2 Medium-Fat Meat

Baked Salmon with Cilantro

4 SERVINGS

Easy Fish and Vegetable Packets

4 mild-flavored fish fillets, such as cod, flounder, sole or walleye pike (about 4 ounces each)

I bag (1 pound) frozen broccoli, cauliflower and carrots (or other combination), thawed and drained

I tablespoon chopped fresh or I teaspoon dried dill weed

1/2 teaspoon salt

1/4 teaspoon pepper

1/4 cup dry white wine or chicken broth

1 Heat oven to 450°. Place each fish fillet on 12-inch square of aluminum foil. Top each fish fillet with one-fourth of the vegetables. Sprinkle with dill weed, salt and pepper. Drizzle 1 tablespoon wine over each mound of vegetables.

2 Fold up sides of foil to make a tent; fold top edges to seal. Fold in sides, making a packet; fold to seal. Place packets on ungreased cookie sheet.

3 Bake about 20 minutes or until vegetables are crisp-tender and fish flakes easily with fork.

1 SERVING: Calories 130 (Calories from Fat 20); Fat 2g (Saturated 0g); Cholesterol 60mg; Sodium 420mg; Carbohydrate 6g (Dietary Fiber 3g); Protein 24g • **% DAILY VALUE:** Vitamin A 62%; Vitamin C 30%; Calcium 6%; Iron 4% • **DIET EXCHANGES:** 3 Very Lean Meat, I Vegetable

prep: **15 min**
cook: **10 min**

Pecan-Crusted Fish Fillets

I cup finely chopped pecans (not ground)

1/4 cup dry bread crumbs

2 teaspoons grated lemon peel

I egg

I tablespoon milk

I pound sole, walleye pike or other delicate-texture fish fillets, about 1/2 inch thick

1/2 teaspoon salt

1/4 teaspoon pepper

2 tablespoons vegetable oil

Lemon wedges

1 Mix pecans, bread crumbs and lemon peel in shallow bowl. Beat egg and milk with wire whisk or fork in another shallow bowl.

2 Cut fish into 4 serving pieces. Sprinkle both sides of fish with salt and pepper. Coat fish with egg mixture, then coat well with pecan mixture, pressing lightly into fish.

3 Heat oil in 12-inch nonstick skillet over medium heat. Add fish. Reduce heat to medium-low. Cook 6 to 10 minutes, turning once carefully with 2 pancake turners, until fish is brown and flakes easily with fork. Serve with lemon wedges.

**COME
&eat!**

Serve this fish with a quick, tasty side dish of noodles tossed with browned butter and chopped fresh parsley. To brown butter (do not use margarine or spreads), heat in a heavy saucepan or skillet over medium heat, stirring occasionally, just until butter begins to turn golden to light brown in color and starts to foam. Watch carefully because butter can brown and burn quickly.

1 SERVING: Calories 350 (Calories from Fat 235); Fat 26g (Saturated 3g); Cholesterol 105mg; Sodium 450mg; Carbohydrate 10g (Dietary Fiber 2g); Protein 21g • **% DAILY VALUE:** Vitamin A 2%; Vitamin C 0%; Calcium 4%; Iron 8% • **DIET EXCHANGES:** 1/2 Starch, 3 Very Lean Meat, 3 Fat

4 SERVINGS

Lemony Fish over Vegetables and Rice

1 package (6.2 ounces) fried rice (rice and vermicelli mix with almonds and Oriental seasonings)

2 tablespoons butter or margarine

2 cups water

1/2 teaspoon grated lemon peel

1 bag (1 pound) frozen corn, broccoli and red peppers (or other combination)

1 pound cod, haddock or other mild-flavored fish fillets, about 1/2 inch thick

1/2 teaspoon lemon pepper or 1/8 teaspoon pepper

1 tablespoon lemon juice

2 tablespoons chopped fresh parsley

1 Cook rice and butter in 12-inch nonstick skillet over medium heat about 2 minutes, stirring occasionally, until rice is golden brown. Stir in water, seasoning packet from rice mix and lemon peel. Heat to boiling; reduce heat. Cover and simmer 10 minutes.

2 Stir in frozen vegetables. Heat to boiling, stirring occasion-ally. Cut fish into 4 serving pieces; arrange on rice mixture. Sprinkle fish with lemon pepper; drizzle with lemon juice.

3 Reduce heat. Cover and simmer about 8 minutes or until fish flakes easily with fork and vegetables are tender. Sprinkle with parsley.

1 SERVING: Calories 255 (Calories from Fat 70); Fat 8g (Saturated 4g); Cholesterol 75mg; Sodium 330mg; Carbohydrate 23g (Dietary Fiber 3g); Protein 26g • **% DAILY VALUE:** Vitamin A 64%; Vitamin C 72%; Calcium 4%; Iron 8% • **DIET EXCHANGES:** 1 1/2 Starch, 3 Very Lean Meat, 1 Fat

Lemony Fish over Vegetables and Rice

Pantry Recipes

If you have a well-stocked pantry (see pages 6–7), you'll be able to make this recipe anytime, even when there's no time to shop.

Fantastic Fruited Fish

**1 pound halibut or other
mild-flavored fish steaks**

1/2 cup apricot preserves

2 tablespoons white vinegar

**1 1/2 teaspoons chopped fresh or
1/2 teaspoon dried tarragon leaves**

Set oven control to broil. Spray broiler pan rack with cooking spray. Place **fish** on rack in broiler pan. Broil with tops about 4 inches from heat 4 minutes; turn. Broil about 4 minutes longer or until fish flakes easily with fork. Meanwhile, mix **preserves, vinegar** and **tarragon;** spoon onto fish. Broil 1 minute longer. MAKES 4 SERVINGS IN 15 MINUTES

serve it 3 ways!

1 Salad
Cut cooked fish into pieces. Serve over spinach or other greens, and drizzle with raspberry vinaigrette.

2 Sandwich
Cut cooked fish into pieces. Place fish on tortilla, add a spoonful of fruit salsa, apricot or peach preserves and roll up.

3 Main Course
Cut cooked fish into pieces. Add to cooked rice and sauce mix, and serve with steamed snow peas.

prep: **10 min**
bake: **15 min**

Ranch Halibut with Lemon-Parsley Tartar Sauce

1 envelope (1 ounce) ranch dressing mix

16 round buttery crackers, crushed (3/4 cup)

2 tablespoons butter or margarine, melted

1 teaspoon lemon juice

1 pound halibut, marlin or other firm fish fillets, about 1 inch thick, skin removed

1/2 cup tartar sauce

2 tablespoons chopped fresh parsley

1 teaspoon grated lemon peel

1 Heat oven to 450°. Line rectangular pan, 13 × 9 × 2 inches, with aluminum foil; spray foil with cooking spray. Mix dressing mix (dry) and crackers in shallow bowl. Mix butter and lemon juice in another shallow bowl.

2 Cut fish into 4 serving pieces. Dip fish into butter, then coat with cracker mixture. Place in pan.

3 Bake uncovered 10 to 15 minutes or until fish flakes easily with fork. While fish is baking, mix tartar sauce, parsley and lemon peel. Serve tartar sauce with fish.

COME **&eat!**

For a speedy fish 'n' chips supper, frozen French fries can go in the oven with the fish. While the fish and fries are baking, toss together coleslaw mix and bottled coleslaw dressing.

1 SERVING: Calories 375 (Calories from Fat 245); Fat 27g (Saturated 7g); Cholesterol 75mg; Sodium 760mg; Carbohydrate 13g (Dietary Fiber 0g); Protein 20g • **% DAILY VALUE:** Vitamin A 8%; Vitamin C 4%; Calcium 4%; Iron 6% • **DIET EXCHANGES:** 1 Starch, 2 1/2 High-Fat Meat, 1 Fat

4 SERVINGS

Halibut-Asparagus Stir-Fry

1 pound halibut, swordfish or tuna fillets, cut into 1-inch pieces

1 medium onion, thinly sliced

3 cloves garlic, finely chopped

1 teaspoon finely chopped gingerroot

1 package (10 ounces) frozen asparagus cuts, thawed and drained

1 package (8 ounces) sliced mushrooms (3 cups)

1 medium tomato, cut into thin wedges

2 tablespoons reduced-sodium soy sauce

1 tablespoon lemon juice

1 Spray 10-inch nonstick skillet with cooking spray; heat over medium-high heat. Add fish, onion, garlic, gingerroot and asparagus; stir-fry 2 to 3 minutes or until fish almost flakes with fork.

2 Carefully stir in remaining ingredients. Cook until heated through and fish flakes easily with fork. Serve with additional soy sauce if desired.

1 SERVING: Calories 140 (Calories from Fat 20); Fat 2g (Saturated 0g); Cholesterol 50mg; Sodium 350mg; Carbohydrate 11g (Dietary Fiber 3g); Protein 22g • % **DAILY VALUE:** Vitamin A 8%; Vitamin C 22%; Calcium 4%; Iron 10% • **DIET EXCHANGES:** 2 1/2 Very Lean Meat, 2 Vegetable

Halibut-Asparagus Stir-Fry

4 SERVINGS

Gremolata-Topped Sea Bass

IT'S **a**
snap!
To save time, use
purchased bread
crumbs that contain
garlic. If the brand
you find doesn't list
garlic on the label,
add 1/4 teaspoon
garlic powder to the
bread crumb mixture.

1/4 cup Italian-style dry bread crumbs

1/4 cup chopped fresh parsley

Grated peel of 1 lemon (1 1/2 to 3 teaspoons)

1 tablespoon butter or margarine, melted

1 pound sea bass, mahimahi or other medium-firm fish fillets

1/4 teaspoon seasoned salt

1 tablespoon lemon juice

1 Heat oven to 425°. Line rectangular pan, 13 × 9 × 2 inches, with aluminum foil; spray foil with cooking spray. Mix bread crumbs, parsley, lemon peel and butter.

2 Cut fish into 4 serving pieces. Place fish in pan. Sprinkle with seasoned salt. Drizzle with lemon juice. Spoon crumb mixture over each piece; press lightly.

3 Bake uncovered 15 to 20 minutes or until fish flakes easily with fork.

1 SERVING: Calories 150 (Calories from Fat 35); Fat 4g (Saturated 2g); Cholesterol 65mg; Sodium 170mg; Carbohydrate 6g (Dietary Fiber 0g); Protein 22g • **% DAILY VALUE:** Vitamin A 4%; Vitamin C 4%; Calcium 4%; Iron 4% • **DIET EXCHANGES:** 3 Very Lean Meat, 1 Fat

Gremolata-Topped Sea Bass

C O M E
&eat!

Need to eat dinner
on the go? This
recipe is ready to
roll in minutes. Fill
buns or rolls with
the tuna patties, top
with sauce, and
wrap in aluminum
foil packets. Foil
works best because
it keeps sandwiches
warm as well
as neat.

4 SERVINGS

Tuna Patties with Sour Cream Dill Sauce

Sour Cream Dill Sauce (below)

2 cans (6 ounces each) water-packed tuna, drained

3 cups cornflakes, crushed to crumbs (1 1/2 cups)

1/4 cup mayonnaise or salad dressing

2 medium green onions, sliced (2 tablespoons)

1 teaspoon yellow mustard

1 egg

1 tablespoon vegetable oil

1 Make Sour Cream Dill Sauce.

2 Mix tuna, 1 cup of the cornflake crumbs, mayonnaise, onions, mustard and egg. Shape mixture into four 4-inch patties. Coat patties with remaining 1/2 cup cornflake crumbs, pressing lightly to coat both sides.

3 Heat oil in 10-inch nonstick skillet over medium-high heat. Cook patties in oil 2 to 3 minutes, turning once, until light golden brown. Serve with sauce.

Sour Cream Dill Sauce

1/4 cup sour cream

1/4 cup mayonnaise or salad dressing

1 teaspoon dried dill weed

Mix all ingredients.

1 SERVING: Calories 395 (Calories from Fat 260); Fat 29g (Saturated 6g); Cholesterol 105mg; Sodium 590mg; Carbohydrate 11g (Dietary Fiber 1g); Protein 24g • **% DAILY VALUE:** Vitamin A 14%; Vitamin C 4%; Calcium 4%; Iron 28% • **DIET EXCHANGES:** 1 Starch, 3 Lean Meat, 3 1/2 Fat

prep: **5** min
cook: **13** min
stand: **2** min

4 SERVINGS

Cheesy Tuna Broccoli Skillet Casserole

1 medium onion, chopped (1/2 cup)

1 can (10 3/4 ounces) condensed cream of broccoli soup

2 cups milk

2 cups uncooked mafalda (mini-lasagna noodle) pasta (4 ounces)

1 1/2 cups frozen broccoli cuts

1 can (6 ounces) tuna, drained

1/2 cup bite-size square crisp cheese crackers, crushed (1/4 cup)

1/2 cup shredded Cheddar cheese (2 ounces)

IT'S **a**
snap!

For easy substitutions, use Cheddar cheese soup or cream of asparagus soup instead of broccoli soup and frozen asparagus cuts for the broccoli. You can vary the ingredients to make this quick comfort skillet casserole a little different every time!

1 Spray 12-inch nonstick skillet with cooking spray; heat over medium-high heat. Cook onion in skillet 2 minutes, stirring occasionally, until crisp-tender. Stir in soup and milk. Heat to boiling, stirring constantly. Stir in pasta and frozen broccoli. Heat to boiling; reduce heat to medium. Cover and cook 5 minutes.

2 Stir in tuna. Cover and cook about 5 minutes, stirring occasionally, until pasta is tender.

3 Mix crackers and cheese; sprinkle over tuna mixture. Cover and let stand 1 to 2 minutes or until cheese is melted.

1 SERVING: Calories 375 (Calories from Fat 115); Fat 13g (Saturated 6g); Cholesterol 40mg; Sodium 820mg; Carbohydrate 42g (Dietary Fiber 4g); Protein 26g • % DAILY VALUE: Vitamin A 24%; Vitamin C 28%; Calcium 34%; Iron 14% • DIET EXCHANGES: 3 Starch, 2 1/2 Lean Meat

4 SERVINGS

Shrimp Florentine Stir-Fry

1 tablespoon olive or vegetable oil

1 pound uncooked peeled deveined medium shrimp, thawed if frozen

4 cups lightly packed spinach leaves

1 can (14 ounces) baby corn nuggets, drained

1/4 cup coarsely chopped drained roasted red bell peppers (from 7-ounce jar)

1 1/2 teaspoons chopped fresh or 1/2 teaspoon dried tarragon leaves

1/2 teaspoon garlic salt

Lemon wedges

1 Heat wok or 12-inch nonstick skillet over medium-high heat. Add oil; rotate wok to coat side.

2 Add shrimp; stir-fry 2 to 3 minutes or until shrimp are pink and firm. Add spinach, corn, bell peppers, tarragon and garlic salt; stir-fry 2 to 4 minutes or until spinach is wilted. Serve with lemon wedges.

1 SERVING: Calories 175 (Calories from Fat 45); Fat 5g (Saturated 1g); Cholesterol 105mg; Sodium 480mg; Carbohydrate 20g (Dietary Fiber 3g); Protein 15g • **% DAILY VALUE:** Vitamin A 32%; Vitamin C 26%; Calcium 6%; Iron 18% • **DIET EXCHANGES:** 1 Medium-Fat Meat, 4 Vegetable

prep: **10 min**
cook: **3 min**

Scampi with Fettuccine

2 tablespoons olive or
vegetable oil

1 1/2 pounds uncooked peeled
deveined medium shrimp,
thawed if frozen

2 medium green onions,
thinly sliced (2 tablespoons)

2 cloves garlic, finely chopped

1 tablespoon chopped fresh or
1/2 teaspoon dried basil leaves

1 tablespoon chopped
fresh parsley

2 tablespoons lemon juice

1/4 teaspoon salt

4 cups hot cooked fettuccine

1   Heat oil in 10-inch skillet over medium heat. Cook
remaining ingredients except fettuccine in oil 2 to 3 minutes,
stirring frequently, until shrimp are pink and firm; remove
from heat.

2   Toss fettuccine with shrimp mixture in skillet.

IT'S **a**
snap!

Peeling and devein-
ing shrimp is quite
time consuming—
and unnecessary!
Fortunately for us,
somebody else has
done this laborious
task. Look for fresh
or frozen shrimp
that has already
been peeled and
deveined.

1 SERVING: Calories 330 (Calories from Fat 70); Fat 8g (Saturated 1g); Cholesterol 210mg; Sodium 350mg; Carbohydrate 41g (Dietary Fiber 2g); Protein 25g • **% DAILY VALUE:** Vitamin A 6%; Vitamin C 4%; Calcium 6%; Iron 28% • **DIET EXCHANGES:** 3 Starch, 2 Lean Meat

4 SERVINGS

Garlic Shrimp

1 tablespoon vegetable oil	1 large carrot, cut into thin strips (1 cup)
3 large cloves garlic, finely chopped (about 1 tablespoon)	2 tablespoons chopped fresh cilantro
1 pound uncooked peeled deveined medium shrimp, thawed if frozen	Hot cooked noodles or rice, if desired

1 Heat wok or 12-inch skillet over medium-high heat. Add oil; rotate wok to coat side.

2 Add garlic; stir-fry 1 minute. Add shrimp; stir-fry 1 minute. Add carrot; stir-fry about 3 minutes or until shrimp are pink and firm and carrot is crisp-tender. Stir in cilantro.

3 Serve over noodles.

1 SERVING: Calories 95 (Calories from Fat 35); Fat 4g (Saturated 1g); Cholesterol 105mg; Sodium 130mg; Carbohydrate 3g (Dietary Fiber 1g); Protein 12g • **% DAILY VALUE:** Vitamin A 30%; Vitamin C 2%; Calcium 2%; Iron 10% • **DIET EXCHANGES:** 1 1/2 Very Lean Meat, 1 Vegetable, 1/2 Fat

Garlic Shrimp

6 SERVINGS

Seafood and Tomatoes with Rice

**I package (8 ounces)
sliced mushrooms (3 cups)**

**I can (14 1/2 ounces) fat-free
chicken broth**

**1/2 cup sliced drained
roasted red bell peppers
(from 7-ounce jar)**

**3 roma (plum) tomatoes,
cut into fourths and sliced
(I 1/2 cups)**

**1/2 pound uncooked peeled
deveined small shrimp,
thawed if frozen**

**1/2 pound cod or other
mild-flavored fish fillets, cubed**

6 ounces bay scallops

**1/2 cup white wine or
chicken broth**

1/2 teaspoon salt

**1/4 to 1/2 teaspoon red pepper
sauce**

1/4 cup chopped fresh cilantro

4 cups hot cooked rice

1 Heat mushrooms and broth to boiling in 3-quart saucepan.
Stir in remaining ingredients except cilantro and rice. Heat
to boiling; reduce heat.

2 Cover and simmer 5 to 7 minutes or until shrimp are pink
and firm. Stir in cilantro. Divide rice among 6 bowls. Top
with seafood mixture.

1 SERVING: Calories 245 (Calories from Fat 20); Fat 2g (Saturated 0g); Cholesterol 80mg;
Sodium 480mg; Carbohydrate 35g (Dietary Fiber 1g); Protein 22g • **% DAILY VALUE:**
Vitamin A 26%; Vitamin C 28%; Calcium 4%; Iron 20% • **DIET EXCHANGES:** 2 Starch,
2 Very Lean Meat, 1 Vegetable

4 SERVINGS

prep: **10 min**
cook: **10 min**

Savory Shrimp and Scallops

2 tablespoons olive or vegetable oil

1 clove garlic, finely chopped

2 medium green onions, sliced (2 tablespoons)

2 medium carrots, thinly sliced (1 cup)

1 tablespoon chopped fresh parsley or 1 teaspoon parsley flakes

1 pound uncooked peeled deveined medium shrimp, thawed if frozen

1 pound sea scallops, cut in half

1/2 cup dry white wine or chicken broth

1 tablespoon lemon juice

1/4 to 1/2 teaspoon crushed red pepper

IT'S **a**
snap!

For this recipe pick up the sea scallops, the larger ones that measure up to 1 1/2 inches, and cut in half. You can also use bay scallops, which are much smaller (only 1/2 inch) but don't cut them. Sea scallops will have a more tender texture for this dish.

1 Heat oil in 10-inch skillet over medium heat. Cook garlic, onions, carrots and parsley in oil about 5 minutes, stirring occasionally, until carrots are crisp-tender.

2 Stir in remaining ingredients. Cook 4 to 5 minutes, stirring frequently, until shrimp are pink and firm and scallops are white.

1 **SERVING:** Calories 185 (Calories from Fat 65); Fat 7g (Saturated 1g); Cholesterol 125mg; Sodium 350mg; Carbohydrate 6g (Dietary Fiber 1g); Protein 25g • **% DAILY VALUE:** Vitamin A 54%; Vitamin C 6%; Calcium 10%; Iron 20% • **DIET EXCHANGES:** 3 Lean Meat, 1 Vegetable

4 SERVINGS

Marinara Shrimp and Vegetable Bowls

1 package (7 ounces) vermicelli

1 tablespoon olive or vegetable oil

2 cloves garlic, finely chopped

1/2 cup red onion wedges

1 medium zucchini, cut into 2 × 1/4-inch strips

1 medium yellow summer squash, cut into 2 × 1/4-inch strips

1/4 teaspoon salt

1 pound uncooked peeled deveined medium or large shrimp, thawed if frozen

1 cup marinara sauce

2 tablespoons chopped fresh or 1/2 teaspoon dried basil leaves

1 Cook and drain vermicelli as directed on package. While vermicelli is cooking, heat oil in 10-inch skillet over medium heat. Cook garlic and onion in oil 2 to 3 minutes, stirring frequently, until onion is crisp-tender. Stir in zucchini, yellow squash and salt. Cook 2 to 3 minutes, stirring frequently, just until squash is tender; remove vegetables from skillet.

2 Add shrimp to skillet. Cook and stir 1 to 2 minutes or until shrimp are pink and firm. Meanwhile heat marinara sauce in 1-quart saucepan over medium heat until hot.

3 Divide vermicelli among 4 bowls; toss each serving with about 2 tablespoons marinara sauce. Top with vegetables and shrimp. Drizzle with remaining marinara sauce. Sprinkle with basil.

1 SERVING: Calories 350 (Calories from Fat 65); Fat 7g (Saturated 1g); Cholesterol 105mg; Sodium 580mg; Carbohydrate 56g (Dietary Fiber 4g); Protein 20g • **% DAILY VALUE:** Vitamin A 20%; Vitamin C 18%; Calcium 6%; Iron 26% • **DIET EXCHANGES:** 3 Starch, 1 Very Lean Meat, 2 Vegetable, 1 Fat

Marinara Shrimp and Vegetable Bowls

4 SERVINGS

Crab and Spinach Casserole

2 cups uncooked gemelli (twist) pasta (4 ounces)

1 package (1.8 ounces) leek soup mix

2 cups milk

1 package (8 ounces) refrigerated imitation crabmeat chunks

2 cups baby spinach leaves, stems removed

1/4 cup freshly shredded Parmesan cheese

1 Heat oven to 350°. Spray 1 1/2-quart casserole or square baking dish, 8 × 8 × 2 inches, with cooking spray. Cook and drain pasta as directed on package.

2 While pasta is cooking, mix soup mix and milk in 1-quart saucepan. Heat to boiling, stirring constantly. Cut up larger pieces of crabmeat if desired. Mix pasta, crabmeat and spinach in casserole.

3 Pour soup mixture over pasta mixture; stir gently to mix. Spread evenly. Sprinkle with cheese. Bake uncovered about 20 minutes or until bubbly and light golden brown.

1 SERVING: Calories 345 (Calories from Fat 55); Fat 6g (Saturated 2g); Cholesterol 25mg; Sodium 960mg; Carbohydrate 55g (Dietary Fiber 4g); Protein 22g • **% DAILY VALUE:** Vitamin A 66%; Vitamin C 14%; Calcium 18%; Iron 18% • **DIET EXCHANGES:** 3 Starch, 1 Very Lean Meat, 1 Vegetable, 1/2 Skim Milk

Crab and Spinach Casserole

4 SERVINGS

Creamy Crab au Gratin

2 tablespoons butter or margarine

1 1/2 cups sliced mushrooms (4 ounces)

2 medium stalks celery, sliced (1 cup)

1 can (14 1/2 ounces) chicken broth

3/4 cup half-and-half

3 tablespoons all-purpose flour

1/2 teaspoon red pepper sauce

2 packages (8 ounces each) refrigerated imitation crabmeat chunks or 2 cups chopped cooked crabmeat

1 cup soft bread crumbs (about 1 1/2 slices bread)

1 Heat oven to 400°. Spray rectangular baking dish, 11 × 7 × 1 1/2 inches, with cooking spray. Melt butter in 10-inch skillet over medium-high heat. Cook mushrooms and celery in butter about 4 minutes, stirring frequently, until celery is tender. Stir in broth. Heat to boiling; reduce heat to medium.

2 Beat half-and-half, flour and pepper sauce with wire whisk until smooth; stir into vegetable mixture. Heat to boiling, stirring constantly. Boil and stir 1 minute. Stir in crabmeat.

3 Spoon crabmeat mixture into baking dish. Top with bread crumbs. Bake uncovered about 15 minutes or until heated through.

1 SERVING: Calories 285 (Calories from Fat 45); Fat 12g (Saturated 6g); Cholesterol 60mg; Sodium 1580mg; Carbohydrate 22g (Dietary Fiber 1g); Protein 23g • **% DAILY VALUE:** Vitamin A 10%; Vitamin C 2%; Calcium 8%; Iron 8% • **DIET EXCHANGES:** 1 Starch, 3 Very Lean Meat, 1 Vegetable, 1/2 Fat

Crab Cakes

super
express

prep: **10 min**
cook: **10 min**

1/4 cup mayonnaise or salad dressing	1/8 teaspoon pepper
1 egg	2 medium green onions, chopped (2 tablespoons)
1 1/4 cups soft bread crumbs (about 2 slices bread)	2 cans (6 ounces each) crabmeat, drained and flaked*
1 teaspoon ground mustard	2 tablespoons vegetable oil
1/4 teaspoon salt	1/4 cup dry bread crumbs

1 Mix mayonnaise and egg in medium bowl. Stir in remaining ingredients except oil and dry bread crumbs. Shape mixture into 6 patties, about 3 inches in diameter.

2 Heat oil in 12-inch skillet over medium heat. Coat each patty with dry bread crumbs. Cook in oil about 10 minutes, turning once, until golden brown and hot in center. Reduce heat if crab cakes brown too quickly.

✴ **HOW TO flake crabmeat:** Flake crabmeat with a fork and remove any tiny pieces of shell.

COME
&eat!

How about a different kind of burger tonight? Thaw on-hand buns from the freezer while the crab cakes are cooking and make Crab Cake Sandwiches; top with tartar sauce and serve with oven-baked French fries.

1 SERVING: Calories 305 (Calories from Fat 170); Fat 19g (Saturated 3g); Cholesterol 135mg; Sodium 650mg; Carbohydrate 12g (Dietary Fiber 0g); Protein 21g • % DAILY VALUE: Vitamin A 2%; Vitamin C 2%; Calcium 12%; Iron 10% • DIET EXCHANGES: 1 Starch, 2 1/2 Lean Meat, 2 Fat

4 SERVINGS

Easy Seafood Risotto

1 tablespoon olive or vegetable oil

1 medium onion, chopped (1/2 cup)

1 can (14 1/2 ounces) chicken broth

1 cup uncooked medium or long-grain white rice

1 cup baby-cut carrots, cut lengthwise in half

1/2 cup water

1/2 teaspoon garlic pepper

2 cups prewashed fresh baby spinach leaves

1 package (8 ounces) refrigerated imitation crabmeat chunks

1/4 cup shredded Parmesan cheese

1 Heat oil in 12-inch nonstick skillet over medium-high heat. Cook onion in oil 2 to 3 minutes, stirring occasionally, until crisp-tender. Stir in broth; heat to boiling. Stir in rice; reduce heat. Cover and simmer 10 minutes without stirring.

2 Stir in carrots, water and garlic pepper. Cover and simmer 8 to 10 minutes without stirring until rice is tender.

3 Stir in spinach until wilted. Stir in crabmeat and cheese.

1 SERVING: Calories 330 (Calories from Fat 65); Fat 7g (Saturated 2g); Cholesterol 20mg; Sodium 1080mg; Carbohydrate 50g (Dietary Fiber 2g); Protein 18g • **% DAILY VALUE:** Vitamin A 60%; Vitamin C 6%; Calcium 12%; Iron 14% • **DIET EXCHANGES:** 3 Starch, 1 Medium-Fat Meat, 1 Vegetable

Easy Seafood Risotto

prep: **10 min**
cook: **10 min**

6 SERVINGS

Corn and Crab Quesadillas

I package (8 ounces) cream cheese, softened

I can (11 ounces) whole kernel corn, drained

I jar (2 ounces) diced pimientos, drained

1/2 cup chopped fresh cilantro or parsley

4 medium green onions, chopped (1/4 cup)

1/2 teaspoon pepper

1/4 teaspoon ground red pepper (cayenne)

I pound chopped cooked crabmeat or imitation crabmeat (2 cups)

6 flour tortillas (8 to 10 inches in diameter)

I tablespoon butter or margarine, melted

Sour cream and additional chopped fresh cilantro, if desired

1 Mix cream cheese, corn, pimientos, cilantro, onions, pepper and red pepper in medium bowl. Fold in crabmeat. Spread 2/3 cup of the crabmeat mixture over each tortilla; fold tortilla in half, pressing lightly. Brush both sides of each tortilla with butter.

2 Cook 3 tortillas at a time in 12-inch skillet over medium-high heat about 5 minutes, turning once, until light brown. Garnish with sour cream and additional cilantro.

1 SERVING: Calories 400 (Calories from Fat 180); Fat 20g (Saturated 10g); Cholesterol 120mg; Sodium 690mg; Carbohydrate 34g (Dietary Fiber 2g); Protein 23g • **% DAILY VALUE:** Vitamin A 18%; Vitamin C 12%; Calcium 16%; Iron 18% • **DIET EXCHANGES:** 2 Starch, 2 Lean Meat, 1 Vegetable, 3 Fat

8 Vegetarian Main Dishes

🕐 = *super express* ready in 20 minutes or less

1-Step Recipes

Vegetarian Main Dishes
Here are some great ideas for pumping up the vegetables, grains and beans in your diet. Turn to these quick vegetarian dishes when you want a meatless meal.

1 Rice and Bean Roll-Ups
Mix cooked rice with salsa, black beans, and corn. Spoon over spinach- or herb-flavor flour tortillas; sprinkle with Mexican 4-cheese blend.

2 Ravioli with Tomato and Basil
Layer cooked cheese-filled ravioli, warmed crushed tomatoes, chopped fresh or dried basil leaves and shredded mozzarella cheese; heat until cheese is melted.

3 "Meatball" Pizza
Top pizza crust with pizza sauce, vegetable "meat-balls" (shape thawed vegetable burgers into balls), sliced ripe olives and mozzarella and Cheddar cheeses.

4 Vegetable and Soybean Stir-Fry
Stir-fry a bag of frozen stir-fry bell peppers and onions with a bag of frozen soybeans. Serve over hot cooked rice.

5 Caesar Salad Wrap-Ups
Toss Caesar dressing with chopped romaine, chopped red onion, sliced hard-cooked eggs and sliced roma tomatoes; sprinkle with Parmesan cheese and roll in tortillas.

6 Chowder in Bread Bowls
Cut off tops of hard rolls and remove soft bread in middle. Fill rolls with potato soup heated with frozen potatoes, sweet peas and carrots and drained canned kidney beans.

7 Vegetable Chili
Cook potatoes, onions and bell peppers; stir in tomato sauce, chili powder, ground cumin, tomatoes, garbanzo beans, black beans and zucchini.

8 Italian Grinders
Fill hot dog buns with cooked vegetable burgers. Top with onion and green pepper slices. Dip in heated pasta sauce.

9 Onion and Cheese Wedges
Cook sliced onions in butter. Sprinkle shredded mozzarella cheese and crumbled Gorgonzola cheese over bottom half of split focaccia bread; top with onions and top of focaccia. Cut into wedges.

10 Cheesy Quesadillas
Sprinkle flour tortilla with shredded Cheddar cheese, seeded and chopped tomato, sliced green onions, chopped chilies and cilantro. Top with another tortilla and heat.

Pasta and Bean Skillet

prep: **10 min**
cook: **18 min**

1 cup salsa

2/3 cup uncooked elbow macaroni (2 ounces)

3/4 cup water

2 teaspoons chili powder

1 can (15 to 16 ounces) kidney beans, rinsed and drained

1 can (8 ounces) tomato sauce

1/2 cup shredded Cheddar cheese (2 ounces)

1 Heat all ingredients except cheese to boiling in 10-inch nonstick skillet; reduce heat to low.

2 Cover and simmer about 15 minutes, stirring frequently, until macaroni is just tender. Sprinkle with cheese.

C O M E
&eat!

For an all-time favorite kids meal, use 3 ounces uncooked wagon wheel pasta or small pasta shells instead of the elbow maca-roni and a 15-ounce can of pork and beans in place of the kidney beans. Adults and kids alike will enjoy crusty bread-sticks and lettuce wedges drizzled with a favorite dressing on the side.

1 SERVING: Calories 280 (Calories from Fat 55); Fat 6g (Saturated 3g); Cholesterol 15mg; Sodium 990mg; Carbohydrate 49g (Dietary Fiber 9g); Protein 17g • **% DAILY VALUE:** Vitamin A 20%; Vitamin C 6%; Calcium 14%; Iron 28% • **DIET EXCHANGES:** 2 Starch, 4 Vegetable, 1/2 Fat

4 SERVINGS

Creamy Corn and Garlic Risotto

3 3/4 cups vegetable or chicken broth

4 cloves garlic, finely chopped

1 cup uncooked Arborio or regular medium-grain white rice

3 cups frozen whole kernel corn

1/2 cup grated Parmesan cheese

1/3 cup shredded mozzarella cheese

1/4 cup chopped fresh parsley

1 Heat 1/3 cup of the broth to boiling in 10-inch skillet. Cook garlic in broth 1 minute, stirring occasionally. Stir in rice and frozen corn. Cook 1 minute, stirring occasionally.

2 Stir in remaining broth. Heat to boiling; reduce heat to medium. Cook uncovered 15 to 20 minutes, stirring occasionally, until rice is tender and creamy; remove from heat.

3 Stir in cheeses and parsley.

1 SERVING: Calories 400 (Calories from Fat 70); Fat 8g (Saturated 4g); Cholesterol 15mg; Sodium 1250mg; Carbohydrate 66g (Dietary Fiber 4g); Protein 20g • **% DAILY VALUE:** Vitamin A 14%; Vitamin C 8%; Calcium 28%; Iron 16% • **DIET EXCHANGES:** 4 1/2 Starch, 1 Lean Meat

Creamy Corn and Garlic Risotto

prep: **7 min**

cook: **8 min**

C O M E

&eat!

For a change of
pace, wrap up this
stir-fry in tortillas so
everyone can enjoy
dinner on the go!

4 SERVINGS

Southern Stir-Fry

1 cup cooked white rice

1 cup frozen whole kernel corn

1 1/2 teaspoons chopped fresh or 1/2 teaspoon dried thyme leaves

1/2 teaspoon garlic salt

1/8 teaspoon ground red pepper (cayenne)

1 can (15 to 16 ounces) black-eyed peas, rinsed and drained

2 cups lightly packed spinach leaves

1 Spray 12-inch nonstick skillet with cooking spray; heat over medium-high heat.

2 Cook all ingredients except spinach in skillet, stirring occasionally, until hot. Stir in spinach. Cook until spinach begins to wilt.

1 SERVING: Calories 180 (Calories from Fat 10); Fat 1g (Saturated 0g); Cholesterol 0mg; Sodium 360mg; Carbohydrate 41g (Dietary Fiber 8g); Protein 10g • **% DAILY VALUE:** Vitamin A 28%; Vitamin C 4%; Calcium 4%; Iron 20% • **DIET EXCHANGES:** 2 Starch, 2 Vegetable

Mediterranean Couscous and Beans

prep: **10 min**
cook: **3 min**
stand: **5 min**

3 cups vegetable or chicken broth

2 cups uncooked couscous

1/2 cup raisins or currants

1/4 teaspoon pepper

1/8 teaspoon ground red pepper (cayenne)

1 small tomato, chopped (1/2 cup)

1 can (15 to 16 ounces) garbanzo beans, rinsed and drained

1/3 cup crumbled feta cheese

1 Heat broth to boiling in 3-quart saucepan. Stir in remaining ingredients except cheese; remove from heat.

2 Cover and let stand about 5 minutes or until liquid is absorbed; stir gently.

3 Sprinkle each serving with cheese.

IT'S **a**

snap!

Couscous is small pasta, but it's often shelved near the boxes of rice and grains in the supermarket. Check out all the different flavored couscous now available— and try a new one in this recipe.

1 SERVING: Calories 550 (Calories from Fat 55); Fat 6g (Saturated 2g); Cholesterol 10mg; Sodium 1050mg; Carbohydrate 115g (Dietary Fiber 14g); Protein 23g • **% DAILY VALUE:** Vitamin A 14%; Vitamin C 6%; Calcium 14%; Iron 26% • **DIET EXCHANGES:** 7 Starch

4 SERVINGS

Vegetable Curry with Couscous

IT'S **a**
snap!

If you'd like to add chicken to this fragrant curry dish, just add 2 boneless, skinless chicken breasts, cut into 3/4-inch pieces, with the bell pepper in step 1. Cook until chicken is no longer pink in center and continue as directed.

1 tablespoon vegetable oil	**1 bag (1 pound) frozen broccoli, carrots and cauliflower (or other combination)**
1 medium red bell pepper, cut into thin strips	**1/2 cup raisins**
1/4 cup vegetable or chicken broth	**1/3 cup chutney**
1 tablespoon curry powder	**2 cups hot cooked couscous or rice**
1 teaspoon salt	**1/4 cup chopped peanuts**

1 Heat oil in 12-inch skillet over medium-high heat. Cook bell pepper in oil, stirring frequently, until tender.

2 Stir in broth, curry powder, salt and frozen vegetables. Heat to boiling. Boil about 4 minutes, stirring frequently, until vegetables are crisp-tender.

3 Stir in raisins and chutney. Serve over couscous. Sprinkle with peanuts.

1 SERVING: Calories 290 (Calories from Fat 70); Fat 8g (Saturated 1g); Cholesterol 0mg; Sodium 940mg; Carbohydrate 53g (Dietary Fiber 7g); Protein 9g • **% DAILY VALUE:** Vitamin A 98%; Vitamin C 80%; Calcium 6%; Iron 8% • **DIET EXCHANGES:** 3 Starch, 1 Vegetable, 1/2 Fat

Vegetable Curry with Couscous

prep: **5 min**
cook: **10 min**
stand: **5 min**

IT'S **a**
snap!

To make Vegetable-
Chicken Paella to
satisfy the meat-
eaters in the family,
remove half of the
paella from the
skillet; keep warm.
Stir I cup of cubed
cooked chicken or
turkey into remain-
ing paella in skillet;
heat through.

4 SERVINGS

Vegetable Paella

**2 tablespoons olive or
vegetable oil**

2 cloves garlic, finely chopped

**I large red onion, cut into
thin wedges**

**I cup uncooked quick-cooking
brown rice**

**I cup vegetable or
chicken broth**

**I can (14 1/2 ounces)
stewed tomatoes, undrained**

**1/2 teaspoon saffron threads,
crushed**

**I bag (I pound) frozen petite
peas, baby whole carrots,
snow peas and baby cob corn
(or other combination)**

1 Heat oil in 12-inch nonstick skillet over medium-high heat.
Cook garlic and onion in oil, stirring frequently, until
onion is tender.

2 Stir in remaining ingredients. Heat to boiling; reduce heat
to medium-low. Cover and cook 5 minutes, stirring occasionally; remove from heat. Let stand covered 5 minutes.

1 SERVING: Calories 270 (Calories from Fat 70); Fat 8g (Saturated Ig); Cholesterol 0mg;
Sodium 600mg; Carbohydrate 50g (Dietary Fiber 8g); Protein 8g • **% DAILY VALUE:**
Vitamin A 100%; Vitamin C 26%; Calcium 8%; Iron 12% • **DIET EXCHANGES:** 3 Starch,
I Vegetable

6 SERVINGS

Broccoli, Rice and Chili Beans

prep: **5 min**
cook: **10 min**
stand: **5 min**

I cup uncooked instant rice

2 cans (16 ounces each) spicy chili beans in sauce, undrained

I bag (I pound) frozen broccoli cuts, thawed and drained

I cup shredded process cheese (4 ounces)

1 Place rice, beans and broccoli in skillet. Heat to boiling; reduce heat to medium.

2 Cover and simmer 5 minutes; remove from heat. Sprinkle with cheese. Cover and let stand about 5 minutes or until liquid is absorbed and cheese is melted.

COME
&eat!

Start with rice, add some beans, broccoli and cheese, and what do you have? An easy, tasty skillet meal with only one pan to clean after dinner.

1 SERVING: Calories 265 (Calories from Fat 65); Fat 7g (Saturated 4g); Cholesterol 20mg; Sodium 1380mg; Carbohydrate 43g (Dietary Fiber 8g); Protein 15g • **% DAILY VALUE:** Vitamin A 38%; Vitamin C 34%; Calcium 18%; Iron 22% • **DIET EXCHANGES:** 2 Starch, 3 Vegetable, 1/2 Fat

IT'S **a**
snap!
To save on chopping time, you can use 1 cup of well-drained canned or frozen (thawed) whole kernel corn instead of the zucchini.

4 SERVINGS

Skillet Nachos

1 tablespoon olive or vegetable oil

1 medium green bell pepper, chopped (1 cup)

1 small zucchini, chopped (1 cup)

1 cup chili beans in chili sauce (from 15-ounce can)

1 cup thick-and-chunky salsa

4 ounces tortilla chips

1 1/2 cups shredded Monterey Jack cheese (6 ounces)

Sliced ripe olives, if desired

1 Heat oil in 12-inch skillet over high heat. Add bell pepper and zucchini; stir-fry about 2 minutes or until vegetables are crisp-tender. Stir in beans and 1/2 cup of the salsa; cook until hot. Remove mixture from skillet.

2 Wipe skillet clean. Arrange tortilla chips in single layer in skillet. Spoon vegetable mixture onto chips. Sprinkle with cheese.

3 Cover and cook over medium-high heat about 5 minutes or until cheese is melted. Sprinkle with olives. Serve with remaining 1/2 cup salsa.

1 SERVING: Calories 385 (Calories from Fat 200); Fat 22g (Saturated 9g); Cholesterol 40mg; Sodium 1180mg; Carbohydrate 35g (Dietary Fiber 6g); Protein 17g • **% DAILY VALUE:** Vitamin A 30%; Vitamin C 36%; Calcium 36%; Iron 18% • **DIET EXCHANGES:** 1 Starch, 1 High-Fat Meat, 1 Vegetable, 2 Fat

Skillet Nachos

Pantry Recipes

If you have a well-stocked pantry (see pages 6–7), you'll be able to make this recipe anytime, even when there's no time to shop.

Savory Vegetable Stew

2 cups frozen stir-fry bell peppers and onions (from 1-pound bag)

1 can (14 1/2 ounces) diced tomatoes with mild green chilies

1 teaspoon chopped fresh or 1/4 teaspoon dried thyme leaves

Spray 12-inch nonstick skillet with cooking spray; heat over medium-high heat. Stir-fry **vegetables** in skillet about 3 minutes or until crisp-tender. Stir in **tomatoes**, undrained, and **thyme**. Heat to boiling; reduce heat. Cover and simmer 8 to 10 minutes, stirring occasionally, until heated through. MAKES 4 SERVINGS IN 20 MINUTES

serve it 3 ways!

1 Sandwich
Spread soft chèvre (goat) cheese with herbs over bottom halves of 4 crusty Italian or French rolls, fill with vegetable mixture and add tops of rolls.

2 Pasta
Add any cooked pasta or rice with the vegetables; stir-fry about 5 minutes or until vegetables are crisp-tender and pasta or rice is heated through. Continue as directed.

3 Main Course
Add 1 pound uncooked peeled deveined medium shrimp (thawed if frozen) with the tomatoes. Continue as directed, cooking until shrimp are pink and firm.

4 SERVINGS

Cheesy Vegetable-Rice Skillet

prep: **5 min**
cook: **9 min**

1 can (14 1/2 ounces) vegetable broth

2 tablespoons butter or margarine

1 bag (1 pound) frozen cauliflower, carrots and asparagus (or other combination)

1 package (6.2 ounces) fast-cooking long-grain and wild rice mix

3/4 cup shredded Cheddar cheese (3 ounces)

IT'S **a**
snap!
Vegetable broth, a pantry staple, adds great flavor to this cheesy veggie and rice dinner.

1 Heat broth and butter to boiling in 10-inch skillet. Stir in frozen vegetables, rice mix and contents of seasoning packet. Heat to boiling; reduce heat.

2 Cover and simmer 5 to 6 minutes or until vegetables and rice are tender. Sprinkle with cheese.

1 SERVING: Calories 215 (Calories from Fat 115); Fat 13g (Saturated 8g); Cholesterol 35mg; Sodium 650mg; Carbohydrate 19g (Dietary Fiber 4g); Protein 9g • % DAILY VALUE: Vitamin A 76%; Vitamin C 32%; Calcium 16%; Iron 6% • DIET EXCHANGES: 1 Starch, 1/2 High-Fat Meat, 1 Vegetable, 1 Fat

prep: **10 min**
cook: **5 min**
stand: **5 min**

IT'S **a**
snap!

For even more
fiesta flavor, use
the new jalapeño-
and cilantro-flavored
flour tortillas
available in the
supermarket.

4 SERVINGS

Salsa-Rice Burritos

1 1/2 cups salsa, plus additional, if desired

1 1/2 teaspoons chili powder

1 cup uncooked instant rice

1 can (15 ounces) black beans, rinsed and drained

1 can (11 ounces) whole kernel corn with red and green peppers, undrained

1 1/2 cups shredded Cheddar cheese (6 ounces)

8 flour tortillas (8 inches in diameter)

1 Heat 1 1/2 cups salsa and the chili powder to boiling in 10-inch skillet. Stir in rice; remove from heat. Cover and let stand 5 minutes. Stir in beans, corn and cheese.

2 Spoon about 1/2 cup rice mixture onto center of each tortilla. Fold up bottom of each tortilla; fold over sides. Secure with toothpick if necessary. Serve with additional salsa.

1 SERVING: Calories 750 (Calories from Fat 200); Fat 22g (Saturated 10g); Cholesterol 45mg; Sodium 1530mg; Carbohydrate 119g (Dietary Fiber 14g); Protein 33g • **% DAILY VALUE:** Vitamin A 20%; Vitamin C 24%; Calcium 46%; Iron 44% • **DIET EXCHANGES:** 7 Starch, 3 Vegetable, 3 Fat

Salsa-Rice Burritos

4 SERVINGS

Wild Rice and White Bean Medley

**1 can (14 1/2 ounces) vegetable
or chicken broth**

**1 package (6.2 ounces)
fast-cooking long-grain and
wild rice mix**

**1 can (15 to 16 ounces)
cannellini or great northern
beans, rinsed and drained**

**1 can (8 ounces) sliced
water chestnuts, drained**

**6 medium green onions, sliced
(6 tablespoons)**

1 Heat broth and seasoning packet from rice mix to boiling in 3-quart saucepan, stirring occasionally; reduce heat.

2 Stir in rice mix and remaining ingredients. Cover and simmer about 5 minutes or until rice is tender and beans are heated through.

1 SERVING: Calories 220 (Calories from Fat 10); Fat 1g (Saturated 0g); Cholesterol 0mg; Sodium 470mg; Carbohydrate 47g (Dietary Fiber 9g); Protein 13g • **% DAILY VALUE:** Vitamin A 8%; Vitamin C 6%; Calcium 12%; Iron 28% • **DIET EXCHANGES:** 2 Starch, 1 Very Lean Meat, 3 Vegetable

super
express

prep: **10 min**
cook: **10 min**

Wild Rice–Pecan Patties

2 cups cooked wild rice

I cup soft bread crumbs (about I I/2 slices bread)

I/3 cup chopped pecans

I/2 teaspoon garlic salt

2 eggs

I jar (2 I/2 ounces) mushroom pieces and stems, drained and finely chopped

I jar (2 ounces) diced pimientos, drained

2 tablespoons vegetable oil

1 Mix all ingredients except oil.

2 Heat oil in 10-inch skillet over medium heat. Scoop wild rice mixture by 1/3 cupfuls into skillet; flatten to 1/2 inch. Cook about 3 minutes on each side or until light brown. Remove patties from skillet; cover and keep warm while cooking remaining patties.

COME
&eat!

Beef burgers beware! These patties are absolutely delicious served in sandwich buns with cranberry sauce. On the side try steamed broccoli with melted butter and fresh fruit for dessert.

2 PATTIES: Calories 340 (Calories from Fat 150); Fat 17g (Saturated 2g); Cholesterol 105mg; Sodium 450mg; Carbohydrate 41g (Dietary Fiber 4g); Protein 11g • % DAILY VALUE: Vitamin A 22%; Vitamin C 4%; Calcium 8%; Iron 16% • DIET EXCHANGES: 2 Starch, 2 Vegetable, 3 Fat

6 SERVINGS

Stacked Enchilada Bake

IT'S **a**

snap!

Use kitchen scissors to snip the tortillas into bite-size pieces—it's even quicker than cutting them with a knife.

12 corn tortillas (5 or 6 inches in diameter), torn into bite-size pieces

2 cans (15 to 16 ounces each) chili beans in sauce, undrained

1 can (10 ounces) enchilada sauce

1 1/2 cups shredded Monterey Jack cheese (6 ounces)

3 medium green onions, sliced (3 tablespoons)

1 Heat oven to 400°. Spray 2-quart casserole with cooking spray.

2 Place half of the tortilla pieces in casserole; top with 1 can of beans. Repeat layers. Pour enchilada sauce oven beans and tortilla pieces. Sprinkle with cheese and onions.

3 Bake uncovered about 20 minutes or until bubbly around edge.

1 SERVING: Calories 300 (Calories from Fat 90); Fat 10g (Saturated 6g); Cholesterol 25mg; Sodium 910mg; Carbohydrate 45g (Dietary Fiber 8g); Protein 16g • **% DAILY VALUE:** Vitamin A 26%; Vitamin C 14%; Calcium 32%; Iron 22% • **DIET EXCHANGES:** 3 Starch, 1 Lean Meat

Stacked Enchilada Bake

prep: **10 min**
cook: **10 min**

4 SERVINGS

Black Bean and Rice Burgers

**IT'S a
snap!**

What's the fastest
way to mash a can
of beans? Reach
for your potato
masher. No need to
dirty the blender or
food processor for
this recipe.

**I can (I5 to I6 ounces)
black beans, rinsed and drained**

I cup cooked rice

**I small onion, finely chopped
(I/4 cup)**

2 tablespoons salsa

I/4 cup sour cream

I/4 cup salsa

4 hamburger buns, split

Lettuce leaves

1 Mash beans. Mix beans, rice, onion and 2 tablespoons salsa.

2 Spray 10-inch skillet with cooking spray; heat over medium-high heat. Spoon bean mixture by 1/2 cupfuls into skillet; flatten to 1/2 inch. Cook 4 to 5 minutes on each side or until light brown. Remove patties from skillet; cover and keep warm while cooking remaining patties.

3 Mix sour cream and 1/4 cup salsa; spread on buns. Top with burgers and lettuce.

1 SERVING: Calories 340 (Calories from Fat 55); Fat 6g (Saturated 2g); Cholesterol 10mg; Sodium 760mg; Carbohydrate 65g (Dietary Fiber 9g); Protein 15g • **% DAILY VALUE:** Vitamin A 10%; Vitamin C 6%; Calcium 16%; Iron 26% • **DIET EXCHANGES:** 4 Starch, 1/2 Fat

Cheesy Soy Burgers

Horseradish Sauce (below)

I can (15 ounces) soybeans, rinsed and drained

1/2 cup shredded Cheddar cheese (2 ounces)

1/4 cup dry bread crumbs

1 teaspoon Worcestershire sauce

1/4 teaspoon pepper

1/8 teaspoon salt

2 medium green onions, finely chopped (2 tablespoons)

I egg white or 2 tablespoons fat-free cholesterol-free egg product

4 hamburger buns, split and toasted

4 slices tomato

4 lettuce leaves

prep: **15 min**
cook: **10 min**

1 Make Horseradish Sauce. Mash soybeans in medium bowl. Mix in cheese, bread crumbs, Worcestershire sauce, pepper, salt, onions and egg white. Shape mixture into 4 patties.

2 Spray 10-inch nonstick skillet with cooking spray; heat over medium heat. Cook patties in skillet about 10 minutes, turning once, until light brown. Serve on buns with sauce, tomato and lettuce.

Horseradish Sauce

1/2 cup plain fat-free yogurt

2 teaspoons prepared horseradish

Mix ingredients. Cover and refrigerate until ready to use.

IT'S **a**
snap!

The ingredient list may be daunting, but don't let that stop you—this recipe is super-easy. But on those nights when there's *really* no time to cook, frozen soy burgers are a terrific option, especially when they're topped with this 30-second horseradish sauce.

1 SERVING: Calories 365 (Calories from Fat 155); Fat 17g (Saturated 5g); Cholesterol 15mg; Sodium 770mg; Carbohydrate 42g (Dietary Fiber 8g); Protein 29g • **% DAILY VALUE:** Vitamin A 12%; Vitamin C 8%; Calcium 32%; Iron 42% • **DIET EXCHANGES:** 3 Starch, 2 1/2 Lean Meat

Sometimes it's called Peking sauce, but either way, hoisin sauce is a sweet, reddish brown sauce made of soybeans, chilies and spices. For increased hoisin flavor, spread each pancake with extra hoisin sauce before adding vegetables.

6 SERVINGS (2 PANCAKES EACH)

Mou Shu Vegetables with Asian Pancakes

I tablespoon vegetable oil

I bag (16 ounces) coleslaw mix

I cup canned drained bean sprouts or I bag (8 ounces) fresh bean sprouts

I package (8 ounces) sliced mushrooms (3 cups)

I tablespoon grated gingerroot

3 tablespoons hoisin sauce

I 1/4 cups Original Bisquick

I 1/4 cups milk

I egg

8 green onions, chopped (1/2 cup)

Additional hoisin sauce, if desired

1 Heat oil in 4-quart Dutch oven over medium-high heat. Cook coleslaw mix, bean sprouts, mushrooms and gingerroot in oil about 10 minutes, stirring frequently, until vegetables are tender. Stir in 3 tablespoons hoisin sauce. Reduce heat; keep warm.

2 Beat Bisquick, milk and egg in medium bowl with wire whisk or hand beater until well blended. Stir in onions. Spray 10-inch skillet with cooking spray; heat over medium-high heat. For each pancake, pour slightly less than 1/4 cup batter into skillet; rotate skillet to make a thin pancake, 5 to 6 inches in diameter. Cook until bubbles break on surface; turn. Cook other side until golden brown. Keep warm while making remaining pancakes.

3 Spoon about 1/3 cup vegetable mixture onto each pancake; roll up. Serve with additional hoisin sauce.

1 SERVING: Calories 225 (Calories from Fat 80); Fat 9g (Saturated 2g); Cholesterol 40mg; Sodium 540mg; Carbohydrate 30g (Dietary Fiber 3g); Protein 9g • **% DAILY VALUE:** Vitamin A 10%; Vitamin C 26%; Calcium 16%; Iron 14% • **DIET EXCHANGES:** 1 Starch, 3 Vegetable, 1 1/2 Fat

Mou Shu Vegetables with Asian Pancakes

prep: **10 min**

cook: **10 min**

4 SERVINGS

New Mexican Black Bean Burritos

IT'S **a**
snap!
Use a garlic press
to quickly crush the
garlic instead of
chopping it. Look
for the self-cleaning
type—it presses all
the garlic through
the holes instead of
leaving pieces
behind.

1 tablespoon butter or margarine

1 large onion, chopped (1 cup)

6 cloves garlic, finely chopped

1 can (15 ounces) black beans, rinsed, drained and mashed

1 to 2 teaspoons finely chopped chipotle chilies in adobo sauce (from 7-ounce can), drained

4 flour tortillas (6 or 8 inches in diameter)

1/2 cup shredded mozzarella cheese (2 ounces)

1 large tomato, chopped (1 cup)

1 Melt butter in 10-inch nonstick skillet. Cook onion and garlic in butter over medium-high heat about 5 minutes, stirring occasionally, until onion is tender but not brown. Stir in beans and chilies. Cook 3 to 5 minutes, stirring occasionally, until hot.

2 Place one-fourth of the bean mixture on center of each tortilla. Top with cheese and tomato and roll up tortilla to enclose filling.

1 BURRITO: Calories 290 (Calories from Fat 70); Fat 8g (Saturated 4g); Cholesterol 15mg; Sodium 620mg; Carbohydrate 49g (Dietary Fiber 9g); Protein 16g • **% DAILY VALUE:** Vitamin A 12%; Vitamin C 10%; Calcium 22%; Iron 20% • **DIET EXCHANGES:** 3 Starch, 2 Vegetable

Crunchy Bean Skillet

super
express

prep: **10 min**
cook: **10 min**

**3 cans (15 to 16 ounces each)
cannellini beans, rinsed and
drained**

**1 jar (14 ounces) tomato
pasta sauce (any variety)**

**2 medium stalks celery, sliced
(1 cup)**

**4 medium green onions, sliced
(1/4 cup)**

1 teaspoon parsley flakes

1 teaspoon dried basil leaves

**1/2 teaspoon dried
oregano leaves**

**1 cup shredded mozzarella
cheese (4 ounces)**

**1/2 cup coarsely chopped
walnuts, toasted* if desired**

1 Mix all ingredients except cheese and walnuts in 10-inch
nonstick skillet. Heat to boiling; reduce heat. Sprinkle with
cheese.

2 Cover and simmer 3 to 5 minutes or just until cheese is
melted. Sprinkle with walnuts.

* **HOW TO toast nuts:** Cook nuts in ungreased heavy skillet over
medium-low heat 5 to 7 minutes, stirring frequently until browning
begins, then stirring constantly until golden brown. Or bake uncovered
in ungreased shallow pan in 350° oven about 10 minutes, stirring
occasionally, until golden brown.

**COME
&eat!**

This skillet dish also
looks great if you
use several varieties
of beans. A colorful
combination to try
is one can each of
cannellini, kidney
and black beans.

1 SERVING: Calories 435 (Calories from Fat 100); Fat 11g (Saturated 3g); Cholesterol 10mg;
Sodium 650mg; Carbohydrate 70g (Dietary Fiber 17g); Protein 31g • **% DAILY VALUE:**
Vitamin A 32%; Vitamin C 26%; Calcium 40%; Iron 54% • **DIET EXCHANGES:** 4 Starch,
2 Lean Meat, 2 Vegetable

4 SERVINGS

Warm Tuscan Bean Salad

C O M E
&eat!

If you want to make Tuscan Bean and Chicken Salad, omit 1 can of cannellini beans and add 1 1/2 cups cubed cooked chicken or turkey with the beans in step 2.

1 tablespoon olive or vegetable oil

2 medium carrots, sliced (1 cup)

1 medium onion, chopped (1/2 cup)

2 cans (15 to 16 ounces each) cannellini beans, drained and 1/2 cup liquid reserved

1 1/2 teaspoons chopped fresh or 1/2 teaspoon dried oregano leaves

1/4 teaspoon pepper

4 cups bite-size pieces spinach leaves

1/4 cup red wine vinaigrette or Italian dressing

2 tablespoons bacon flavor bits

1 Heat oil in 12-inch skillet over medium heat. Cook carrots and onion in oil 5 to 7 minutes, stirring occasionally, until vegetables are crisp-tender.

2 Stir in beans, 1/2 cup reserved liquid, the oregano and pepper. Cook 5 minutes, stirring occasionally.

3 Line large platter with spinach. Top with bean mixture. Pour vinaigrette over salad. Sprinkle with bacon bits.

1 SERVING: Calories 385 (Calories from Fat 100); Fat 11g (Saturated 2g); Cholesterol 5mg; Sodium 230mg; Carbohydrate 63g (Dietary Fiber 16g); Protein 24g • **% DAILY VALUE:** Vitamin A 72%; Vitamin C 22%; Calcium 24%; Iron 50% • **DIET EXCHANGES:** 3 Starch, 1 Medium-Fat Meat, 3 Vegetable, 1 Fat

Warm Tuscan Bean Salad

Grilling Vegetables

Grilling is a favorite cooking method for vegetables, imparting a distinctive and delicious flavor. Follow the guidelines that came with your grill for more information.

1. Place rack of outdoor grill 4 to 5 inches above heat. Start grill. If using charcoal grill, wait until coals are covered with ash (medium heat).

2. Clean and cut vegetables. (Some vegetables should be partially cooked in boiling water 5 to 10 minutes or just until crisp-tender before grilling.)

3. Brush grill rack with vegetable oil or spray with cooking spray. Grill vegetables for times shown in chart, brushing occasionally with melted butter or margarine, olive or vegetable oil, or your favorite bottled or homemade salad dressing, to prevent vegetables from drying out.

Timetable for Grilling Vegetables

Time	Vegetable
10 minutes	Carrots, small whole, partially cooked*
	Cherry tomatoes, whole
	Mushrooms, whole
	Onions, cut into 1/2-inch slices
	Potatoes, cut into 1-inch wedges, partially cooked*
15 minutes	Bell peppers, cut into 1-inch strips
	Eggplant, cut into 1/4-inch slices
	Green beans, whole
	Pattypan squash, whole
	Zucchini, cut into 3/4-inch pieces
20 minutes	Asparagus spears, whole
	Broccoli spears, cut lengthwise in half
	Cauliflowerets, cut lengthwise in half
	Corn on the cob, husked and wrapped in aluminum foil

Before grilling, cook in boiling water 5 to 10 minutes or just until crisp-tender

super
express

prep: **5 min**
cook: **12 min**

Indian Peas
with Cauliflower

1 tablespoon vegetable oil

1 teaspoon curry powder

2 jalapeño chilies, seeded and finely chopped

3 cups cauliflowerets (1 pound)

1/4 cup vegetable or chicken broth

2 cups frozen green peas

1 can (15 ounces) black beans, rinsed and drained

1 Heat oil in 10-inch skillet over medium-high heat. Cook curry powder and chilies in oil 2 minutes, stirring occasionally.

2 Stir in cauliflowerets and broth. Cover and cook 3 to 4 minutes or until cauliflowerets are tender.

3 Stir in peas and beans. Cook about 5 minutes, stirring occasionally, until hot.

IT'S **a**
snap!

Don't worry, the amount of curry makes this vegetarian dish perfectly mild. If you love Indian flavors, increase the curry or turn up the heat with another jalapeño. A dollop of chutney on the side adds even more Indian flair.

1 SERVING: Calories 230 (Calories from Fat 45); Fat 5g (Saturated 1g); Cholesterol 0mg; Sodium 740mg; Carbohydrate 44g (Dietary Fiber 13g); Protein 15g • % DAILY VALUE: Vitamin A 10%; Vitamin C 50%; Calcium 12%; Iron 24% • DIET EXCHANGES: 2 Starch, 3 Vegetable

5 SERVINGS

Quick Pepper and Bean Stir-Fry

IT'S a snap!

You can use a 10-ounce package of frozen green peas instead of the frozen soybeans.

I tablespoon vegetable oil

I tablespoon curry powder

I bag (I pound) frozen stir-fry bell peppers and onions

I bag (12 ounces) frozen soybeans

4 cloves garlic, finely chopped

I cup unsweetened coconut milk

2 cups hot cooked jasmine or brown rice

1/2 cup salted roasted cashews

Chopped fresh cilantro or parsley, if desired

1 Heat oil in 12-inch nonstick skillet over medium-high heat. Add curry powder; cook and stir 1 minute. Stir in frozen vegetables, soybeans and garlic; stir-fry 2 minutes. Cover and cook about 3 minutes longer or until vegetables are tender.

2 Stir in coconut milk; reduce heat. Simmer uncovered 2 minutes, stirring occasionally.

3 Serve vegetable mixture over rice. Sprinkle with cashews and cilantro.

1 SERVING: Calories 300 (Calories from Fat 100); Fat 10g (Saturated 8g); Cholesterol 0mg; Sodium 510mg; Carbohydrate 40g (Dietary Fiber 8g); Protein 17g • **% DAILY VALUE:** Vitamin A 54%; Vitamin C 76%; Calcium 10%; Iron 30% • **DIET EXCHANGES:** 2 Starch, 1 High-Fat Meat, 2 Vegetable

super
express
prep: **10 min**
cook: **10 min**

Savory Black-Eyed Peas

1 cup vegetable or chicken broth

3 medium carrots, thinly sliced (1 1/2 cups)

2 medium stalks celery, sliced (1 cup)

1 large onion, chopped (1 cup)

1 1/2 tablespoons chopped fresh or 1 1/2 teaspoons dried savory or basil leaves

1 clove garlic, finely chopped

1 can (15 to 16 ounces) black-eyed peas, rinsed and drained

1/2 cup shredded reduced-fat Monterey Jack cheese (2 ounces)

1 Heat broth, carrots, celery, onion, savory and garlic to boiling in 10-inch nonstick skillet; reduce heat to medium. Cook 8 to 10 minutes, stirring occasionally, until vegetables are tender.

2 Stir in peas. Cook, stirring occasionally, until hot. Sprinkle with cheese.

IT'S **a**
snap!

The mild, peppery flavor of fresh savory is a cross between mint and thyme. Fresh herbs add a wonderful flavor to your dishes, but if you don't have any on hand, dried savory or basil from your cupboard will work just fine in this easy recipe.

1 SERVING: Calories 175 (Calories from Fat 25); Fat 3g (Saturated 2g); Cholesterol 10mg; Sodium 610mg; Carbohydrate 32g (Dietary Fiber 9g); Protein 14g • **% DAILY VALUE:** Vitamin A 100%; Vitamin C 6%; Calcium 16%; Iron 16% • **DIET EXCHANGES:** 2 Starch, 1 Very Lean Meat

5 SERVINGS

Potatoes, Green Beans and Tomatoes with Tofu

2 tablespoons olive or vegetable oil

1/2 cup coarsely chopped red onion

5 small red potatoes, sliced (2 1/2 cups)

2 cups frozen cut green beans

1/2 teaspoon Italian seasoning

1/2 teaspoon garlic salt

1 package (14 ounces) firm tofu, cut into 1/2-inch cubes

2 roma (plum) tomatoes, thinly sliced

1 hard-cooked egg, chopped

1 Heat oil in 12-inch skillet over medium-high heat. Cook onion in oil 2 minutes, stirring frequently. Stir in potatoes; reduce heat to medium-low. Cover and cook about 10 minutes, stirring occasionally, until potatoes are tender.

2 Stir in green beans, Italian seasoning and garlic salt. Cover and cook about 6 minutes, stirring occasionally, until beans are tender and potatoes are light golden brown.

3 Stir in tofu and tomatoes. Cook about 2 minutes, stirring occasionally and gently, just until hot. Sprinkle each serving with egg.

1 SERVING: Calories 205 (Calories from Fat 100); Fat 11g (Saturated 2g); Cholesterol 85mg; Sodium 140mg; Carbohydrate 20g (Dietary Fiber 3g); Protein 10g • **% DAILY VALUE:** Vitamin A 12%; Vitamin C 10%; Calcium 12%; Iron 12% • **DIET EXCHANGES:** 1 Starch, 1 Very Lean Meat, 1 Vegetable, 1 1/2 Fat

Potatoes, Green Beans and Tomatoes with Tofu

prep: **15 min**
cook: **5 min**

IT'S **a**
snap!

This dish is super-fast to prepare if you have leftover baked potatoes. Just reheat in the microwave on High for 40 seconds to 1 minute or until hot. Split open and top with the warm beans and cottage cheese topping.

4 SERVINGS

Chili Baked Potatoes

4 large baking potatoes

1 can (15 to 16 ounces) chili beans, undrained

1/4 cup grated Parmesan cheese

Salt and pepper to taste

Cottage Cheese Topping (below) or sour cream

1 Pierce potatoes with fork. Microwave potatoes on High 12 to 14 minutes or until tender. Let stand until cool enough to handle. Make Cottage Cheese Topping.

2 While potatoes are cooking, heat chili beans in 2-quart saucepan over medium heat until hot. Split open potatoes; top with beans. Sprinkle with cheese, salt and pepper. Serve with topping.

Cottage Cheese Topping

1 1/2 cups cottage cheese

1 tablespoon lemon juice

1 to 2 tablespoons milk

Place all ingredients in blender. Cover and blend on medium-high speed, stopping blender occasionally to scrape sides, until smooth. Add additional milk if necessary to achieve desired creaminess.

1 SERVING: Calories 315 (Calories from Fat 55); Fat 6g (Saturated 4g); Cholesterol 15mg; Sodium 1210mg; Carbohydrate 50g (Dietary Fiber 6g); Protein 21g • **% DAILY VALUE:** Vitamin A 12%; Vitamin C 24%; Calcium 18%; Iron 14% • **DIET EXCHANGES:** 2 Starch, 1 Very Lean Meat, 1 Vegetable, 1 Skim Milk

4 SERVINGS

Sweet Potatoes and Black Beans

3 sweet potatoes, peeled and cut into 3/4-inch cubes (3 cups)

3/4 cup orange juice

2 teaspoons cornstarch

1 teaspoon pumpkin pie spice, apple pie spice or ground cinnamon

1/4 teaspoon ground cumin

1 can (15 ounces) black beans, rinsed and drained

1 cup cooked rice

1 Place sweet potatoes in 2-quart saucepan; add enough water just to cover. Heat to boiling; reduce heat. Cover and simmer 10 to 12 minutes or until tender; drain and set aside in a bowl.

2 Mix orange juice, cornstarch, pie spice and cumin in same saucepan. Heat to boiling. Boil about 1 minute, stirring constantly, until thickened.

3 Stir in sweet potatoes, beans and rice. Cook about 2 minutes or until hot.

C O M E
&eat!

The tantalizing aromas from this black-and-orange stovetop dish will entice the whole family into the kitchen. Round out dinner with a salad topped with avocado and sliced tropical fruit.

1 SERVING: Calories 285 (Calories from Fat 10); Fat 1g (Saturated 0g); Cholesterol 0mg; Sodium 420mg; Carbohydrate 66g (Dietary Fiber 9g); Protein 12g • **% DAILY VALUE:** Vitamin A 100%; Vitamin C 30%; Calcium 10%; Iron 20% • **DIET EXCHANGES:** 4 Starch

6 SERVINGS

Creamy Quinoa Primavera

1 1/2 cups uncooked quinoa

3 cups vegetable or chicken broth

1 package (3 ounces) cream cheese

1 tablespoon chopped fresh or 1 teaspoon dried basil leaves

2 teaspoons butter or margarine

2 cloves garlic, finely chopped

5 cups thinly sliced or bite-size pieces assorted uncooked vegetables (such as asparagus, broccoli, carrot, zucchini)

2 tablespoons grated Romano cheese

COME
& eat!

You can use whatever vegetables you have on hand in this tasty, colorful skillet dinner. Serve a salad tossed with sliced apples or pears and crunchy walnuts on the side and follow with Strawberry-Rhubarb Frozen-Yogurt Parfaits (page 397) for dessert.

1 Rinse quinoa thoroughly; drain. Heat quinoa and broth to boiling in 2-quart saucepan; reduce heat. Cover and simmer 10 to 15 minutes or until all broth is absorbed. Stir in cream cheese and basil.

2 Melt butter in 10-inch nonstick skillet over medium-high heat. Cook garlic in butter about 30 seconds, stirring frequently, until golden. Stir in vegetables. Cook about 2 minutes, stirring frequently, until vegetables are crisp-tender.

3 Toss vegetables and quinoa mixture. Sprinkle with Romano cheese.

1 SERVING: Calories 265 (Calories from Fat 90); Fat 10g (Saturated 5g); Cholesterol 20mg; Sodium 630mg; Carbohydrate 37g (Dietary Fiber 5g); Protein 12g • **% DAILY VALUE:** Vitamin A 100%; Vitamin C 22%; Calcium 10%; Iron 28 • **DIET EXCHANGES:** 1 Starch, 4 Vegetable, 2 Fat

Creamy Quinoa Primavera

6 SERVINGS

Polenta with Italian Vegetables

I cup yellow cornmeal

3/4 cup cold water

2 1/2 cups boiling water

1/2 teaspoon salt

2/3 cup shredded Swiss cheese

2 teaspoons olive or
vegetable oil

2 medium zucchini or yellow
summer squash, sliced (4 cups)

I medium red bell pepper,
chopped (I cup)

I small onion, chopped
(1/4 cup)

I clove garlic, finely chopped

1/4 cup chopped fresh or
I tablespoon dried basil leaves

I can (about 14 ounces)
artichoke hearts, drained

1 Beat cornmeal and cold water in 2-quart saucepan with
wire whisk. Stir in boiling water and salt. Cook over medium-
high heat, stirring constantly, until mixture thickens and
boils; reduce heat. Cover and simmer 10 minutes, stirring
occasionally. Stir in cheese until smooth; keep polenta warm.

2 Heat oil in 10-inch nonstick skillet over medium-high heat.
Cook zucchini, bell pepper, onion and garlic in oil about
5 minutes, stirring occasionally, until vegetables are crisp-
tender. Stir in basil and artichoke hearts. Serve vegetable
mixture over polenta.

1 SERVING: Calories 175 (Calories from Fat 45); Fat 5g (Saturated 2g); Cholesterol 10mg;
Sodium 430mg; Carbohydrate 30g (Dietary Fiber 7g); Protein 9g • **% DAILY VALUE:**
Vitamin A 40%; Vitamin C 42%; Calcium 16%; Iron 12% • **DIET EXCHANGES:** I Starch,
3 Vegetable, 1/2 Fat

Polenta with Italian Vegetables

4 SERVINGS

Barley, Corn and Lima Bean Sauté

2 2/3 cups water

1 1/3 cups uncooked
quick-cooking barley

1 tablespoon butter or
margarine

1 large onion, chopped (1 cup)

1 clove garlic, finely chopped

2 tablespoons chopped fresh or
2 teaspoons dried thyme leaves

1/2 teaspoon salt

1 bag (1 pound) frozen
whole kernel corn, thawed
and drained

1 package (10 ounces) frozen
lima beans, thawed and drained

1 Heat water to boiling in a medium saucepan. Stir in barley.
Reduce heat to low. Cover and simmer 10 to 12 minutes.
Let stand covered 5 minutes.

2 Melt butter in 10-inch skillet over medium-high heat.
Cook onion and garlic in butter about 2 minutes, stirring
occasionally, until onion is crisp-tender.

3 Stir in barley and remaining ingredients. Cook about
5 minutes, stirring occasionally, until hot.

1 SERVING: Calories 350 (Calories from Fat 35); Fat 4g (Saturated 2g); Cholesterol 5mg;
Sodium 370mg; Carbohydrate 81g (Dietary Fiber 15g); Protein 13g • **% DAILY VALUE:**
Vitamin A 12%; Vitamin C 12%; Calcium 4%; Iron 16% • **DIET EXCHANGES:** 5 Starch

9 Great Grilling

= *super express* ready in 20 minutes or less

1-Step Recipes

Great Grilling Secrets These grilling "top secrets" shouldn't remain a mystery. They will save you loads of time in the long run, so check them out before heading to the grill.

1 Brush grill rack with vegetable oil or spray with cooking spray before heating the grill to prevent food from sticking.

2 Turn food with tongs instead of piercing with a fork to retain food juices.

3 Use long-handled barbecue tools to allow a safe distance between you and the intense heat of the grill.

4 Keep the heat as even as possible throughout the grilling time by placing thicker foods on the center of the grill rack and smaller pieces on the edges.

5 Enhance grilled flavor by using wood chips and covering the grill.

6 Brush sauces on foods but only during only the last few minutes of cooking to prevent overbrowning.

7 Place a sheet of heavy-duty aluminum foil across the firebox and press it down to mold to the firebox before adding briquettes for easy grill cleanup.

8 Use grill helpers such as perforated aluminum foil sheets, grill baskets, smoker bags and long-handled tools.

9 Let cooked meat stand a few minutes after grilling for heightened flavor and juicer meat.

10 Clean grill as soon as possible after using for easier cleanup.

prep: **15 min**
grill: **12 min**

Tuscan Grilled Chicken Pockets

8 large boneless, skinless chicken breasts halves (about 2 1/2 pounds)

1/2 cup herb-and-garlic spreadable cheese

4 ounces thinly sliced prosciutto or fully cooked ham

1/2 cup zesty Italian dressing

1 Heat coals or gas grill for direct heat. Carefully cut a horizontal slit in each chicken breast half, making a pocket when top of chicken is lifted back.

2 Spread 1 tablespoon cheese inside each chicken pocket. Top with folded slices of prosciutto. Close chicken around filling, being sure that most of the filling is enclosed. Brush dressing on chicken.

3 Cover and grill chicken 4 to 5 inches from medium-high heat 10 to 12 minutes, brushing occasionally with dressing and turning once, until juice of chicken is no longer pink when centers of thickest pieces are cut.

IT'S **a** snap!

A large, long-handled grill spatula comes in handy for turning the chicken pieces instead of a fork or tongs, which might squeeze out the cheese filling.

1 SERVING: Calories 285 (Calories from Fat 135); Fat 15g (Saturated 5g); Cholesterol 110mg; Sodium 400mg; Carbohydrate 2g (Dietary Fiber 0g); Protein 35g • **% DAILY VALUE:** Vitamin A 4%; Vitamin C 0%; Calcium 2%; Iron 8% • **DIET EXCHANGES:** 5 Lean Meat

prep: **5 min**
grill: **15 min**

6 SERVINGS

Raspberry-Glazed Chicken

1/2 cup raspberry jam

1 tablespoon Dijon mustard

6 boneless, skinless chicken breast halves (about 1 3/4 pounds)

1 1/2 cups fresh or frozen (thawed and drained) raspberries

1 Brush grill rack with vegetable oil. Heat coals or gas grill for direct heat. Mix jam and mustard.

2 Cover and grill chicken 4 to 5 inches from medium heat 12 to 15 minutes, brushing occasionally with jam mixture and turning once, until juice of chicken is no longer pink when centers of thickest pieces are cut. Discard any remaining jam mixture.

3 Serve chicken topped with raspberries.

1 SERVING: Calories 195 (Calories from Fat 35); Fat 4g (Saturated 1g); Cholesterol 75mg; Sodium 120mg; Carbohydrate 15g (Dietary Fiber 2g); Protein 27g • **% DAILY VALUE:** Vitamin A 0%; Vitamin C 8%; Calcium 2%; Iron 6% • **DIET EXCHANGES:** 3 Very Lean Meat, 1 Fruit, 1/2 Fat

Raspberry-Glazed Chicken

IT'S **a**
snap!
Cleanup? Nothing's
easier! Make your
own foil packet with
two 18 × 15-inch
sheets of heavy-duty
aluminum foil. Place
vegetable mixture
on one sheet of foil;
top with chicken.
Cover with the
other sheet of foil
and tightly seal
the edges.

6 SERVINGS

Spanish Chicken Supper

3 medium unpeeled baking potatoes, cut into 1/2-inch cubes (4 cups)

2 medium green or red bell peppers, chopped (2 cups)

1 large onion, coarsely chopped (1 cup)

12 large pimiento-stuffed olives, coarsely chopped

1 can (14 1/2 ounces) diced tomatoes with roasted garlic, undrained

1 tablespoon all-purpose flour

3 teaspoons chili powder

1 teaspoon salt

1 1/2 pounds chicken breast tenders (not breaded)

1 Heat coals or gas grill for direct heat. Mix potatoes, bell peppers, onion, olives and tomatoes in large bowl. Stir in flour, 2 teaspoons of the chili powder and 1/2 teaspoon of the salt. Spoon mixture into heavy-duty aluminum foil bag.

2 Sprinkle remaining 1 teaspoon chili powder and 1/2 teaspoon salt over chicken. Arrange chicken on top of vegetables. Double-fold open end of bag. Slide foil bag onto cookie sheet to carry to grill.

3 Slide foil bag onto grill. Grill uncovered 4 to 5 inches from medium-high heat about 20 minutes or until potatoes are tender and chicken is no longer pink in center. Place bag on serving plate. Cut large X across top of packet; fold back foil.

1 SERVING: Calories 240 (Calories from Fat 45); Fat 5g (Saturated 1g); Cholesterol 70mg; Sodium 800mg; Carbohydrate 25g (Dietary Fiber 4g); Protein 28g • **% DAILY VALUE:** Vitamin A 22%; Vitamin C 46%; Calcium 6%; Iron 14% • **DIET EXCHANGES:** 1 Starch, 3 Very Lean Meat, 2 Vegetable

Peanutty Chicken Kabobs

prep: **15 min**
grill: **15 min**

1 pound boneless, skinless chicken breast halves or thighs, cut into 1 1/2-inch pieces

Spicy Peanut Sauce (below)

Chopped peanuts, if desired

1 Brush grill rack with vegetable oil. Heat coals or gas grill for direct heat. Thread chicken pieces on four 10- to 12-inch metal skewers, leaving space between each piece.

2 Make Spicy Peanut Sauce; reserve 1/2 cup sauce to serve with cooked kabobs. Brush chicken with half of the remaining sauce.

3 Cover and grill kabobs 4 to 5 inches from medium heat about 15 minutes, turning and brushing occasionally with remaining sauce, until chicken is no longer pink in center. Serve kabobs with reserved sauce and the peanuts.

Spicy Peanut Sauce

1/3 cup crunchy peanut butter

1/3 cup boiling water

1 tablespoon grated gingerroot or 1 teaspoon ground ginger

1 tablespoon lemon juice

1/8 teaspoon crushed red pepper

Mix all ingredients.

COME

& eat!

For a quick side dish, double the peanut sauce and toss half with cooked Chinese noodles or spaghetti and chopped green onions.

1 SERVING: Calories 260 (Calories from Fat 125); Fat 14g (Saturated 3g); Cholesterol 60mg; Sodium 160mg; Carbohydrate 5g (Dietary Fiber 1g); Protein 30g • % DAILY VALUE: Vitamin A 0%; Vitamin C 0%; Calcium 2%; Iron 6% • DIET EXCHANGES: 4 Lean Meat, 1 Fat

4 SERVINGS

Cheddar-Stuffed Chicken Breasts

**4 boneless, skinless
chicken breast halves
(about 1 1/4 pounds)**

1/4 teaspoon salt

1/4 teaspoon pepper

3 ounces Cheddar cheese

**1 tablespoon butter or
margarine, melted**

1/4 cup salsa

1 Heat coals or gas grill for direct heat. Flatten each chicken
breast half to 1/4-inch thickness between sheets of plastic
wrap or waxed paper. Sprinkle with salt and pepper.

2 Cut cheese into 4 slices, about 3 × 1 × 1/4 inch. Place
1 slice cheese on center of each chicken piece. Roll chicken
around cheese, folding in sides. Brush rolls with butter.

3 Cover and grill chicken rolls, seam sides down, 4 to 5 inches
from medium heat about 15 minutes, turning after 10 minutes, until juice of chicken is no longer pink in center. Serve
with salsa.

1 SERVING: Calories 250 (Calories from Fat 115); Fat 13g (Saturated 7g); Cholesterol 100mg;
Sodium 400mg; Carbohydrate 1g (Dietary Fiber 0g); Protein 32g • **% DAILY VALUE:**
Vitamin A 8%; Vitamin C 2%; Calcium 12%; Iron 6% • **DIET EXCHANGES:** 4 1/2 Lean Meat

Cheddar-Stuffed Chicken Breasts

Pantry Recipes

If you have a well-stocked pantry (see pages 6–7), you'll be able to make this recipe anytime, even when there's no time to shop.

Great Grilled Chicken

1/2 cup ranch dressing

2 tablespoons French or Catalina dressing

6 boneless, skinless chicken breast halves (about 1 3/4 pounds)

Heat coals or gas grill for direct heat. Mix **dressings** together. Cover and grill **chicken** 4 to 6 inches from medium heat 15 to 20 minutes, brushing frequently with dressing mixture and turning once, until juice of chicken is no longer pink when centers of thickest pieces are cut. Discard any remaining dressing mixture.

6 SERVINGS IN 25 MINUTES

serve it 3 ways!

1 Sandwich
Place grilled chicken in buns with lettuce leaves, tomatoes and mustard.

2 Salad
Cut grilled chicken into strips. Add to romaine, and drizzle with raspberry vinaigrette or your favorite salad dressing.

3 Light Meal
Cut grilled chicken into bite-size pieces. Mix with mayonnaise, chopped celery and onion, salt and pepper. Use as a sandwich filling, to stuff tomatoes or to serve with cut-up fresh vegetables or fruits.

prep: **10 min**
grill: **15 min**

Grilled Parmesan– Turkey Burgers

1 pound ground turkey

1/3 cup grated Parmesan cheese

1 tablespoon chopped fresh chives

1/4 teaspoon pepper

1/8 teaspoon salt

4 hamburger buns, split and toasted

Red onion rings, if desired

1 Brush grill rack with vegetable oil. Heat coals or gas grill for direct heat. Mix all ingredients except buns and onion. Shape mixture into 4 patties, about 1/2 inch thick.

2 Cover and grill patties 4 to 6 inches from medium heat 12 to 15 minutes, turning once, until no longer pink in center.

3 Serve patties on buns with grilled or raw onion rings.

TO BROIL: Set oven control to broil. Place patties on rack in broiler pan. Broil with tops 4 to 6 inches from heat 12 to 15 minutes, turning once, until no longer pink in center.

IT'S **a**
snap!

Low in fat, turkey patties may stick to the grill unless it is well oiled first. For safety's sake, always brush oil on the grill rack or spray with cooking spray before lighting the coals or turning on the gas.

1 SERVING: Calories 310 (Calories from Fat 100); Fat 11g (Saturated 4g); Cholesterol 80mg; Sodium 540mg; Carbohydrate 22g (Dietary Fiber 1g); Protein 32g • % DAILY VALUE: Vitamin A 2%; Vitamin C 0%; Calcium 18%; Iron 14% • DIET EXCHANGES: 1 1/2 Starch, 4 Very Lean Meat, 1 Fat

4 SERVINGS

Sesame-Ginger Turkey Slices

2 tablespoons teriyaki sauce

I tablespoon sesame seed, toasted*

I teaspoon ground ginger

I pound uncooked turkey breast slices, about 1/4 inch thick

4 cups hot cooked rice, if desired

1 Brush grill rack with vegetable oil. Heat coals or gas grill for direct heat. Mix teriyaki sauce, sesame seed and ginger.

2 Cover and grill turkey 4 to 6 inches from medium heat 15 to 20 minutes, brushing frequently with sauce mixture and turning after 10 minutes, until no longer pink in center. Discard any remaining sauce mixture.

3 Serve turkey with rice.

✳ **HOW TO toast sesame seed:** Heat sesame seed in ungreased skillet over medium heat about 2 minutes, stirring occasionally, until golden brown.

COME
& eat!

For a dinner with Asian flair, accompany this tender turkey with rice and a shredded lettuce and cucumber salad with Asian dressing. Then, scoop lemon sherbet and top with fresh blueberries for a refreshing dessert.

1 SERVING: Calories 120 (Calories from Fat 20); Fat 2g (Saturated 0g); Cholesterol 75mg; Sodium 350mg; Carbohydrate 1g (Dietary Fiber 0g); Protein 27g • **% DAILY VALUE:** Vitamin A 0%; Vitamin C 0%; Calcium 2%; Iron 8% • **DIET EXCHANGES:** 4 Very Lean Meat

Strip Steaks with Chipotle Peach Glaze

1/2 cup peach preserves

1/4 cup lime juice

1 chipotle chili in adobo sauce (from 7-ounce can), seeded and chopped

1 teaspoon adobo sauce (from can of chilies)

2 tablespoons chopped fresh cilantro

8 beef boneless strip steaks (about 3 pounds)

1 teaspoon garlic pepper

1/2 teaspoon ground cumin

1/2 teaspoon salt

4 peaches, cut in half and pitted, if desired

Cilantro sprigs, if desired

IT'S **a**
snap!
You can use 1/2 tea-spoon garlic powder and 1/2 teaspoon coarsely ground black pepper instead of the 1 teaspoon garlic pepper.

1 Heat coals or gas grill for direct heat. Mix preserves, lime juice, chili and adobo sauce in 1-quart saucepan. Heat over low heat, stirring occasionally, until preserves are melted. Stir in chopped cilantro; set aside. Sprinkle each beef steak with garlic pepper, cumin and salt.

2 Cover and grill beef 4 to 6 inches from medium heat 8 to 10 minutes for medium doneness, turning once or twice and brushing with preserves mixture during last 2 minutes of grilling. Add peach halves to grill for last 2 to 3 minutes of grilling just until heated.

3 Heat any remaining preserves mixture to boiling; boil and stir 1 minute. Serve with beef and peaches. Garnish with cilantro sprigs.

1 SERVING: Calories 315 (Calories from Fat 110); Fat 12g (Saturated 5g); Cholesterol 95mg; Sodium 250mg; Carbohydrate 14g (Dietary Fiber 0g); Protein 37g • % DAILY VALUE: Vitamin A 0%; Vitamin C 6%; Calcium 2%; Iron 8% • DIET EXCHANGES: 5 Lean Meat, 1 Fruit

4 SERVINGS

Rosemary-Dijon Steaks

1/4 cup Dijon mustard

2 teaspoons chopped fresh or
1/2 teaspoon dried rosemary
leaves, crumbled

1 teaspoon coarsely ground
pepper

2 cloves garlic, finely chopped

4 beef boneless top loin steaks,
about 1 inch thick (about
1 pound)

1 Heat coals or gas grill for direct heat. Mix mustard, rosemary, pepper and garlic; spread on both sides of beef.

2 Grill beef uncovered 4 to 5 inches from medium heat 1 minute on each side to seal in juices. Cover and grill 8 to 9 minutes longer for medium doneness, turning once.

1 SERVING: Calories 165 (Calories from Fat 80); Fat 9g (Saturated 3g); Cholesterol 65mg; Sodium 430mg; Carbohydrate 1g (Dietary Fiber 0g); Protein 25g • **% DAILY VALUE:** Vitamin A 2%; Vitamin C 0%; Calcium 0%; Iron 12% • **DIET EXCHANGES:** 3 Lean Meat

Rosemary-Dijon Steaks

prep: **5 min**
grill: **14 min**

4 SERVINGS

Grilled Steak, Florentine Style

1/4 cup chopped fresh parsley
1/4 cup olive or vegetable oil
4 cloves garlic, cut into pieces
4 beef T-bone steaks, about 1 inch thick (about 2 pounds)

1 teaspoon salt
1/2 teaspoon freshly ground pepper

1 Brush grill rack with olive or vegetable oil. Heat coals or gas grill for direct heat. Place parsley, oil and garlic in food processor or blender. Cover and process until smooth.

2 Cut outer edge of fat on beef steaks diagonally at 1-inch intervals to prevent curling (do not cut into beef).

3 Cover and grill beef 3 to 4 inches from medium heat 5 minutes for medium-rare or 7 minutes for medium doneness, brushing frequently with oil mixture. Turn; brush generously with oil mixture. Grill 5 to 7 minutes longer or until desired doneness. Sprinkle with salt and pepper. Discard any remaining oil mixture.

TO BROIL: Set oven control to broil. Brush broiler pan rack with olive or vegetable oil. Cut outer edge of fat on beef steaks diagonally at 1-inch intervals to prevent curling (do not cut into beef). Place beef on rack in broiler pan; brush with oil mixture. Broil with tops 3 to 4 inches from heat 5 minutes for medium-rare or 7 minutes for medium doneness. Turn; brush generously with oil mixture. Broil 5 to 8 minutes longer or until desired doneness.

1 SERVING: Calories 305 (Calories from Fat 180); Fat 20g (Saturated 5g); Cholesterol 75mg; Sodium 500mg; Carbohydrate 1g (Dietary Fiber 0g); Protein 30g • % DAILY VALUE: Vitamin A 6%; Vitamin C 4%; Calcium 2%; Iron 14% • DIET EXCHANGES: 4 Medium-Fat Meat

Southwest Steak and Salsa Sandwiches

1-pound beef boneless sirloin steak, 1 inch thick

1/2 teaspoon seasoned salt

1/2 teaspoon garlic pepper

1/2 teaspoon chili powder

1/2 teaspoon dried oregano leaves

6 hoagie buns, split

3/4 cup thick-and-chunky salsa

1 medium avocado, pitted, peeled and thinly sliced

6 slices (1 ounce each) Colby-Monterey Jack cheese

1 Heat coals or gas grill for direct heat. Sprinkle both sides of beef with seasoned salt, garlic pepper, chili powder and oregano.

2 Cover and grill beef 4 to 6 inches from medium heat 8 to 9 minutes, turning once or twice, until desired doneness. Add buns, cut sides down, for last 4 minutes of grilling or until toasted.

3 Cut beef crosswise into thin slices. Spread about 2 tablespoons salsa on bottom of each bun. Top with beef, avocado, cheese and tops of buns.

IT'S **a**
snap!

Spice things up! To save some time, just use your favorite pre-mixed Southwest seasoning blend instead of the spices called for here. Also, you can use 1/4 teaspoon garlic powder and 1/4 teaspoon coarsely ground pepper instead of the garlic pepper.

1 SERVING: Calories 400 (Calories from Fat 170); Fat 19g (Saturated 8g); Cholesterol 70mg; Sodium 720mg; Carbohydrate 33g (Dietary Fiber 4g); Protein 28g • **% DAILY VALUE:** Vitamin A 14%; Vitamin C 14%; Calcium 24%; Iron 22% • **DIET EXCHANGES:** 2 Starch, 3 Medium-Fat Meat, 1 Vegetable

4 SERVINGS

Vidalia-Topped Caesar Burgers

I pound ground beef	**I small Vidalia onion,** cut into 1/4- to 1/2-inch slices
2 tablespoons chopped fresh parsley	**I 1/2 cups shredded romaine**
1/2 cup Caesar dressing	**2 tablespoons freshly shredded Parmesan cheese**
1/2 teaspoon peppered seasoned salt	**4 sandwich buns, split**

1   Heat coals or gas grill for direct heat. Mix beef, parsley, 2 tablespoons of the dressing and the peppered seasoned salt. Shape mixture into 4 patties, about 1/2 inch thick.

2   Cover and grill patties 4 to 6 inches from medium heat 12 to 15 minutes, turning once, until patties are no longer pink in center and juice of beef is clear. Add onion slices to grill for last 8 to 10 minutes of grilling, brushing with 2 tablespoons of the dressing and turning once, until crisp-tender.

3   Toss romaine, remaining 1/4 cup dressing and the cheese. Layer romaine, burger and onion in each bun.

1 SERVING: Calories 480 (Calories from Fat 260); Fat 29g (Saturated 9g); Cholesterol 70mg; Sodium 920mg; Carbohydrate 27g (Dietary Fiber 2g); Protein 27g • **% DAILY VALUE:** Vitamin A 12%; Vitamin C 14%; Calcium 12%; Iron 20% • **DIET EXCHANGES:** 1 1/2 Starch, 3 High-Fat Meat, 1 Vegetable, 1 Fat

Vidalia-Topped Caesar Burgers

6 SERVINGS

Two-Tomato Italian Burgers

12 sun-dried tomato halves
(not in oil)

1 pound ground beef

1/2 pound bulk Italian sausage

6 slices (1 ounce each)
provolone cheese, cut in half

12 slices tomato, cut in half

12 fresh basil leaves, if desired

1 loaf (1 pound) ciabatta bread
or other Italian flatbread,
cut into 12 slices

1 Heat coals or gas grill for direct heat. Place sun-dried tomatoes in small bowl. Pour enough boiling water over tomatoes to cover. Let stand 10 minutes.

2 Drain tomatoes. Mix beef, sausage and drained tomatoes. Shape mixture into 6 oblong patties, about 1/2 inch thick.

3 Grill patties uncovered 4 to 5 inches from medium-high heat 10 to 12 minutes, turning once, until no longer pink in center and juice is clear. Top each burger with cheese slice for last 2 minutes of grilling. Top burgers with tomato and basil. Serve burgers between slices of bread.

1 SERVING: Calories 555 (Calories from Fat 260); Fat 29g (Saturated 12g); Cholesterol 90mg; Sodium 1080mg; Carbohydrate 42g (Dietary Fiber 3g); Protein 34g • **% DAILY VALUE:** Vitamin A 10%; Vitamin C 8%; Calcium 28%; Iron 24% • **DIET EXCHANGES:** 2 Starch, 3 1/2 High-Fat Meat, 2 Vegetable

Supreme Burgers

2 pounds ground beef

**1/2 package (2-ounce size)
onion soup mix (1 envelope)**

1 cup sour cream

1/2 cup dry bread crumbs

1/8 teaspoon pepper

1 Heat coals or gas grill for direct heat. Mix all ingredients. Shape mixture into 8 patties, about 3/4 inch thick.

2 Grill patties uncovered 4 to 6 inches from medium heat 10 to 15 minutes, turning once, until no longer pink in center and juice is clear.

TO BROIL: Set oven control to broil. Place patties on rack in broiler pan. Broil with tops 4 to 6 inches from heat 10 to 15 minutes, turning once, until no longer pink in center and juice is clear.

COME
&eat!

No one will ever guess the secret ingredients! Sour cream and soup mix add zip and juiciness. All you have to add is a bun and lettuce and tomato for serving.

1 BURGER: Calories 325 (Calories from Fat 200); Fat 22g (Saturated 10g); Cholesterol 85mg; Sodium 580mg; Carbohydrate 9g (Dietary Fiber 0g); Protein 23g • **% DAILY VALUE:** Vitamin A 4%; Vitamin C 2%; Calcium 6%; Iron 12% • **DIET EXCHANGES:** 1/2 Starch, 3 High-Fat Meat

COME
&eat!

Couscous goes won-
derfully with lamb,
with sliced cucum-
bers on the side. If
you have extra fresh
mint, sprinkle it over
the cucumbers too.

4 SERVINGS

Mint-Smoked Lamb Chops

2 tablespoons dry white wine or chicken broth

2 tablespoons honey

1 tablespoon butter or margarine, melted

1 teaspoon chopped fresh mint leaves

1/4 teaspoon salt

1/8 teaspoon pepper

1 cup whole fresh mint leaves

8 lamb rib or loin chops, about 1 inch thick (about 2 pounds)

1 Brush grill rack with vegetable oil. Heat coals or gas grill for direct heat.

2 Mix all ingredients except 1 cup mint and the lamb.

3 Sprinkle 1 cup mint over hot coals or lava rock. Immediately cover and grill lamb 4 to 5 inches from hot heat 6 minutes. Brush with wine mixture. Turn lamb; brush with wine mixture. Cover and grill about 6 minutes longer for medium doneness. Discard any remaining wine mixture.

1 SERVING: Calories 390 (Calories from Fat 200); Fat 22g (Saturated 9g); Cholesterol 140mg; Sodium 260mg; Carbohydrate 6g (Dietary Fiber 0g); Protein 41g • **% DAILY VALUE:** Vitamin A 2%; Vitamin C 0%; Calcium 2%; Iron 16% • **DIET EXCHANGES:** 6 Lean Meat, 1/2 Fruit, 1 Fat

Mint-Smoked Lamb Chops

4 SERVINGS

Honey-Mustard Pork Chops

Honey-Mustard Glaze   **4 pork butterfly loin chops,**
(below)   **1 inch thick (about 1 pound)**

1   Brush grill rack with vegetable oil. Heat coals or gas grill for direct heat. Make Honey-Mustard Glaze.

2   Cover and grill pork 4 to 5 inches from medium heat 14 to 16 minutes, brushing occasionally with glaze and turning once, until slightly pink in center. Discard any remaining glaze.

Honey-Mustard Glaze

1/4 cup honey

2 tablespoons Dijon mustard

1 tablespoon orange juice

1 teaspoon chopped fresh or
1/4 teaspoon dried tarragon leaves

1 teaspoon balsamic or cider vinegar

1/2 teaspoon white Worcestershire sauce

Dash of onion powder

Mix all ingredients.

1 SERVING: Calories 235 (Calories from Fat 70); Fat 8g (Saturated 3g); Cholesterol 65mg; Sodium 230mg; Carbohydrate 18g (Dietary Fiber 0g); Protein 23g • **% DAILY VALUE:** Vitamin A 0%; Vitamin C 0%; Calcium 0%; Iron 6% • **DIET EXCHANGES:** 3 Lean Meat, 1 Fruit

6 SERVINGS

Zesty Pork Chops

2/3 cup packed brown sugar

1/4 cup prepared horseradish

1 tablespoon lemon juice

6 fully cooked smoked pork chops, about 1/2 inch thick (about 1 1/4 pounds)

1 Heat coals or gas grill for direct heat. Heat brown sugar, horseradish and lemon juice to boiling in 1-quart saucepan, stirring constantly. Brush on pork.

2 Cover and grill pork 4 to 6 inches from medium-high heat about 15 minutes, turning once, until hot. Serve remaining sauce with pork.

TO BROIL: Set oven control to broil. Place pork on rack in broiler pan. Broil with tops 4 to 6 inches from heat 3 minutes; turn. Broil 3 to 5 minutes longer or until hot.

COME
&eat!

For a complete grilled meal, cut zucchini lengthwise in half, brush with oil, season with salt and pepper and grill with the pork chops. Add buttered French bread for the last 3 to 5 minutes of grilling.

1 SERVING: Calories 220 (Calories from Fat 55); Fat 6g (Saturated 2g); Cholesterol 40mg; Sodium 1050mg; Carbohydrate 25g (Dietary Fiber 0g); Protein 16g • **% DAILY VALUE:** Vitamin A 0%; Vitamin C 2%; Calcium 2%; Iron 8% • **DIET EXCHANGES:** 1 Starch, 2 Very Lean Meat, 1/2 Fruit, 1 Fat

6 SERVINGS

Latin Grilled Halibut with Green Sauce

6 small halibut or sea bass steaks, about 3/4 inch thick (about 2 1/2 pounds)

I tablespoon olive or vegetable oil

I teaspoon seasoned salt

I jar (16 ounces) green salsa (salsa verde) (2 cups)

I ripe avocado, pitted, peeled and chopped

2 tablespoons chopped ripe olives

Sour cream, if desired

Fresh cilantro leaves, if desired

1 Heat coals or gas grill for direct heat. Brush fish lightly with oil; sprinkle with seasoned salt.

2 Grill fish uncovered 4 to 5 inches from medium-high heat about 10 minutes, turning once, until fish flakes easily with fork.

3 Mix salsa, avocado and olives. Serve over fish. Garnish with sour cream and cilantro.

1 SERVING: Calories 290 (Calories from Fat 125); Fat 14g (Saturated 3g); Cholesterol 90mg; Sodium 560mg; Carbohydrate 6g (Dietary Fiber 3g); Protein 38g • **% DAILY VALUE:** Vitamin A 18%; Vitamin C 16%; Calcium 8%; Iron 16% • **DIET EXCHANGES:** 5 1/2 Lean Meat

Latin Grilled Halibut with Green Sauce

6 SERVINGS

Swordfish with Strawberry Salsa

1/3 cup balsamic vinegar

1 1/2 pounds swordfish steaks, 1 to 1 1/2 inches thick

Strawberry Salsa (below)

1 Heat coals or gas grill for direct heat. Place vinegar in shallow nonmetal dish or resealable plastic food-storage bag. Add fish, turning to coat with vinegar. Make Strawberry Salsa.

2 Drain fish; discard vinegar. Cover and grill fish 4 inches from medium heat 10 to 15 minutes, turning once, until fish flakes easily with fork. Remove fish to platter. Immediately top with salsa.

Strawberry Salsa

1/3 cup coarsely chopped strawberries

1 tablespoon dried cranberries or golden raisins

1 tablespoon red wine vinegar

2 teaspoons chopped fresh cilantro

1/4 teaspoon grated lime peel

1 green onion, finely chopped (1 tablespoon)

Mix all ingredients.

1 SERVING: Calories 120 (Calories from Fat 45); Fat 5g (Saturated 1g); Cholesterol 55mg; Sodium 55mg; Carbohydrate 2g (Dietary Fiber 1g); Protein 19g • % DAILY VALUE: Vitamin A 2%; Vitamin C 14%; Calcium 0%; Iron 4% • **DIET EXCHANGES:** 2 1/2 lean meat

Sole Fillets with Spinach

prep: **15 min**
grill: **10 min**

1 pound spinach

1 teaspoon poultry seasoning

1/2 teaspoon chili powder

1/2 teaspoon salt

1 to 1 1/2 pounds sole, flounder or red snapper fillets, 1/4 to 1/2 inch thick

2 tablespoons butter or margarine, melted

Lemon wedges

IT'S a snap!

Is it done yet? Save time by knowing when the fish is ready to serve. To test fish for doneness, place a fork in the thickest part and gently twist. The fish will flake easily when it's cooked through.

1 Heat coals or gas grill for direct heat. Spray 13 × 9-inch aluminum foil pan with cooking spray. Rinse spinach; shake off excess water, but do not dry. Place about three-fourths of the spinach leaves in pan, covering bottom completely.

2 Mix poultry seasoning, chili powder and salt. Lightly rub into both sides of fish. Place fish on spinach, folding thin tail ends under and, if necessary, overlapping thin edges slightly. Drizzle with butter. Cover fish completely with remaining spinach.

3 Cover and grill fish and spinach 4 inches from medium heat 8 to 10 minutes or until fish flakes easily with fork. Check after about 3 minutes; if top layer of spinach is charring, sprinkle with about 1/4 cup water. Serve fish and spinach from pan with a slotted spoon. Serve with lemon wedges.

1 SERVING: Calories 150 (Calories from Fat 65); Fat 7g (Saturated 4g); Cholesterol 70mg; Sodium 580mg; Carbohydrate 3g (Dietary Fiber 2g); Protein 21g • **% DAILY VALUE:** Vitamin A 100%; Vitamin C 18%; Calcium 10%; Iron 14% • **DIET EXCHANGES:** 3 Very Lean Meat, 1 Fat

6 SERVINGS

Mexican Fish in Foil

**1 1/2 pounds halibut fillets,
1/2 to 3/4 inch thick**

**1/4 cup sliced pimiento-stuffed
olives**

2 teaspoons capers

**1 medium tomato, seeded and
coarsely chopped (3/4 cup)**

**3 medium green onions,
thinly sliced (3 tablespoons)**

1 clove garlic, finely chopped

2 tablespoons lemon juice

1/4 teaspoon salt

1/8 teaspoon pepper

Lemon wedges

1 Heat coals or gas grill for direct heat. If fish fillets are
large, cut into 6 serving pieces. Place fish in heavy-duty
aluminum foil bag.

2 Mix olives, capers, tomato, green onions and garlic; spoon
over fish. Drizzle with lemon juice. Sprinkle with salt and
pepper. Double-fold open end of bag. Slide foil bag onto
cookie sheet to carry to grill.

3 Slide foil bag onto grill. Cover and grill 5 to 6 inches from
medium heat about 15 minutes or until fish flakes easily
with fork. Place bag on serving plate. Cut large X across
top of packet; fold back foil. Serve fish with lemon wedges.

1 SERVING: Calories 95 (Calories from Fat 20); Fat 2g (Saturated 0g); Cholesterol 50mg;
Sodium 350mg; Carbohydrate 2g (Dietary Fiber 1g); Protein 18g • **% DAILY VALUE:**
Vitamin A 2%; Vitamin C 6%; Calcium 2%; Iron 2% • **DIET EXCHANGES:** 2 1/2 Very
Lean Meat

Grilled Antipasto Pizza

super express

prep: **10 min**
grill: **10 min**

1/4 pound small whole mushrooms (1 1/2 cups)

1 medium yellow bell pepper, cut into 8 pieces

1/4 cup Italian dressing

1 package (16 ounces) ready-to-serve original Italian pizza crust (12 inches in diameter)

1 cup shredded mozzarella cheese (4 ounces)

2 roma (plum) tomatoes, thinly sliced

4 medium green onions, sliced (1/4 cup)

1/4 cup sliced ripe olives

IT'S **a**
snap!

If you don't have a grill basket, take a sheet of heavy-duty aluminum foil and poke a few holes in it. It works fine instead.

1 Heat coals or gas grill for direct heat. Toss mushrooms, bell pepper and 2 tablespoons of the dressing. Place vegetables in grill basket. Cover and grill vegetables 4 to 5 inches from medium heat 4 to 6 minutes, shaking grill basket occasionally to turn vegetables, until bell pepper is crisp-tender. Coarsely chop vegetables.

2 Brush pizza crust with remaining 2 tablespoons dressing. Sprinkle with 1/2 cup of the cheese. Arrange tomatoes on cheese. Top with grilled vegetables, onions, olives and remaining 1/2 cup cheese.

3 Place pizza directly on grill. Cover and grill 4 to 5 inches from medium heat 8 to 10 minutes or until crust is crisp and cheese is melted.

1 SERVING: Calories 240 (Calories from Fat 90); Fat 10g (Saturated 3g); Cholesterol 10mg; Sodium 440mg; Carbohydrate 32g (Dietary Fiber 2g); Protein 8g • % DAILY VALUE: Vitamin A 4%; Vitamin C 26%; Calcium 12%; Iron 12% • DIET EXCHANGES: 2 Starch, 2 Fat

6 SERVINGS

Grilled Portabella and Bell Pepper Sandwiches

6 fresh medium portabella mushroom caps

1 large bell pepper, cut into 1/4-inch slices

1 large red onion, sliced

1 tablespoon olive or vegetable oil

1/2 teaspoon seasoned salt

1 round focaccia bread (8 or 9 inches in diameter)

1/4 cup mayonnaise or salad dressing

1/4 cup basil pesto

4 leaf lettuce leaves

1 Heat coals or gas grill for direct heat. Brush mushrooms, bell pepper and onion with oil. Sprinkle with seasoned salt. Place vegetables in grill basket.

2 Cover and grill vegetables 4 to 5 inches from medium heat 10 to 12 minutes, shaking grill basket occasionally to turn vegetables, until bell pepper and onion are crisp-tender and mushrooms are just tender.

3 Cut bread horizontally in half. Mix mayonnaise and pesto; spread over cut sides of bread. Layer lettuce and grilled vegetables on bottom half of bread. Add top of bread. Cut into 6 wedges.

1 SERVING: Calories 290 (Calories from Fat 170); Fat 19g (Saturated 3g); Cholesterol 5mg; Sodium 690mg; Carbohydrate 26g (Dietary Fiber 2g); Protein 5g • **% DAILY VALUE:** Vitamin A 10%; Vitamin C 24%; Calcium 4%; Iron 12% • **DIET EXCHANGES:** 1 Starch, 2 Vegetable, 4 Fat

Grilled Portabella and Bell Pepper Sandwiches

Grilled Herbed
New Potatoes

**2 tablespoons olive or
vegetable oil**

**1 tablespoon chopped fresh or
1/2 teaspoon dried rosemary
leaves, crumbled**

**1 tablespoon chopped fresh or
1/2 teaspoon parsley flakes**

1/2 teaspoon lemon pepper

1/4 teaspoon salt

**8 small red potatoes,
cut into fourths**

Sour Cream Sauce (below)

1 Heat coals or gas grill for direct heat. Mix oil, rosemary, parsley, lemon pepper and salt in medium bowl. Add potatoes; toss. Place potatoes in grill basket.

2 Cover and grill potatoes 4 to 6 inches from medium heat 10 to 15 minutes, shaking grill basket occasionally to turn potatoes, until tender.

3 Make Sour Cream Sauce. Serve with potatoes.

Sour Cream Sauce

1/3 cup sour cream

**1 tablespoon chopped fresh or
1/2 teaspoon dried rosemary leaves,
crumbled**

1/4 teaspoon lemon pepper

1/8 teaspoon garlic powder

Mix all ingredients.

1 SERVING: Calories 290 (Calories from Fat 100); Fat 11g (Saturated 3g); Cholesterol 10mg; Sodium 220mg; Carbohydrate 47g (Dietary Fiber 5g); Protein 5g • **% DAILY VALUE:** Vitamin A 2%; Vitamin C 20%; Calcium 4%; Iron 14% • **DIET EXCHANGES:** 3 Starch, 1 Fat

10 Speedy Sides, Vegetables and Breads

= *super express* ready in 20 minutes or less

1-Step Recipes

Ready-in-a-Minute Sides

No need to get stuck in the same-sides-again rut. It's easy to vary your veggies with these high-flavor, super-quick and easy sides.

1 Seasoned Mashed Potatoes
Stir prepared horseradish or chopped garlic into creamy mashed potatoes.

2 Super-Stuffed Spuds
Fill baked potatoes with sliced cooked mushrooms, chopped cooked ham, sliced green onions, sour cream and shredded cheese.

3 Seasoned Southwest Vegetables
Stir salsa, sliced olives and bell pepper into cooked corn.

4 Zippy zucchini
Toss cooked zucchini and summer squash with Italian dressing and balsamic vinegar.

5 Crunchy winter squash
Sprinkle toasted chopped soy nuts, almonds, peanuts or walnuts over baked acorn or butternut squash.

6 Herbed Peas
Toss cooked baby peas or a mix of baby peas and pearl onions with butter and chopped fresh or dried mint, rosemary or sage leaves.

7 Orange- or Lemon-Glazed Vegetables
Stir melted butter, orange or lemon juice and grated peel, ground ginger and salt into cooked carrots, green beans or pea pods.

8 Sweet Potato Topper
Mix 1 tablespoon molasses, 1/4 teaspoon ground cinnamon and 2 tablespoons orange juice; pour over baked sweet potatoes.

9 Lemon Rice
Stir lemon juice and grated peel into cooked rice.

10 Creamy Quinoa or Couscous
Stir softened cream cheese and grated Romano or Parmesan cheese into cooked quinoa or couscous.

prep: **15 min**
cook: **15 min**

Mushroom, Tomato and Basil Orzo Pilaf

1 1/3 cups uncooked rosamarina (orzo) pasta (8 ounces)

1/4 cup pine nuts

2 teaspoons olive or vegetable oil

1 clove garlic, finely chopped

1 cup sliced mushrooms (3 ounces)

4 medium green onions, sliced (1/4 cup)

1 cup sliced roma (plum) tomatoes

2 tablespoons chopped fresh or 2 teaspoons dried basil leaves

1/4 teaspoon salt

1 teaspoon olive or vegetable oil

1 Cook and drain pasta as directed on package. While pasta is cooking, cook nuts in 12-inch skillet over medium heat 2 to 3 minutes, stirring constantly, until toasted. Remove from skillet.

2 Add 2 teaspoons oil and the garlic to skillet. Cook and stir over medium-high heat 1 minute. Stir in mushrooms and onions. Cook about 2 minutes, stirring occasionally, until onions are crisp-tender.

3 Stir in tomatoes, pasta, basil, salt and remaining teaspoon oil. Cook over medium heat, stirring occasionally, until heated through. Spoon into serving dish; sprinkle with nuts.

IT'S **a** snap!

To make ahead, cook the pasta, removing it from heat 1 or 2 minutes before it is completely cooked; drain and rinse with cold water. Toss pasta with a teaspoon of olive oil. Refrigerate, tightly covered, up to 5 days. When making pilaf, add pasta to the skillet after cooking mushrooms and onions; stir in remaining ingredients and heat through.

1 SERVING: Calories 135 (Calories from Fat 25); Fat 3g (Saturated 1g); Cholesterol 0mg; Sodium 80mg; Carbohydrate 25g (Dietary Fiber 2g); Protein 4g • **% DAILY VALUE:** Vitamin A 2%; Vitamin C 4%; Calcium 0%; Iron 8% • **DIET EXCHANGES:** 1 Starch, 2 Vegetable, 1/2 Fat

4 SERVINGS

Spinach Orzo

1 teaspoon butter or margarine

1 clove garlic, finely chopped

1/2 cup coarsely shredded carrot (1 small)

2 cups chicken broth

1 cup uncooked rosamarina (orzo) pasta (6 ounces)

1 1/2 cups thinly sliced fresh spinach

2 tablespoons grated Parmesan cheese

1 tablespoon chopped fresh or 1 teaspoon dried basil leaves

Salt and pepper to taste

1 Melt butter in 3-quart saucepan over medium heat. Cook garlic and carrot in butter about 2 minutes, stirring occasionally, until carrot is tender.

2 Stir in broth, pasta and spinach. Heat to boiling; reduce heat. Cover and simmer 15 to 20 minutes, stirring occasionally, until broth is absorbed. Stir in remaining ingredients before serving.

IT'S **a**

snap!

A 10-ounce package of frozen chopped spinach, thawed and squeezed to drain, can be substituted for the fresh spinach.

1 SERVING: Calories 100 (Calories from Fat 35); Fat 4g (Saturated 2g); Cholesterol 10mg; Sodium 950mg; Carbohydrate 10g (Dietary Fiber 2g); Protein 8g • **% DAILY VALUE:** Vitamin A 88%; Vitamin C 4%; Calcium 6%; Iron 6% • **DIET EXCHANGES:** 1 Starch, 1/2 Very Lean Meat

Spinach Orzo

C O M E
&eat!

For a heartier
meal, slice 3 fully
cooked mild Italian
sausages (1/2 pound
total) and cook with
the garlic about
2 minutes or until
lightly browned.

4 SERVINGS

Fresh Tomato and Garlic Penne

8 ounces uncooked penne pasta

1 tablespoon olive or vegetable oil

3 cloves garlic, finely chopped

2 pounds roma (plum) tomatoes (12 medium), coarsely chopped

2 tablespoons chopped fresh basil leaves

1/2 teaspoon salt

1/4 teaspoon freshly ground pepper

1 Cook and drain pasta as directed on package.

2 While pasta is cooking, heat oil in 10-inch skillet over medium-high heat. Cook garlic in oil 30 seconds, stirring frequently. Stir in tomatoes. Cook 5 to 8 minutes, stirring frequently, until tomatoes are soft and sauce is slightly thickened.

3 Stir in basil, salt and pepper. Cook 1 minute. Serve sauce over pasta.

1 SERVING: Calories 340 (Calories from Fat 45); Fat 5g (Saturated 1g); Cholesterol 0mg; Sodium 320mg; Carbohydrate 67g (Dietary Fiber 5g); Protein 12g • **% DAILY VALUE:** Vitamin A 12%; Vitamin C 32%; Calcium 2%; Iron 20% • **DIET EXCHANGES:** 3 1/2 Starch, 2 Vegetable

super
express

prep: **10 min**
cook: **10 min**

Spaetzle in Herbed Tomato Cream Sauce

1 teaspoon olive or vegetable oil	**1 tablespoon chopped fresh or 1 teaspoon dried basil leaves**
4 roma (plum) tomatoes, cut into fourths and sliced (2 cups)	**1/4 cup sour cream**
2 cloves garlic, finely chopped	**2 tablespoons mayonnaise or salad dressing**
2 tablespoons chopped fresh chives	**1 package (12 ounces) frozen cooked spaetzle (4 cups)**

1 Heat oil in 10-inch nonstick skillet over medium heat. Cook tomatoes and garlic in oil 5 to 7 minutes, stirring occasionally, until tomatoes are tender; reduce heat to low.

2 Stir in chives, basil, sour cream and mayonnaise. Cook 2 to 3 minutes, stirring occasionally, until sauce is hot.

3 Meanwhile, heat spaetzle as directed on package. Add hot spaetzle to skillet; toss to coat with sauce.

IT'S **a**
snap!

Spaetzle, a German side dish, are tiny noodles or dumplings that you can buy in the frozen foods section of the grocery store. For an even quicker side, toss the spaetzle with warmed bottled spaghetti sauce and add 1/4 cup half-and-half to make it rich and creamy.

1 SERVING: Calories 110 (Calories from Fat 25); Fat 3g (Saturated 1g); Cholesterol 50mg; Sodium 220mg; Carbohydrate 17g (Dietary Fiber 1g); Protein 5g • **% DAILY VALUE:** Vitamin A 8%; Vitamin C 10%; Calcium 6%; Iron 6% • **DIET EXCHANGES:** 1 Starch, 1/2 Fat

6 SERVINGS

Wild Rice Salad with Dried Cherries

C O M E
&eat!

Transform this
side-dish salad into
a main-meal master-
piece. Add 2 cups
chopped cooked
chicken or turkey
breast and 1/2 cup
chopped dried apri-
cots. Turn up the
heat by sprinkling
in 1/4 teaspoon
crushed red pepper.

1 package (6.2 ounces) fast-cooking long-grain and wild rice mix

1 medium unpeeled eating apple, chopped (1 cup)

1 medium green bell pepper, chopped (1 cup)

1 medium stalk celery, chopped (1/2 cup)

1/3 cup dried cherries, chopped

2 tablespoons reduced-sodium soy sauce

2 tablespoons water

2 teaspoons sugar

2 teaspoons cider vinegar

1/3 cup dry-roasted peanuts

1 Cook rice mix as directed on package—except omit butter. Spread rice evenly in thin layer on large cookie sheet. Let stand 10 minutes, stirring occasionally, until cool.

2 Mix apple, bell pepper, celery and cherries in large bowl. Mix soy sauce, water, sugar and vinegar in small bowl until sugar is dissolved. Add rice and soy sauce mixture to apple mixture. Gently toss until coated. Add peanuts; gently toss.

1 SERVING: Calories 130 (Calories from Fat 35); Fat 4g (Saturated 1g); Cholesterol 0mg; Sodium 220mg; Carbohydrate 22g (Dietary Fiber 2g); Protein 4g • **% DAILY VALUE:** Vitamin A 2%; Vitamin C 16%; Calcium 2%; Iron 4% • **DIET EXCHANGES:** 1 Starch, 1/2 Fruit, 1/2 Fat

Wild Rice Salad with Dried Cherries

8 SERVINGS

Garden Medley Salad

Caraway Vinaigrette (below)

1 medium cucumber

8 cups bite-size pieces salad greens

1 medium tomato, cut into wedges

4 medium green onions, sliced (1/4 cup)

1 Make Caraway Vinaigrette. Cut cucumber lengthwise in half; scrape out seeds. Cut halves diagonally into 1/2-inch-wide pieces.

2 Toss salad greens, tomato, onions, cucumber and vinaigrette.

Caraway Vinaigrette

1/4 cup olive or vegetable oil

1 tablespoon chopped fresh parsley

2 tablespoons red wine vinegar

1/2 teaspoon caraway seed

1/2 teaspoon salt

1 clove garlic, finely chopped

Shake all ingredients in tightly covered container. Shake before using.

1 SERVING: Calories 75 (Calories from Fat 65); Fat 7g (Saturated 1g); Cholesterol 0mg; Sodium 160mg; Carbohydrate 4g (Dietary Fiber 2g); Protein 1g • **% DAILY VALUE:** Vitamin A 40%; Vitamin C 26%; Calcium 4%; Iron 6% • **DIET EXCHANGES:** 1 Vegetable, 1 Fat

6 SERVINGS

Spring Greens Fruit Salad

1/4 cup champagne vinegar or white wine vinegar

2 tablespoons olive or vegetable oil

1 tablespoon honey

2 teaspoons chopped fresh or 1/2 teaspoon dried marjoram leaves

Dash of salt

3 cups mixed baby greens

1 cup sliced strawberries

1 peach, pitted and thinly sliced

1/2 cup diced Gouda cheese (2 ounces)

1/4 cup hazelnuts, toasted* and coarsely chopped

1 Mix vinegar, oil, honey, marjoram and salt.

2 Mix baby greens, strawberries, peach and cheese in large serving bowl. Add dressing mixture; toss. Sprinkle with hazelnuts.

* **HOW TO toast hazelnuts:** Cook hazelnuts in an ungreased heavy skillet over medium-low heat 5 to 7 minutes, stirring frequently until browning begins, then stirring constantly until golden brown.

IT'S **a**
snap!
Use strawberries as soon as possible after buying them. If storing them for a day or two, place in a single layer in a jelly roll pan lined with paper towels. Cover the berries with paper towels and refrigerate.

1 SERVING: Calories 145 (Calories from Fat 100); Fat 11g (Saturated 3g); Cholesterol 10mg; Sodium 110mg; Carbohydrate 9g (Dietary Fiber 2g); Protein 4g • **% DAILY VALUE:** Vitamin A 6%; Vitamin C 32%; Calcium 10%; Iron 2% • **DIET EXCHANGES:** 1/2 High-Fat Meat, 1/2 Fruit, 1 1/2 Fat

6 SERVINGS

Pineapple Fruit and Rice Salad

1 cup uncooked instant rice

**1/2 cup pineapple or
piña colada low-fat yogurt**

1/4 teaspoon ground cinnamon

**1 cup frozen (thawed)
whipped topping**

**1 medium unpeeled eating
apple, coarsely chopped**

**1 medium unpeeled pear,
coarsely chopped**

1 cup seedless grape halves

1 Cook rice as directed on package. Place cooked rice in wire mesh strainer or colander with small holes. Rinse with cold water to chill; drain well.

2 Mix yogurt and cinnamon in medium bowl. Fold in whipped topping. Gently stir in rice and remaining ingredients.

1 SERVING: Calories 165 (Calories from Fat 25); Fat 3g (Saturated 1g); Cholesterol 0mg; Sodium 15mg; Carbohydrate 34g (Dietary Fiber 2g); Protein 3g • **% DAILY VALUE:** Vitamin A 0%; Vitamin C 8%; Calcium 4%; Iron 4% • **DIET EXCHANGES:** 1/2 Starch, 2 Fruit

Pineapple Fruit and Rice Salad

prep: **10 min**
cook: **5 min**

COME
&eat!

Here's a quick-
cooking side dish
that's delicious for
an Asian-inspired
dinner. Try serving
with Apricot-Glazed
Pork (page 224) and
hot cooked rice.

6 SERVINGS

Sesame Pea Pods

1 tablespoon sesame oil

**1/2 pound snow (Chinese)
pea pods (2 cups)**

1 tablespoon sesame seed

**1 medium red or yellow
bell pepper, cut into thin strips**

1 Heat oil in 10-inch skillet over medium-high heat. Add
pea pods and sesame seed. Cook about 2 minutes, stirring
frequently, until pea pods are crisp-tender.

2 Stir in bell pepper. Cook about 2 minutes, stirring frequently,
until bell pepper is crisp-tender.

1 SERVING: Calories 45 (Calories from Fat 25); Fat 3g (Saturated 0g); Cholesterol 0mg;
Sodium 0mg; Carbohydrate 4g (Dietary Fiber 1g); Protein 2g • **% DAILY VALUE:**
Vitamin A 26%; Vitamin C 44%; Calcium 2%; Iron 4% • **DAILY EXCHANGES:** 1 Vegetable,
1/2 Fat

super
express

prep: 5 min
cook: 12 min

Orange-Glazed Snap Peas with Carrot

1 bag (1 pound) frozen snap pea pods

1 medium carrot, shredded (2/3 cup)

1/2 cup orange juice

1 1/2 teaspoons cornstarch

1/2 teaspoon grated orange peel

1/4 teaspoon ground ginger

1/8 teaspoon salt

1 Cook pea pods as directed on package, with carrot.

2 While pea pods and carrot are cooking, heat remaining ingredients to boiling in 1-quart saucepan, stirring constantly. Boil and stir 1 minute.

3 Drain vegetables. Pour sauce over vegetables; toss.

IT'S **a**

snap!

Snap pea pods are sweeter than snow peas and have more rounded and fully developed peas inside. You'll find them fresh in your supermarket during the spring and fall. At other times, use the convenient frozen ones. They save you extra time since you don't have to string them.

1 SERVING: Calories 55 (Calories from Fat 0); Fat 0g (Saturated 0g); Cholesterol 0mg; Sodium 85mg; Carbohydrate 13g (Dietary Fiber 3g); Protein 4g • **% DAILY VALUE:** Vitamin A 24%; Vitamin C 50%; Calcium 4%; Iron 12% • **DIET EXCHANGES:** 1/2 Starch, 1 Vegetable

prep: **10 min**
cook: **10 min**

IT'S **a**
snap!

This convenient
succotash, made
with frozen vegeta-
bles, can be enjoyed
year-round. In the
summer months, it's
even more delicious
if you use fresh corn
cut off the cob.

5 SERVINGS

Creamy Confetti Succotash

I tablespoon butter or margarine

I small red or green bell pepper, chopped (1/2 cup)

2 medium green onions, sliced (2 tablespoons)

I package (10 ounces) frozen whole kernel corn or 2 cups fresh whole kernel corn

I cup frozen baby lima beans

1/4 cup half-and-half

2 teaspoons chopped fresh or 1/2 teaspoon dried marjoram leaves

1/4 teaspoon salt

1/8 teaspoon pepper

1 Melt butter in 8-inch skillet over medium-high heat. Cook bell pepper and onions in butter 2 to 3 minutes, stirring occasionally, until crisp-tender.

2 Stir in remaining ingredients; reduce heat to medium-low. Cover and cook 5 to 6 minutes, stirring occasionally, until vegetables are tender.

1 SERVING: Calories 115 (Calories from Fat 35); Fat 4g (Saturated 2g); Cholesterol 10mg; Sodium 4160mg; Carbohydrate 20g (Dietary Fiber 4g); Protein 4g • **% DAILY VALUE:** Vitamin A 8%; Vitamin C 16%; Calcium 2%; Iron 4% • **DIET EXCHANGES:** 1 Starch, 1/2 Fat

Creamy Confetti Succotash

Pantry Recipes

If you have a well-stocked pantry (see pages 6–7), you'll be able to make this recipe anytime, even when there's no time to shop.

Pesto Vegetables

1 bag (1 pound) frozen broccoli, cauliflower and carrots (or other combination)

1/3 cup basil pesto

Grated Parmesan cheese

Cook and drain **vegetables** as directed on package. Toss vegetables with **pesto** and sprinkle with **cheese**. MAKES 5 SERVINGS IN 15 MINUTES

serve it 3 ways!

1 Salad
Add vegetable mixture to salad greens and drizzle with any creamy dressing.

2 Sandwich
Slice 1 round focaccia bread horizontally in half. Spread vegetable mixture over bottom half; sprinkle with mozzarella cheese. Add top of focaccia and cut into wedges.

3 Pasta
Serve over hot cooked rice, pasta, couscous or quinoa.

super
express

prep: **10 min**
cook: **10 min**

Ginger Glazed Carrots

6 medium carrots, thinly sliced (3 cups)

2 tablespoons packed brown sugar

2 tablespoons butter or margarine

1/2 teaspoon ground ginger

1 Heat 1 inch water to boiling in 3-quart saucepan. Add carrots. Heat to boiling; reduce heat to medium. Cover and simmer about 5 minutes or until crisp-tender; drain and set aside.

2 Cook brown sugar, butter and ginger in same saucepan over medium heat, stirring constantly, until bubbly. Stir in carrots. Cook over low heat 2 to 4 minutes, stirring occasionally, until carrots are glazed and hot.

IT'S **a**
snap!
Skip the peeling and chopping—use convenient already-peeled baby carrots in this easy, tasty side dish.

1 SERVING: Calories 75 (Calories from Fat 35); Fat 4g (Saturated 2g); Cholesterol 10mg; Sodium 50mg; Carbohydrate 11g (Dietary Fiber 2g); Protein 1g • **% DAILY VALUE:** Vitamin A 100%; Vitamin C 4%; Calcium 2%; Iron 2% • **DIET EXCHANGES:** 1 Vegetable, 1/2 Fruit, 1/2 Fat

6 SERVINGS

Warm Caramelized Vegetables

2 pounds small red potatoes, cut into 1-inch pieces

1/2 teaspoon salt

1 pound asparagus, cut into 2-inch pieces

1/3 cup butter or margarine

1 large onion, chopped (1 cup)

1/4 cup balsamic vinegar

1/4 cup packed brown sugar

1/4 teaspoon salt

Freshly ground pepper, if desired

1 Heat 1 inch water to boiling in 3-quart saucepan. Add potatoes and 1/2 teaspoon salt. Heat to boiling; reduce heat to medium. Cover and cook about 12 minutes or until tender; drain and set aside.

2 While potatoes are cooking, heat 1 inch water to boiling in 2-quart saucepan. Add asparagus. Heat to boiling; reduce heat to medium. Cover and cook about 5 minutes or until crisp-tender; drain and set aside.

3 While vegetables are cooking, melt butter in 10-inch skillet over medium-high heat. Cook onion in butter about 5 minutes, stirring occasionally, until golden brown. Stir in vinegar, brown sugar and 1/4 teaspoon salt. Pour onion mixture over potatoes and asparagus; stir until coated. Sprinkle with pepper.

1 SERVING: Calories 275 (Calories from Fat 100); Fat 11g (Saturated 6g); Cholesterol 25mg; Sodium 380mg; Carbohydrate 44g (Dietary Fiber 4g); Protein 4g • **% DAILY VALUE:** Vitamin A 10%; Vitamin C 22%; Calcium 4%; Iron 12% • **DIET EXCHANGES:** 2 Vegetable, 2 Starch, 2 Fat

Warm Caramelized Vegetables

prep: **2 min**
cook: **7 min**

6 SERVINGS

Caesar Vegetable Medley

2 tablespoons olive or vegetable oil

2 bags (1 pound each) frozen cauliflower, carrots and snow pea pods (or other combination)

1 envelope (1.2 ounces) Caesar dressing mix

1 Heat oil in 10-inch nonstick skillet over medium-high heat.

2 Cover and cook frozen vegetables and dressing mix (dry) in oil 5 to 7 minutes, stirring frequently, until vegetables are crisp-tender.

1 SERVING: Calories 85 (Calories from Fat 45); Fat 5g (Saturated 1g); Cholesterol 0mg; Sodium 380mg; Carbohydrate 13g (Dietary Fiber 6g); Protein 3g • **% DAILY VALUE:** Vitamin A 100%; Vitamin C 32%; Calcium 12%; Iron 24% • **DIET EXCHANGES:** 1/2 Starch, 1 Vegetable, 1/2 Fat

8 SERVINGS

Asparagus with Maple-Mustard Sauce

prep: **10 min**
cook: **5 min**

**2 pounds asparagus, cut into
2 inch pieces**

**2 tablespoons real maple syrup
or maple-flavored syrup**

2 tablespoons Dijon mustard

**2 tablespoons olive or
vegetable oil**

1 Heat 1 inch water (salted if desired) to boiling in 12-inch skillet or Dutch oven. Add asparagus. Heat to boiling; reduce heat to medium. Cover and cook 4 to 5 minutes or until asparagus is crisp-tender; drain.

2 Mix maple syrup, mustard and oil. Drizzle over asparagus.

IT'S **a**
snap!

Here's a really speedy way to trim the tough ends from asparagus: Just break off the end by gently bending the stalk as far down as it snaps easily.

1 SERVING: Calories 65 (Calories from Fat 35); Fat 4g (Saturated 1g); Cholesterol 0mg; Sodium 50mg; Carbohydrate 6g (Dietary Fiber 1g); Protein 2g • **% DAILY VALUE:** Vitamin A 4%; Vitamin C 10%; Calcium 2%; Iron 2% • **DIET EXCHANGES:** 1 Vegetable, 1 Fat

prep: **10** min
microwave: **4** min
stand: **2** min

4 SERVINGS

Pesto-Stuffed Tomatoes

4 medium tomatoes
(1 1/4 to 1 1/2 pounds)

3 tablespoons shredded
Parmesan cheese

2 tablespoons pine nuts

2 tablespoons chopped fresh or
2 teaspoons dried basil leaves

1 1/2 teaspoons olive or
vegetable oil

1/2 teaspoon garlic salt

1/4 teaspoon pepper

2 slices bread, torn into crumbs

1 Cut 1/4-inch slice from stem end of each tomato; scoop out pulp. Discard seeds; chop pulp. Mix pulp, 2 tablespoons of the cheese, the nuts, basil, oil, garlic salt and pepper. Gently stir in bread crumbs. Fill tomatoes with mixture.

2 Place each tomato in 6-ounce custard cup, or arrange tomatoes in circle in shallow round microwavable dish. Cover loosely with waxed paper.

3 Microwave on High 3 to 4 minutes or until tender. Sprinkle with remaining 1 tablespoon cheese. Cover and let stand about 2 minutes or until cheese is melted.

1 SERVING: Calories 120 (Calories from Fat 55); Fat 6g (Saturated 2g); Cholesterol 5mg; Sodium 290mg; Carbohydrate 13g (Dietary Fiber 2g); Protein 5g • **% DAILY VALUE:** Vitamin A 8%; Vitamin C 20%; Calcium 8%; Iron 6% • **DIET EXCHANGES:** 3 Vegetable, 1 Fat

Pesto-Stuffed Tomatoes

4 SERVINGS

Caramelized Onion and Sweet Potato Skillet

1 tablespoon vegetable oil

**1/4 large sweet onion
(Bermuda, Maui, Spanish or
Vidalia), sliced**

**3 medium sweet potatoes,
peeled and sliced (3 1/2 cups)**

**2 tablespoons packed
brown sugar**

1/2 teaspoon jerk seasoning

**1 tablespoon chopped
fresh parsley**

1 Heat oil in 10-inch skillet over medium heat. Cook onion and sweet potatoes in oil about 5 minutes, stirring occasionally, until light brown; reduce heat to low. Cover and cook 10 to 12 minutes, stirring occasionally, until potatoes are tender.

2 Stir in brown sugar and jerk seasoning. Cook uncovered about 3 minutes, stirring occasionally, until glazed. Sprinkle with parsley.

1 SERVING: Calories 115 (Calories from Fat 10); Fat 1g (Saturated 0g); Cholesterol 0mg; Sodium 10mg; Carbohydrate 28g (Dietary Fiber 3g); Protein 2g • **% DAILY VALUE:** Vitamin A 100%; Vitamin C 18%; Calcium 2%; Iron 2% • **DIET EXCHANGES:** 1/2 Starch, 1 Vegetable, 1 Fruit

Sweet Potato Surprise

prep: **15 min**
bake: **10 min**

I can (18 ounces) vacuum-pack sweet potatoes

I tablespoon packed brown sugar

6 large marshmallows

I tablespoon butter or margarine, melted

1/3 cup cornflake crumbs

1 Heat oven to 450°. Grease bottom and sides of square pan, 8 × 8 × 2 inches, with shortening. Mash sweet potatoes and brown sugar. Shape 1/3 cup potato mixture around each marshmallow into a ball.

2 Brush 1 sweet potato ball at a time with butter; roll in cornflake crumbs to coat. Place in pan. Bake uncovered 8 to 10 minutes or until coating is light brown.

COME
&eat!

Here's a yummy surprise—melted marshmallows hidden inside balls of mashed sweet potato, covered in a buttery-crisp coating! What kid could possibly resist these veggies?

1 SERVING: Calories 135 (Calories from Fat 20); Fat 2g (Saturated 1g); Cholesterol 5mg; Sodium 80mg; Carbohydrate 28g (Dietary Fiber 1g); Protein 2g • **% DAILY VALUE:** Vitamin A 100%; Vitamin C 18%; Calcium 2%; Iron 6% • **DIET EXCHANGES:** 1 Starch, 2 Vegetable

IT'S **a**
snap!
If you don't have
enough room on the
grill for the corn,
cook them indoors
instead. Remove
the husks; do not
spread corn with
Chili-Lime Spread.
Heat cold water to
boiling. Add corn.
Cover and cook 6 to
8 minutes or until
tender. Serve with
spread on the side.

8 SERVINGS

Grilled Corn with Chili-Lime Spread

Chili-Lime Spread (below)
8 ears corn (with husks)

1 Heat coals or gas grill for direct heat. Make Chili-Lime Spread.

2 Remove large outer husks from each ear of corn; gently pull back inner husks and remove silk. Spread each ear of corn with about 2 teaspoons Chili-Lime Spread; reserve remaining spread. Pull husks up over ears; tie with fine wire to secure.

3 Grill corn uncovered 3 inches from medium heat 10 to 15 minutes, turning frequently, until tender. Let stand 5 minutes. Serve corn with remaining spread.

Chili-Lime Spread

1/2 cup butter or margarine, softened
1/2 teaspoon grated lime peel
3 tablespoons lime juice
1 to 2 teaspoons ground red chilies or chili powder

Mix all ingredients.

1 SERVING: Calories 205 (Calories from Fat 100); Fat 11g (Saturated 6g); Cholesterol 25mg; Sodium 85mg; Carbohydrate 26g (Dietary Fiber 3g); Protein 3g • **% DAILY VALUE:** Vitamin A 8%; Vitamin C 4%; Calcium 8%; Iron 10% • **DIET EXCHANGES:** 1 1/2 Starch, 2 Fat

Grilled Corn with Chili-Lime Spread

6 SERVINGS

Skillet Cheddar Bread

2 cups all-purpose flour

1/4 cup nonfat dry milk

1 tablespoon sugar

1 teaspoon cream of tartar

1/2 teaspoon baking soda

1/2 teaspoon salt

1/4 cup firm butter or margarine

1/2 cup shredded Cheddar cheese (2 ounces)

3/4 cup water

IT'S **a**
snap!
Save time by making your own baking mix. Start the bread by doing step 1 ahead. Then, when you're ready, go on to the next steps and let it "bake."

1 Mix flour, dry milk, sugar, cream of tartar, baking soda and salt in resealable plastic food-storage bag.

2 Pour flour mixture into medium bowl. Cut in butter, using pastry blender or crisscrossing 2 knives, until mixture looks like cornmeal. Gently stir in cheese. Stir in water just until dough forms (do not overmix).

3 Grease 10-inch cast-iron skillet. Press dough into 3/4-inch-thick round. Cut into 6 wedges. Place wedges in skillet. Cover with aluminum foil. Cook over low heat about 10 minutes or until puffed and bottom is light brown. Turn wedges; cook about 10 minutes longer or until cooked through.

1 SERVING: Calories 270 (Calories from Fat 100); Fat 11g (Saturated 7g); Cholesterol 30mg; Sodium 320mg; Carbohydrate 36g (Dietary Fiber 1g); Protein 8g • **% DAILY VALUE:** Vitamin A 8%; Vitamin C 0%; Calcium 8%; Iron 10% • **DIET EXCHANGES:** 2 1/2 Starch, 2 Fat

Irish Yogurt Bread

1 3/4 cups all-purpose flour

1/2 cup currants or raisins

1 1/2 teaspoons baking powder

1/4 teaspoon baking soda

1/4 teaspoon salt

1 container (8 ounces) lemon, orange or plain low-fat yogurt

2 tablespoons vegetable oil

1 Heat oven to 375°. Lightly grease bottom and side of round pan, 9 × 1 1/2 inches, with shortening.

2 Mix flour, currants, baking powder, baking soda and salt in medium bowl. Mix yogurt and oil; stir into flour mixture just until flour is moistened. Spread dough in pan.

3 Bake about 20 minutes or until toothpick inserted in center comes out clean. Cut into wedges. Serve warm or cool.

IT'S **a**
snap!

For a quick, fruity topping for these yogurt wedges, mix equal parts of plain or flavored yogurt with your favorite preserves and drizzle over the top.

1 WEDGE: Calories 185 (Calories from Fat 35); Fat 4g (Saturated 1g); Cholesterol 0mg; Sodium 220mg; Carbohydrate 34g (Dietary Fiber 1g); Protein 4g • **% DAILY VALUE:** Vitamin A 0%; Vitamin C 0%; Calcium 10%; Iron 8% • **DIET EXCHANGES:** 2 Starch, 1 Fat

prep: **5 min**
broil: **4 min**

8 SERVINGS

Texas Toast

1/4 cup butter or margarine,   **1/2 teaspoon seasoned salt**
softened

4 slices thick-cut white bread,
about 1 inch thick

1 Set oven control to broil. Spread butter on both sides of bread slices. Sprinkle with seasoned salt. Place on rack in broiler pan.

2 Broil with tops 4 to 6 inches from heat 2 to 4 minutes, turning once, until lightly toasted.

3 Cut each slice diagonally in half. Serve warm or cool.

IT'S **a**

snap!

**Craving variety?
Add garlic spread
with the butter, or
sprinkle toast with
garlic salt before
serving to make gar-
lic toast. Or sprinkle
with mozzarella
cheese after broiling,
and let stand 1 to 2
minutes to melt.**

1 SLICE: Calories 85 (Calories from Fat 55); Fat 6g (Saturated 4g); Cholesterol 15mg; Sodium 200mg; Carbohydrate 7g (Dietary Fiber 0g); Protein 1g • **% DAILY VALUE:** Vitamin A 4%; Vitamin C 0%; Calcium 2 %; Iron 2% • **DIET EXCHANGES:** 1 1/2 Starch, 1 Fat

12 STICKS

Sour Cream Biscuit Sticks

prep: **10 min**
bake: **12 min**

2 cups all-purpose flour

3 teaspoons baking powder

1/2 teaspoon salt

1/3 cup shortening

2 tablespoons chopped fresh or freeze-dried chives

1 1/4 cups sour cream

2 tablespoons butter or margarine, melted

About 1/4 cup poppy seed, sesame seed or coarse salt

1 Heat oven to 450°. Mix flour, baking powder and salt in large bowl. Cut in shortening, using pastry blender or crisscrossing 2 knives, until mixture looks like fine crumbs. Stir in chives. Stir in sour cream until dough leaves side of bowl and forms a ball.

2 Place dough on lightly floured surface; gently roll in flour to coat. Knead lightly 10 times. Roll or pat into 12 × 8-inch rectangle. Cut rectangle crosswise into 12 strips, 8 × 1 inch. Twist each strip. Place about 1 inch apart on ungreased cookie sheet. Brush strips lightly with butter. Sprinkle with poppy seed.

3 Bake 10 to 12 minutes or until golden brown. Immediately remove from cookie sheet. Serve hot.

IT'S **a**
snap!

To get two different looks from one batch, sprinkle a few sticks with poppy seed and some with sesame seed.

1 STICK: Calories 195 (Calories from Fat 125); Fat 14g (Saturated 6g); Cholesterol 20mg; Sodium 240mg; Carbohydrate 17g (Dietary Fiber 1g); Protein 3g • **% DAILY VALUE:** Vitamin A 4%; Vitamin C 0%; Calcium 14%; Iron 8% • **DIET EXCHANGES:** 1 Starch, 2 1/2 Fat

24 MINI-MUFFINS

Orange-Almond Mini-Muffins

IT'S **a**
snap!

Mini-muffins are really fun to eat, but if you don't have the smaller muffin tin, you can make regular-size muffins. Grease just the bottoms of 12 muffin cups, 2 1/2 × 1 1/4 inches; bake 20 to 25 minutes.

3/4 cup milk

1/3 cup vegetable oil

1/4 cup frozen (thawed) orange juice concentrate

2 teaspoons grated orange peel

1/2 teaspoon almond extract

1 egg, slightly beaten

2 1/4 cups all-purpose flour

1/2 cup granulated sugar

3 teaspoons baking powder

1/4 teaspoon salt

1/3 cup finely chopped blanched almonds

2 tablespoons coarse sugar crystals (decorating sugar), if desired

2 tablespoons finely chopped blanched almonds, if desired

1 Heat oven to 400°. Grease bottoms only of 24 small muffin cups, 1 3/4 × 1 inch, with shortening, or line with paper baking cups.

2 Beat milk, oil, juice concentrate, orange peel, almond extract and egg in large bowl with spoon until blended. Stir in flour, granulated sugar, baking powder and salt all at once just until flour is moistened (batter will be lumpy). Stir in 1/3 cup almonds. Divide batter evenly among cups. Sprinkle with sugar crystals and 2 tablespoons almonds.

3 Bake 10 to 15 minutes or until light golden brown. Immediately remove from pan to wire rack. Serve warm or cool.

1 MUFFIN: Calories 110 (Calories from Fat 45); Fat 5g (Saturated 1g); Cholesterol 10mg; Sodium 95mg; Carbohydrate 15g (Dietary Fiber 1g); Protein 2g • **% DAILY VALUE:** Vitamin A 0%; Vitamin C 2%; Calcium 4%; Iron 4% • **DIET EXCHANGES:** 1 Starch, 1/2 Fat

Orange-Almond Mini-Muffins

8 MUFFINS

Double-Corn Muffins

2/3 cup milk

3 tablespoons vegetable oil

1 egg

3/4 cup all-purpose flour

3/4 cup cornmeal

2 tablespoons sugar

1 teaspoon baking powder

1/2 teaspoon salt

1 can (8 3/4 ounces) whole kernel corn, drained, or 1 cup frozen (thawed) whole kernel corn

C O M E
&eat!

These muffins are great served with chili or any stew or soup. They also keep well; if there are any left, keep tightly covered and enjoy them the next day.

1 Heat oven to 400°. Grease bottoms only of 8 medium muffin cups, 2 1/2 × 1 1/4 inches, with shortening, or line with paper baking cups.

2 Beat milk, oil and egg in medium bowl with spoon. Stir in remaining ingredients except corn just until flour is moistened. Fold in corn. Divide batter evenly among muffin cups (about 3/4 full).

3 Bake 18 to 20 minutes or until golden brown. Immediately remove from pan to wire rack. Serve warm or cool.

1 MUFFIN: Calories 240 (Calories from Fat 65); Fat 7g (Saturated 1g); Cholesterol 30mg; Sodium 290mg; Carbohydrate 40g (Dietary Fiber 2g); Protein 6g • **% DAILY VALUE:** Vitamin A 2%; Vitamin C 2%; Calcium 6%; Iron 12% • **DIET EXCHANGES:** 2 1/2 Starch, 1 Fat

Dried Cherry-Lemon Scones

prep: **10 min**
bake: **15 min**

2 cups all-purpose flour

1/4 cup sugar

2 teaspoons grated lemon peel

1 1/2 teaspoons cream of tartar

3/4 teaspoon baking soda

1/4 teaspoon salt

1/2 cup firm butter or margarine, cut into 8 pieces

1/3 to 1/2 cup buttermilk

1/2 cup dried cherries

2 tablespoons milk

1 Heat oven to 425°. Mix flour, sugar, lemon peel, cream of tartar, baking soda and salt in medium bowl. Cut in butter, using pastry blender or crisscrossing 2 knives, until mixture looks like fine crumbs. Stir in just enough buttermilk so dough leaves sides of bowl and forms a ball. Stir in cherries.

2 Drop dough by about 1/3 cupfuls about 1 inch apart onto ungreased cookie sheet. Brush with milk. Sprinkle with additional sugar if desired.

3 Bake 10 to 15 minutes or until light brown. Immediately remove from cookie sheet to wire rack. Serve warm or cool.

IT'S **a**
snap!
Did you know?
If you don't have buttermilk, you can use plain yogurt with 2 tablespoons milk stirred into it instead.

1 SCONE: Calories 215 (Calories from Fat 90); Fat 10g (Saturated 6g); Cholesterol 25mg; Sodium 220mg; Carbohydrate 31g (Dietary Fiber 3g); Protein 3g • **% DAILY VALUE:** Vitamin A 8%; Vitamin C 6%; Calcium 2%; Iron 6% • **DIET EXCHANGES:** 1 Starch, 1 Fruit, 2 Fat

8 WEDGES

Gingerbread Wedges

2 1/2 cups Original Bisquick   1/2 teaspoon ground cinnamon

1/4 cup packed brown sugar   1/2 teaspoon ground ginger

1/3 cup molasses   1 egg

1/4 cup whipping (heavy) cream   Lemon Glaze (below)

1 Heat oven to 425°. Grease cookie sheet with shortening.

2 Mix all ingredients except Lemon Glaze until soft dough forms. Place on surface sprinkled with additional Bisquick; roll in Bisquick to coat. Shape into ball; knead 10 times. Pat dough into 8-inch circle on cookie sheet. Cut into 8 wedges, but do not separate.

3 Bake 13 to 15 minutes or until set and starting to brown. Make Lemon Glaze; drizzle over warm wedges. Carefully separate wedges. Serve warm.

Lemon Glaze

1 cup powdered sugar

2 tablespoons butter or margarine, melted

1 teaspoon grated lemon peel

1 tablespoon lemon juice

Mix powdered sugar, butter and lemon peel. Stir in lemon juice until smooth enough to drizzle.

1 WEDGE: Calories 325 (Calories from Fat 100); Fat 11g (Saturated 3g); Cholesterol 35mg; Sodium 590mg; Carbohydrate 54g (Dietary Fiber 1g); Protein 4g • **% DAILY VALUE:** Vitamin A 6%; Vitamin C 0%; Calcium 10%; Iron 12% • **DIET EXCHANGES:** Not Recommended

Gingerbread Wedges

8 ROLLS

Caramel Apple Breakfast Rolls

1/2 cup packed dark or light brown sugar

1/2 cup whipping (heavy) cream

1/4 cup chopped pecans

1 can (11 ounces) refrigerated soft breadsticks

1/3 cup cinnamon-flavored applesauce

1 Heat oven to 350°. Mix brown sugar and whipping cream in ungreased round pan, 8 × 1 1/2 inches. Sprinkle with pecans.

2 Unroll breadstick dough, but do not separate into breadsticks. Spread applesauce over dough. Roll up dough from short end; separate at perforations. Place coiled dough in pan.

3 Bake 15 to 20 minutes or until golden brown. Cool 1 minute. Invert pan onto heatproof tray or serving plate; let pan remain on top 1 minute so caramel will drizzle over rolls. Remove pan.

IT'S **a** snap!

Can you smell the goodness? If you want the same great taste, but don't have cinnamon applesauce on hand, use regular applesauce and stir in 1/4 teaspoon ground cinnamon.

1 ROLL: Calories 235 (Calories from Fat 80); Fat 9g (Saturated 3g); Cholesterol 15mg; Sodium 240mg; Carbohydrate 36g (Dietary Fiber 1g); Protein 4g • **% DAILY VALUE:** Vitamin A 2%; Vitamin C 0%; Calcium 4%; Iron 8% • **DIET EXCHANGES:** 1 Starch, 1 1/2 Fruit, 1 1/2 Fat

11 Easy Dreamy Desserts

🌙 = *super express* ready in 20 minutes or less

1-Step Recipes

Easy Dessert Toppings, Sauces and Dippers

Make simple desserts sensational! Here are easy and quick ways to turn plain fruit, ice cream, frozen yogurt, cakes or cookies into delightful treats.

1 Honey-Coffee

Drizzle vanilla ice cream with honey; sprinkle with instant coffee granules.

2 Chocolate Cream

Stir chocolate syrup into whipped cream and spoon over mixed berries and angel or pound cake.

3 Fruity Yogurt

Mix equal parts plain or vanilla yogurt with apricot or peach preserves and drizzle over pineapple slices, sliced strawberries and butter cookies.

4 Tea-Flavored Whipped Cream

Stir instant tea powder into whipped cream and spoon over blueberries and shortbread cookies.

5 Orange Glaze

Melt orange marmalade with orange-flavored liqueur or water and drizzle over chocolate cake and mandarin orange slices.

6 Honey-Citrus Topping

Mix honey with grated lemon, lime or orange peel and juice and pour over sliced bananas and oatmeal cookies.

7 Whole Berry Cranberry Sauce

Spoon over vanilla or orange frozen yogurt and angel food cake.

8 White Chocolate Sauce

Heat chopped white baking chocolate and shortening until melted and drizzle over raspberries and chocolate cookies.

9 Cherry-Berries Topping

Stir sliced strawberries and lemon juice into cherry pie filling; serve warm or cool over cheesecake.

10 Semisweet Chocolate

Melt chocolate chips and drizzle over sliced bananas, graham crackers and marshmallows.

4 SERVINGS

Pound Cake with Maple-Nut Topping

1/2 package (8-ounce size) cream cheese, softened

1/4 cup maple-flavored syrup

1/4 cup coarsely chopped pecans

4 slices pound cake, 1 inch thick

1 Mix cream cheese, maple syrup and pecans.

2 Spoon topping onto cake.

COME

&eat!

Need a tasty dessert that takes only minutes? Make a quick, special topping for cake! You can use angel food, sponge or other prepared cake, butterscotch or caramel topping and any type of nuts that you love!

1 SERVING: Calories 395 (Calories from Fat 235); Fat 26g (Saturated 11g); Cholesterol 75mg; Sodium 140mg; Carbohydrate 36g (Dietary Fiber 1g); Protein 5g • **% DAILY VALUE:** Vitamin A 8%; Vitamin C 0%; Calcium 4%; Iron 6% • **DIET EXCHANGES:** Not Recommended

9 SERVINGS

Fudge Pudding Cake

1 cup all-purpose flour	2 tablespoons vegetable oil
3/4 cup granulated sugar	1 teaspoon vanilla
2 tablespoons baking cocoa	1 cup chopped nuts
2 teaspoons baking powder	1 cup packed brown sugar
1/4 teaspoon salt	1/4 cup baking cocoa
1/2 cup milk	1 3/4 cups boiling water

1 Mix flour, granulated sugar, 2 tablespoons cocoa, the baking powder and salt in 2-quart microwavable casserole.

2 Stir in milk, oil and vanilla. Stir in nuts. Spread evenly in
casserole. Mix brown sugar and 1/4 cup cocoa; sprinkle
over batter. Pour boiling water over batter.

3 Microwave uncovered on Medium (50%) 9 minutes; rotate
casserole 1/2 turn. Microwave uncovered on High 5 to 6
minutes or until top is almost dry. Serve warm with ice
cream or whipped cream.

1 SERVING: Calories 345 (Calories from Fat 180); Fat 13g (Saturated 2g); Cholesterol 0mg;
Sodium 140mg; Carbohydrate 56g (Dietary Fiber 3g); Protein 4g • **% DAILY VALUE:**
Vitamin A 0%; Vitamin C 0%; Calcium 10%; Iron 10% • **DIET EXCHANGES:** Not
Recommended

Fudge Pudding Cake

prep: **15 min**

If you have the time, make this dessert a few hours ahead and refrigerate before serving. The flavors blend together while chilling, making an even more flavorful dessert. If you don't have the time, dig right in— it's incredibly yummy either way.

6 SERVINGS

Easy Banana Cream Trifle

1 package (4-serving size) vanilla instant pudding and pie filling mix

2 cups cold milk

1 package (16 ounces) frozen banana breakfast quick bread loaf or pound cake, thawed and cut into 1-inch cubes (about 6 cups)

3 ripe medium bananas, sliced

1 container (8 ounces) frozen whipped topping, thawed

1 Make pudding mix in large bowl as directed on package for pudding, using 2 cups milk.

2 Layer half of the bread cubes, pudding, banana slices and whipped topping in 2-quart serving bowl. Repeat layers. Store covered in refrigerator.

1 SERVING: Calories 375 (Calories from Fat 90); Fat 10g (Saturated 5g); Cholesterol 45mg; Sodium 490mg; Carbohydrate 68g (Dietary Fiber 3g); Protein 6g • **% DAILY VALUE:** Vitamin A 6%; Vitamin C 14%; Calcium 12%; Iron 6% • **DIET EXCHANGES:** Not Recommended

Chocolate-Cherry Dessert

prep: **10 min**
bake: **11 min**
cool: **5 min**

2/3 cup powdered sugar

1/2 teaspoon almond extract

1 egg

1 package (3 ounces) cream cheese, softened

1 3/4 cups Original Bisquick

2/3 cup miniature semisweet chocolate chips

1 can (21 ounces) cherry pie filling

1/4 cup white baking chips

2 teaspoons shortening

1 Heat oven to 400°. Mix powdered sugar, almond extract, egg and cream cheese in medium bowl. Stir in Bisquick. Roll or pat dough into 12-inch circle on ungreased cookie sheet. Flute edge if desired. Bake 8 to 10 minutes or until crust is light golden brown.

2 Sprinkle chocolate chips over hot crust. Bake about 1 minute or until chips are melted; spread evenly. Cool 5 minutes. Gently loosen and transfer to serving plate.

3 Spread pie filling over chocolate. Heat white baking chips and shortening over low heat, stirring frequently, until smooth; drizzle over pie filling.

IT'S **a**
snap!
This dessert looks just as good as it tastes. Use a fork to easily drizzle the melted white baking chips in a decorative pattern over the cherry pie filling.

1 SERVING: Calories 385 (Calories from Fat 145); Fat 16g (Saturated 9g); Cholesterol 40mg; Sodium 420mg; Carbohydrate 58g (Dietary Fiber 2g); Protein 4g • **% DAILY VALUE:** Vitamin A 4%; Vitamin C 2%; Calcium 8%; Iron 8% • **DIET EXCHANGES:** Not Recommended

6 SERVINGS

Triple-Berry Shortcakes

1 pint (2 cups) strawberries,
sliced

1 cup raspberries

1 cup blueberries

1/3 cup sugar

1/4 cup raspberry- or
orange-flavored liqueur or
orange juice

6 sponge shortcake cups

1 1/2 cups lemon sorbet or
sherbet

1 Toss berries, sugar and liqueur. Let stand 20 minutes.

2 Top each shortcake cup with berries and sorbet.

1 SERVING: Calories 200 (Calories from Fat 10); Fat 1g (Saturated 0g); Cholesterol 40mg;
Sodium 15mg; Carbohydrate 50g (Dietary Fiber 5g); Protein 3g • **% DAILY VALUE:**
Vitamin A 2%; Vitamin C 76%; Calcium 2%; Iron 4% • **DIET EXCHANGES:** 1 Starch,
2 Fruit

Triple-Berry Shortcakes

6 SERVINGS

Quick Cherry Cobbler

I can (21 ounces) cherry or peach pie filling

I cup Original Bisquick

I tablespoon sugar

1/4 cup milk

I tablespoon butter or margarine, softened

Additional sugar, if desired

1 Spread pie filling in ungreased square pan, 8 × 8 × 2 inches; place in cold oven. Heat oven to 400°; let heat 10 minutes. Remove pan from oven.

2 While pie filling is heating, mix Bisquick, 1 tablespoon sugar, milk and butter with fork until soft dough forms. Drop dough by 6 spoonfuls onto warm cherry mixture. Sprinkle with additional sugar.

3 Bake 18 to 20 minutes or until topping is light brown.

IT'S **a**
snap!

Get two things done at once: Heat the filling while the oven heats to the set temperature. Heating the fruit before adding the biscuit topping ensures that the dough bakes through completely.

1 SERVING: Calories 200 (Calories from Fat 45); Fat 5g (Saturated 2g); Cholesterol 5mg; Sodium 300mg; Carbohydrate 38g (Dietary Fiber 1g); Protein 2g • **% DAILY VALUE:** Vitamin A 25%; Vitamin C 0%; Calcium 4%; Iron 4% • **DIET EXCHANGES:** 1/2 Starch, 2 Fruit

6 SERVINGS

Orange-Cream Frosty

1/2 gallon orange, vanilla or peach frozen yogurt

1 cup milk

1 can (6 ounces) frozen (thawed) calcium-fortified or regular orange juice concentrate

1 Place half each of the frozen yogurt, milk and juice concentrate in blender. Cover and blend on medium speed about 45 seconds, stopping blender occasionally to scrape sides, until thick and smooth. Pour into 3 glasses.

2 Repeat with remaining frozen yogurt, milk and juice concentrate.

IT'S **a**

snap!

For another fast, kid-favorite frosty, use grape juice concentrate instead of orange.

1 SERVING: Calories 350 (Calories from fat 25); Fat 3g (Saturated 2g); Cholesterol 10mg; Sodium 170mg; Carbohydrate 69g (Dietary Fiber 1g); Protein 14g • % DAILY VALUE: Vitamin A 8%; Vitamin C 100%; Calcium 46%; Iron 2% • DIET EXCHANGES: 3 Fruit, 2 Skim Milk

Pantry Recipes

If you have a well-stocked pantry (see pages 6–7), you'll be able to make this recipe anytime, even when there's no time to shop.

Perfect Baked Pears

1 can (28 or 29 ounces) pear halves in juice (6 halves)

1/4 cup caramel topping

Ground cinnamon

Heat oven to 350°. Drain pear halves on paper towels. Place **pears**, cut sides down, in pie plate, 9 × 1 1/4 inches. Drizzle **caramel** over pears. Bake 8 to 10 minutes or until warm. Spoon topping in pie plate over pears and sprinkle with **cinnamon**. MAKES 3 SERVINGS IN 15 MINUTES

serve it 3 ways!

1 Fruit
Drizzle pears with 2 tablespoons each chocolate fudge topping and caramel topping before baking.

2 Ice Cream
Spoon scoop of vanilla or cinnamon ice cream into hollow of pear and spoon pear sauce on top.

3 Cake
Spoon pears and sauce over pound or angel food cake.

8 SERVINGS

Strawberry-Rhubarb Frozen-Yogurt Parfaits

4 cups cut-up rhubarb

1/3 cup water

1/2 package (4-serving size) strawberry-flavored gelatin (1/4 cup)

1 cup chopped fresh or frozen (thawed) strawberries

1/2 gallon vanilla frozen yogurt

1 Heat rhubarb and water to boiling in 2-quart saucepan. Boil 5 minutes, stirring occasionally; remove from heat. Stir in gelatin until dissolved. Boil 5 minutes longer, stirring constantly; remove from heat.

2 Stir in strawberries. Serve sauce warm or cold, layering frozen yogurt and sauce in parfait glasses.

prep: **10 min**

cook: **10 min**

COME

&eat!

If you have the time, layer the sauce and frozen yogurt in pretty parfait or wine glasses. It's perfect to serve when you're entertaining friends. In a rush? Just scoop the frozen yogurt into bowls and spoon the sauce over.

1 SERVING: Calories 235 (Calories from Fat 0); Fat 0g (Saturated 0g); Cholesterol 5mg; Sodium 115mg; Carbohydrate 54g (Dietary Fiber 1g); Protein 6g • **% DAILY VALUE:** Vitamin A 8%; Vitamin C 34%; Calcium 30%; Iron 2% • **DIET EXCHANGES:** 1 Starch, 2 Fruit, 1/2 Skim Milk

Many people keep
tortillas on hand
as a pantry staple.
Ever thought of
making them into
dessert? The kids
can help by pressing
the tortillas into the
custard cups.

4 SERVINGS

Blueberry-Nectarine Dessert Tortillas

4 flour tortillas (about 7 inches in diameter)

1/2 cup semisweet chocolate chips

2 teaspoons shortening

I cup blueberries or raspberries

3 medium nectarines or peaches, sliced

1/2 cup peach yogurt

1 Heat each tortilla in warmed skillet or microwave oven 15 to 20 seconds to soften. Press each tortilla into 10-ounce custard cup, forming a shell. Microwave uncovered on High 2 to 3 minutes, rotating cups 1/2 turn after 2 minutes, until tortillas feel dry. Remove from cups.

2 Place chocolate chips and shortening in small bowl. Microwave uncovered on High 1 to 2 minutes or until softened; stir until smooth. Dip edges of tortillas into melted chocolate. Drizzle remaining chocolate on inside of tortillas. Refrigerate about 10 minutes or until chocolate is firm.

3 Mix blueberries and nectarines; spoon into tortillas. Top with yogurt.

1 SERVING: Calories 305 (Calories from Fat 100); Fat 11g (Saturated 5g); Cholesterol 5mg; Sodium 190mg; Carbohydrate 50g (Dietary Fiber 4g); Protein 6g • **% DAILY VALUE:** Vitamin A 4%; Vitamin C 16%; Calcium 12%; Iron 8% • **DIET EXCHANGES:** Not Recommended

Blueberry-Nectarine Dessert Tortillas

6 SERVINGS

Creamy Caramel-Peach Parfaits

2/3 cup caramel topping

1 container (8 ounces) frozen whipped topping, thawed

1 can (29 ounces) sliced peaches, drained and cut into pieces

5 soft molasses cookies, broken up, if desired

1 Fold caramel topping into whipped topping in small bowl.

2 Layer cookies, whipped topping mixture and peaches in 6 parfait or other tall glasses. Sprinkle with cookie crumbs. Serve immediately, or refrigerate until serving.

IT'S **a**
snap!
When peaches are in season, try this recipe with chopped fresh peaches. Vary the recipe by using fresh or canned pears or other soft fruit.

1 SERVING: Calories 300 (Calories from Fat 90); Fat 10g (Saturated 6g); Cholesterol 30mg; Sodium 230mg; Carbohydrate 53g (Dietary Fiber 3g); Protein 3g • **% DAILY VALUE:** Vitamin A 24%; Vitamin C 2%; Calcium 6%; Iron 4% • **DIET EXCHANGES:** Not Recommended

Quick Rice and Raisin Pudding

super express

prep: **5 min**
cook: **2 min**
stand: **5 min**

I cup uncooked instant rice

I cup milk or water

1/4 cup raisins

3 tablespoons sugar

1/4 teaspoon salt

1/4 teaspoon ground cinnamon or nutmeg

1 Mix all ingredients in 2-quart saucepan.

2 Heat to boiling, stirring constantly; remove from heat. Cover and let stand 5 minutes.

COME
& eat!

This pudding works with your schedule—it's delicious right out of the pan, warm, cool or chilled. Leftovers are great for breakfast too!

1 SERVING: Calories 195 (Calories from Fat 10); Fat 1g (Saturated 1g); Cholesterol 5mg; Sodium 170mg; Carbohydrate 43g (Dietary Fiber 0g); Protein 4g • **% DAILY VALUE:** Vitamin A 2%; Vitamin C 0%; Calcium 8%; Iron 6% • **DIET EXCHANGES:** 1 1/2 Starch; 1 1/2 Fruit

C O M E

&eat!

**This delicious
dessert is ready in a
snap! And you can
use whatever fresh
fruit you have on
hand. Blueberries
and sliced straw-
berries are great.
It's also very pretty,
which makes it per-
fect for entertaining.**

4 SERVINGS

Raspberry Stirred Custard

I cup raspberries	2 cups half-and-half
1/3 cup granulated sugar	1/2 teaspoon vanilla
2 tablespoons cornstarch	4 teaspoons packed brown sugar
1/4 teaspoon salt	

1 Divide raspberries evenly among 4 individual serving bowls.

2 Mix granulated sugar, cornstarch and salt in 2-quart sauce-pan. Stir in half-and-half. Heat to boiling over medium heat, stirring frequently. Stir in vanilla.

3 Spoon custard over raspberries. Sprinkle with brown sugar. Serve warm or cool. Store covered in refrigerator.

1 SERVING: Calories 270 (Calories from Fat 125); Fat 14g (Saturated 9g); Cholesterol 45mg; Sodium 200mg; Carbohydrate 34g (Dietary Fiber 2g); Protein 4g • **% DAILY VALUE:** Vitamin A 12%; Vitamin C 14%; Calcium 14%; Iron 2% • **DIET EXCHANGES:** 2 Fruit, 1/2 Skim Milk, 2 1/2 Fat

prep: **10 min**
bake: **10 min per sheet**

super express

Stir-'n-Drop Sugar Cookies

3/4 cup sugar

2/3 cup vegetable oil

2 teaspoons baking powder

2 teaspoons vanilla

1/2 teaspoon salt

2 eggs

2 cups all-purpose flour

Additional sugar

1 Heat oven to 400°. Mix 3/4 cup sugar, the oil, baking powder, vanilla, salt and eggs in large bowl with spoon. Stir in flour.

2 Drop dough by teaspoonfuls about 2 inches apart onto ungreased cookie sheet. Press bottom of glass onto dough to grease, then dip into additional sugar; press on balls of dough to make 1/4 inch thick.

3 Bake 8 to 10 minutes until light brown. Remove from cookie sheet to wire rack.

IT'S **a**
snap!

Go crazy with color! Before baking, dip bottom of glass onto a wet paper towel, then dip into dry fruit-flavored gelatin; press onto dough. Repeat until desired color appears. Bake as directed.

1 COOKIE: Calories 60 (Calories from Fat 25); Fat 3g (Saturated 1g); Cholesterol 10mg; Sodium 45mg; Carbohydrate 7g (Dietary Fiber 0g); Protein 1g • **% DAILY VALUE:** Vitamin A 0%; Vitamin C 0%; Calcium 0%; Iron 2% • **DIET EXCHANGES:** 1/2 Starch, 1/2 Fat

ABOUT 2 DOZEN COOKIES

Double-Chocolate Chunk Cookies

1 bag (24 ounces) semisweet chocolate chips (4 cups)

1 cup butter or margarine, softened

1 cup packed brown sugar

1 teaspoon vanilla

2 eggs

2 1/2 cups all-purpose flour

1 1/2 teaspoons baking soda

1/2 teaspoon salt

1 package (6 ounces) white baking bars (white chocolate), cut into 1/4- to 1/2-inch chunks

1 cup pecan or walnut halves

1 Heat oven to 350°. Melt 1 1/2 cups of the chocolate chips in 1-quart saucepan over low heat, stirring constantly. Cool to room temperature, but do not allow chocolate to become firm.

2 Beat butter, brown sugar and vanilla in large bowl with electric mixer on medium speed until light and fluffy. Beat in eggs and melted chocolate until light and fluffy. Stir in flour, baking soda and salt. Stir in remaining 2 1/2 cups chocolate chips, the white baking bar chunks and pecan halves.

3 Drop dough by level 1/4 cupfuls or #16 cookie/ice-cream scoop about 2 inches apart onto ungreased cookie sheet. Bake 12 to 14 minutes or until set (centers will appear soft and moist). Cool 1 to 2 minutes; remove from cookie sheet to wire rack.

1 COOKIE: Calories 375 (Calories from Fat 200); Fat 22g (Saturated 12g); Cholesterol 40mg; Sodium 200mg; Carbohydrate 42g (Dietary Fiber 2g); Protein 4g • **% DAILY VALUE:** Vitamin A 6%; Vitamin C 0%; Calcium 4%; Iron 10% • **DIET EXCHANGES:** Not Recommended

Double-Chocolate Chunk Cookies

prep: **10 min**
bake: **10 min per sheet**

ABOUT 3 DOZEN COOKIES

Chocolate Kiss–Peanut Butter Cookies

1 can (14 ounces) sweetened condensed milk

3/4 cup peanut butter

2 cups Original Bisquick

1 teaspoon vanilla

Sugar

About 36 milk chocolate kisses or milk chocolate kisses with white chocolate stripes

1 Heat oven to 375°. Stir milk and peanut butter in large bowl until smooth. Stir in Bisquick and vanilla.

2 Shape dough into 1 1/4-inch balls. Roll in sugar. Place 2 inches apart on ungreased cookie sheet.

3 Bake 8 to 10 minutes or until bottoms of cookies just begin to brown. Immediately press chocolate kiss into top of each cookie. Remove from cookie sheet to wire rack.

IT'S **a**
snap!

Vary the look of these easy cookies by using different kinds of chocolate kisses. Or press on miniature peanut butter cups for a tasty alternative to the kisses.

1 COOKIE: Calories 130 (Calories from Fat 55); Fat 6g (Saturated 3g); Cholesterol 5mg; Sodium 140mg; Carbohydrate 17g; (Dietary Fiber 0g); Protein 3g • **% DAILY VALUE:** Vitamin A 0%; Vitamin C 0%; Calcium 6%; Iron 2% • **DIET EXCHANGES:** 1 Starch, 1 Fat

Chocolate Kiss–Peanut Butter Cookies

ABOUT 2 DOZEN COOKIES

Apple Jack Cookies

1 cup packed brown sugar	1 teaspoon ground nutmeg
1/2 cup butter or margarine, softened	1/2 teaspoon salt
1 egg	1/2 teaspoon baking soda
1 1/2 cups all-purpose flour	1 medium apple, chopped (1 cup)

1 Heat oven to 375°. Grease cookie sheet with shortening. Beat brown sugar, butter and egg in large bowl with electric mixer on medium speed until light and fluffy. Stir in flour, nutmeg, salt and baking soda. Stir in apple.

2 Drop dough by rounded teaspoonfuls about 2 inches apart onto cookie sheet.

3 Bake 8 to 10 minutes or until light brown. Remove from cookie sheet to wire rack; cool. Store loosely covered.

1 COOKIE: Calories 115 (Calories from Fat 45); Fat 5g (Saturated 1g); Cholesterol 10mg; Sodium 80mg; Carbohydrate 16g (Dietary Fiber 0g); Protein 1g • **% DAILY VALUE:** Vitamin A 0%; Vitamin C 0%; Calcium 0%; Iron 2% • **DIET EXCHANGES:** 1 Starch, 1 Fat

prep: **15 min**
bake: **15 min per sheet**

Cinnamon-Chocolate Cookie Strips

I 1/3 cups sugar	I teaspoon baking powder
I cup plus 2 tablespoons butter or margarine, softened	I bag (6 ounces) semisweet chocolate chips (I cup)
I teaspoon vanilla	3 tablespoons sugar
2 eggs	3/4 teaspoon ground cinnamon
3 cups all-purpose flour	

1 Heat oven to 350°. Beat 1 1/3 cups sugar, the butter, vanilla and eggs in large bowl with electric mixer on medium speed, or mix with spoon. Stir in flour and baking powder. Stir in chocolate chips.

2 Divide dough into fourths. Shape each fourth into roll, 1 inch in diameter and about 15 inches long, on lightly floured surface. Place rolls about 2 inches apart on ungreased cookie sheet. Flatten with fork to about 5/8-inch thickness. Mix 3 tablespoons sugar and the cinnamon; sprinkle over dough.

3 Bake 13 to 15 minutes or until edges are light brown. Cut diagonally into about 1-inch strips while warm.

IT'S **a**
snap!

Want to save the time of making individual cookies? Place rolls of this cookie dough onto cookie sheets, bake and then slice. These are the same good old chocolate chip cookies that everyone loves, only they're shaped in strips instead of rounds, saving you time in the end.

1 COOKIE: Calories 95 (Calories from Fat 45); Fat 5g (Saturated 3g); Cholesterol 15mg; Sodium 35mg; Carbohydrate 12g (Dietary Fiber 0g); Protein 1g • **% DAILY VALUE:** Vitamin A 2%; Vitamin C 0%; Calcium 0%; Iron 2% • **DIET EXCHANGES:** I Starch, 1/2 Fat

ABOUT 2 DOZEN BARS

Quick Praline Bars

24 graham cracker squares   **1/2 teaspoon vanilla**

1/2 cup packed brown sugar   **1/2 cup chopped pecans**

1/2 cup butter or margarine

1 Heat oven to 350°. Arrange crackers in single layer in ungreased jelly roll pan, 15 1/2 × 10 1/2 × 1 inch.

2 Heat brown sugar and butter to boiling in 2-quart sauce-pan. Boil 1 minute, stirring constantly; remove from heat. Stir in vanilla.

3 Pour sugar mixture over crackers; spread evenly. Sprinkle with pecans. Bake 8 to 10 minutes or until bubbly; cool slightly.

IT'S **a**
snap!

How about adding a quick, irresistible chocolate topping? Sprinkle 1/2 cup semisweet chocolate chips over the crackers immediately after removing them from the oven. When completely melted, "spread" the chips.

1 SQUARE: Calories 95 (Calories from Fat 55); Fat 6g (Saturated 3g); Cholesterol 10mg; Sodium 70mg; Carbohydrate 10g (Dietary Fiber 0g); Protein 0g • **% DAILY VALUE:** Vitamin A 2%; Vitamin C 0%; Calcium 0%; Iron 2% • **DIET EXCHANGES:** 1/2 Starch, 1 Fat

Mini Cookie Pizzas

6 purchased sugar, chocolate chip or peanut butter cookies (4 inches in diameter)

1/2 tub (16-ounce size) chocolate ready-to-spread frosting

1/2 cup assorted candies (such as licorice candy, candy-coated chocolate candies)

1 ounce vanilla-flavored candy coating (almond bark)

1 Frost each cookie with about 2 tablespoons of the frosting. Top with 1 heaping tablespoon of the candies.

2 Melt candy coating in 1-quart saucepan over low heat, stirring constantly, until smooth. Drizzle over cookies.

COME
&eat!

To make these cookies look more like a pizza, use vanilla frosting instead of chocolate and sprinkle the frosting with colored sugar before topping with the candies. The drizzle of candy coating will look like cheese on a pizza if you tint the melted coating orange with 1 part red and 2 parts yellow food color.

1 SERVING: Calories 460 (Calories from Fat 200); Fat 22g (Saturated 13g); Cholesterol 15mg; Sodium 95mg; Carbohydrate 65g (Dietary Fiber 2g); Protein 3g • **% DAILY VALUE:** Vitamin A 0%; Vitamin C 0%; Calcium 4%; Iron 6% • **DIET EXCHANGES:** Not Recommended

24 WANDS

Licorice Wands

6 ounces vanilla-flavored candy coating (almond bark), chopped

24 licorice twists

Candy decorations

1 Place candy coating in 2-cup microwavable measuring cup. Microwave uncovered on High 1 minute to 1 minute 30 seconds, stirring every 15 seconds, until melted.

2 Dip half of each licorice twist into melted candy coating. Sprinkle with candy decorations. Place on waxed paper and let stand about 20 minutes or until coating is firm.

COME

&eat!

Make a "magical" birthday treat: tie colorful narrow ribbon around each individual licorice twist for an extra-festive party look. Or tie several licorice twists together for a party favor.

1 WAND: Calories 85 (Calories from Fat 25); Fat 3g (Saturated 1g); Cholesterol 0mg; Sodium 30mg; Carbohydrate 14g (Dietary Fiber 2g); Protein 1g • **% DAILY VALUE:** Vitamin A 0%; Vitamin C 0%; Calcium 2%; Iron 0% • **DIET EXCHANGES:** 1 Fruit, 1/2 Fat

Licorice Wands

Helpful Nutrition and Cooking Information

Nutrition Guidelines

We provide nutrition information for each recipe that includes calories, fat, cholesterol, sodium, carbohydrate, fiber and protein. Individual food choices can be based on this information.

Recommended intake for a daily diet of 2,000 calories as set by the Food and Drug Administration

Total Fat	Less than 65g
Saturated Fat	Less than 20g
Cholesterol	Less than 300mg
Sodium	Less than 2,400mg
Total Carbohydrate	300g
Dietary Fiber	25g

Criteria Used for Calculating Nutrition Information

- The first ingredient was used wherever a choice is given (such as 1/3 cup sour cream or plain yogurt).
- The first ingredient amount was used wherever a range is given (such as 3- to 3-1/2–pound cut-up broiler-fryer chicken).
- The first serving number was used wherever a range is given (such as 4 to 6 servings).
- "If desired" ingredients and recipe variations were not included (such as sprinkle with brown sugar, if desired).
- Only the amount of a marinade or frying oil that is estimated to be absorbed by the food during preparation or cooking was calculated.

Ingredients Used in Recipe Testing and Nutrition Calculations

- Ingredients used for testing represent those that the majority of consumers use in their homes: large eggs, 2% milk, 80%-lean ground beef, canned ready-to-use chicken broth and vegetable oil spread containing not less than 65 percent fat.
- Fat-free, low-fat or low-sodium products were not used, unless otherwise indicated.
- Solid vegetable shortening (not butter, margarine, nonstick cooking sprays or vegetable oil spread as they can cause sticking problems) was used to grease pans, unless otherwise indicated.

Equipment Used in Recipe Testing

We use equipment for testing that the majority of consumers use in their homes. If a specific piece of equipment (such as a wire whisk) is necessary for recipe success, it is listed in the recipe.

- Cookware and bakeware without nonstick coatings were used, unless otherwise indicated.
- No dark-colored, black or insulated bakeware was used.
- When a pan is specified in a recipe, a metal pan was used; a baking dish or pie plate means ovenproof glass was used.
- An electric hand mixer was used for mixing only when mixer speeds are specified in the recipe directions. When a mixer speed is not given, a spoon or fork was used.

Cooking Terms Glossary

Beat: Mix ingredients vigorously with spoon, fork, wire whisk, hand beater or electric mixer until smooth and uniform.

Boil: Heat liquid until bubbles rise continuously and break on the surface and steam is given off. For rolling boil, the bubbles form rapidly.

Chop: Cut into coarse or fine irregular pieces with a knife, food chopper, blender or food processor.

Cube: Cut into squares 1/2 inch or larger.

Dice: Cut into squares smaller than 1/2 inch.

Grate: Cut into tiny particles using small rough holes of grater (citrus peel or chocolate).

Grease: Rub the inside surface of a pan with shortening, using pastry brush, piece of waxed paper or paper towel, to prevent food from sticking during baking (as for some casseroles).

Julienne: Cut into thin, matchlike strips, using knife or food processor (vegetables, fruits, meats).

Mix: Combine ingredients in any way that distributes them evenly.

Sauté: Cook foods in hot oil or margarine over medium-high heat with frequent tossing and turning motion.

Shred: Cut into long thin pieces by rubbing food across the holes of a shredder, as for cheese, or by using a knife to slice very thinly, as for cabbage.

Simmer: Cook in liquid just below the boiling point on top of the stove; usually after reducing heat from a boil. Bubbles will rise slowly and break just below the surface.

Stir: Mix ingredients until uniform consistency. Stir once in a while for stirring occasionally, often for stirring frequently and continuously for stirring constantly.

Toss: Tumble ingredients (such as green salad) lightly with a lifting motion, usually to coat evenly or mix with another food.

metric conversion chart

Volume

U.S. Units	Canadian Metric	Australian Metric
1/4 teaspoon	1 mL	1 ml
1/2 teaspoon	2 mL	2 ml
1 teaspoon	5 mL	5 ml
1 tablespoon	15 mL	20 ml
1/4 cup	50 mL	60 ml
1/3 cup	75 mL	80 ml
1/2 cup	125 mL	125 ml
2/3 cup	150 mL	170 ml
3/4 cup	175 mL	190 ml
1 cup	250 mL	250 ml
1 quart	1 liter	1 liter
1 1/2 quarts	1.5 liters	1.5 liters
2 quarts	2 liters	2 liters
2 1/2 quarts	2.5 liters	2.5 liters
3 quarts	3 liters	3 liters
4 quarts	4 liters	4 liters

Weight

U.S. Units	Canadian Metric	Australian Metric
1 ounce	30 grams	30 grams
2 ounces	55 grams	60 grams
3 ounces	85 grams	90 grams
4 ounces (1/4 pound)	115 grams	125 grams
8 ounces (1/2 pound)	225 grams	225 grams
16 ounces (1 pound)	455 grams	500 grams
1 pound	455 grams	1/2 kilogram

Measurements

Inches	Centimeters
1	2.5
2	5.0
3	7.5
4	10.0
5	12.5
6	15.0
7	17.5
8	20.5
9	23.0
10	25.5
11	28.0
12	30.5
13	33.0

Temperatures

Fahrenheit	Celsius
32°	0°
212°	100°
250°	120°
275°	140°
300°	150°
325°	160°
350°	180°
375°	190°
400°	200°
425°	220°
450°	230°
475°	240°
500°	260°

Note: The recipes in this cookbook have not been developed or tested using metric measures. When converting recipes to metric, some variations in quality may be noted.

1-Step Recipes

When you know the shortcuts, there's always enough time for great-tasting meals. Start with some favorite pantry staples and add a few more ingredients for dinner in a flash.

Quick Chicken

**START WITH:
4 BONELESS,
SKINLESS
CHICKEN
BREAST HALVES**
(about 1 1/4
pounds), flattened
to 1/2-inch thick-
ness between
sheets of plastic
wrap. (Cook until
juice of chicken is
no longer pink
when centers of
thickest pieces
are cut.)

1 Teriyaki Pineapple Chicken
Spray skillet with cook-ing spray; heat over medium heat. Add chicken and cook about 10 minutes, turning once. Coat chicken with 1/4 cup **teriyaki baste and glaze** and cook until hot. Top with **pineapple rings**.

2 Pesto Chicken
Spray skillet with cook-ing spray; heat over medium heat. Add chicken and cook about 10 minutes, turning once. Spoon **pesto** over each piece and sprinkle with shredded **moz-zarella cheese**; cover skillet until cheese is melted.

3 Italian Chicken and Peppers
Heat 1/4 cup **Italian dressing** (not creamy type) in skillet over medium heat. Add chicken and cook 5 minutes; turn chick-en. Stir in 2 small **bell peppers**, cut into strips and cook about 5 min-utes more.

4 Caesar Chicken with Feta
Heat 1/4 cup **Caesar dressing** in skillet over medium heat. Add chicken and cook about 10 minutes, turning once. Sprinkle chicken with crumbled **feta cheese** and a cut-up **tomato**; cover skillet until cheese is melted.

Quick Main-Dish Salads

**START WITH:
1 bag (about 10
ounces) SALAD
GREENS or
1 bag (16 ounces)
BROCCOLI SLAW.**

1 Grilled Raspberry Chicken Salad
Divide spinach greens salad mix into 4 serv-ings. Top each salad with a grilled **chicken breast**, cut into strips, and fresh **raspberries**; drizzle with **raspberry vinaigrette** and toasted sliced **almonds**.

2 Oriental Chicken Salad
Divide Oriental salad mix into 4 servings. Top each salad with chopped cooked **chick-en or pork** and **man-darin orange segments**.

3 Ham and Cheddar Salad
Mix broccoli slaw with 1 cup cut-up fully cooked **ham**, 1 cup shredded **Cheddar cheese**, 1/2 cup **raisins** and 1/2 cup **ranch dressing**. Top with red **onion** rings and sprin-kle with **sunflower nuts**.

4 Broccoli-Peanut Chicken Salad
Mix broccoli slaw with 2 cups cut-up cooked **chicken** and about 1/3 cup **peanut sauce**. Sprinkle with chopped **peanuts** and **cilantro**.

Quick Fruit Salads

**START WITH:
2 cans (15 to 16
ounces each)
CHUNKY
MIXED FRUIT or
4 cups CUT-UP
FRESH FRUIT**
from the deli.

1 Zesty Fruit Cocktail
Mix drained canned fruit with 2 to 3 tea-spoons finely chopped fresh or canned jalapeño chilies.

2 Lemon-Cream Fruit Salad
Drain canned fruit and mix with equal parts canned **lemon pie filling** and whipped cream or whipped topping.

3 Honey-Lime Fruit Salad
Divide fresh fruit among 4 salad plates. Mix 1/4 cup frozen **limeade or lemonade** concentrate, thawed, and 1/4 cup **honey**; drizzle over fruit.

4 Elegant Orange Fruit
Place fresh fruit in serving bowl. Mix 1 tablespoon **orange-flavored liqueur**, 2 tablespoons **orange juice**, 2 tablespoons **whipping (heavy) cream** and 1 teaspoon **sugar**. Pour over fruit and toss gently.

Just Zap It! Microwave Rescues

The magic of the microwave can soften rock-hard brown sugar, crisp stale pretzels and potato chips, and toast nuts and coconut. Check out this handy chart for other fast and convenient microwave solutions. *Use microwavable utensils only.*

Food and Utensil	Power Level	Amount	Time
Cooking Bacon Put bacon on plate lined with paper towels and cover with paper towels.	High (100%)	1 slice 4 slices 6 slices 8 slices	45 seconds to 2 minutes 3 to 4 minutes 4 to 6 minutes 6 to 8 minutes
Softening Brown Sugar Bowl; uncovered.	High (100%)	Up to 2 cups	1 minute; let stand 2 minu until softened.
Melting Butter or Margarine Remove foil wrapper. Measuring cup or small bowl; covered.	High (100%)	1 to 2 tablespoons 3 to 4 tablespoons 1/3 to 1/2 cup 2/3 to 1 cup	15 to 30 seconds 30 to 45 seconds 45 to 60 seconds 1 to 1 1/2 minutes
Softening Butter or Margarine Remove foil wrapper. Measuring cup or small bowl; uncovered.	Medium-Low (30%)	1 to 3 tablespoons 1/4 to 1 cup	15 to 30 seconds 30 to 45 seconds
Melting Caramels Mixed with 2 tablespoons water. Unwrap. 4-cup glass measuring cup; uncovered.	High (100%)	1 bag (14 ounces) caramels	3 to 4 minutes *Stir every 45 seconds.*
Melting Baking Chocolate (squares) Paper wrapper or bowl; uncovered.	Medium (50%)	1 to 2 ounces	3 or 4 minutes *Stir after 2 minutes.*
Melting Chocolate Chips Bowl or glass measuring cup; uncovered. Chips will not change shape; stir until smooth.	Medium (50%)	1/2 to 1 cup	3 to 4 minutes
Toasting Coconut Shallow bowl or pie plate; uncovered.	High (100%)	1/4 to 1/2 cup 1 cup	1 to 1 1/2 minutes 2 to 2 1/2 minutes *Stir every 30 seconds.*
Softening Cream Cheese Remove foil wrapper. Place on waxed paper or plate; uncovered.	Medium (50%)	3-ounce package 8-ounce package	30 to 45 seconds 1 to 1 1/2 minutes
Heating Hot Dogs Plate or cloth napkins; uncovered.	High (100%)	1 hot dog 2 hot dogs 4 hot dogs	30 to 45 seconds 1 to 1 1/4 minutes 1 1/4 to 1 1/2 minutes *Heat until hot.*
Warming Muffins or Rolls Plate or basket lined with paper or cloth napkins; uncovered.	Medium (50%)	1 muffin/roll 2 muffins/rolls 3 muffins/rolls 4 muffins/rolls	15 to 30 seconds 25 to 40 seconds 35 to 60 seconds 45 seconds to 1 1/4 minu
Toasting Chopped Nuts Mix nuts with 1 teaspoon melted butter or margarine in shallow bowl or pie plate; uncovered.	High (100%)	1/4 cup 1/2 cup	1 1/2 to 2 minutes 2 1/2 to 3 minutes *Stir every 30 seconds.*
Crisping Snacks (popcorn, pretzels, corn chips or potato chips) Basket lined with paper or cloth napkins; uncovered.	High (100%)	2 cups 4 cups	30 to 60 seconds 1 to 2 minutes

Index

Note: *Italicized* page references indicate photographs.

Corn *(cont.)*
  and olive spread, 20
  salsa, taco chicken with,
    156, *157*
Cornmeal Chicken with Fresh
    Peach Salsa, 170, *171*
Cottage Cheese Topping, 310
Country Eggs in Tortilla Chips,
    132, *133*
Countryside Pasta Toss, 98, *99*
Couscous
  and beans, Mediterranean,
    281
  and Sweet Potatoes with
    Pork, 100
  vegetable curry with,
    282, *283*
Crab (crabmeat)
  chopped vegetable and,
    salad, 68, *69*
  Crab Cakes, 273
  corn and, quesadillas, 276
  creamy, au gratin, 272
  and Spinach Casserole,
    270, *271*
Cranberry, apple-, sauce,
    pork chops with, 230
Cream cheese. *See* Cheese,
    cream
Cream of Broccoli Soup, 56
Creamy Caramel-Peach
    Parfaits, 400
Creamy Confetti Succotash,
    362, *363*
Creamy Corn and Garlic
    Risotto, 278, *279*
Creamy Crab au Gratin, 272
Creamy Pesto Dip, 11
Creamy Quinoa Primavera,
    312, *313*
Crispy Baked Catfish, 246
Crostini, roasted pepper–
    tomato, 38, *39*
Crunchy Bean Skillet, 301
Crunchy Chicken Chunks, 29
Curry, vegetable, with couscous,
    282, *283*
Custard, raspberry stirred, 402

D

Desserts, 387–413
Dijon mustard
  bacon-, sauce, sirloin with,
    198
  Parmesan-, chicken, 155
  rosemary-, steaks, 328, *329*
Dill
  lemon-, chicken, 158
  orange and, pan-seared
    tuna, 240, *241*
  sauce, sour cream, 260
Dip
  baked spinach–artichoke, 28
  Caesar vegetable, 13
  creamy pesto, 11
  easy sugar 'n spice, 18, *19*
  five-layer Mexican, 17
  gingered caramel and
    yogurt, with fruit, 14, *15*
  hot Reuben, 27
  salsa and black bean, 12
Dipping sauce, string cheese
    sticks with, 42, *43*
Do-Aheads, delicious, 10
Double-Cheese, Spinach and
    Chicken Pizza, 112, *113*
Double-Chocolate Chunk
    Cookies, 404, *405*
Double-Corn Muffins, 382
Dressing
  hot bacon, spinach-shrimp
    salad with, 66
  lime, 68
  lime, spicy, 61
Dried Cherry-Lemon Scones,
    383

E

Easy Banana Cream Trifle,
    390
Easy Cheesy Vegetable Soup,
    54, *55*
Easy Fish and Vegetable
    Packets, 250
Easy Macaroni and Cheese,
    106

Easy Philly Cheesesteak Pizza,
    118, *119*
Easy Seafood Risotto, 274, *275*
Easy Sugar 'n Spice Dip, 18, *19*
Easy Turkey Fajitas, 190, *191*
Egg dishes
  country, in tortilla chips,
    132, *133*
  frittata, cheese, vegetables
    and, 138
  frittata, fresh spinach and
    new potato, 136, *137*
  omelet, salmon and cream
    cheese, 135
  pepper and, fajitas, 134
  scramble, potato and bacon,
    128, *129*
  scrambled, home-style, 127
  scrambled, suppertime, 130
  smoked salmon and, wraps,
    131
Enchilada bake, stacked, 294,
    295
Enchilada pizzas, chicken, 115
Enchiladas, beef and cheese,
    208

F

Fajita(s)
  beef, bowls, 210, *211*
  pepper and egg, 134
  pizza, 110, *111*
  turkey, easy, 190, *191*
Fantastic Fruited Fish, 254
Fettuccine, scampi with, 263
Fettuccine and Chicken in
    Orange-Cherry Sauce,
    88, *89*
Fiesta Taco Salad, 64, *65*
Fish, 239–76. *See also* Seafood
  baked, with tropical fruit
    salsa, 244, *245*
  fillets, pecan-crusted, 251
  in foil, Mexican, 344
  fruited, fantastic, 254
  lemony, over vegetables and
    rice, 252, *253*

K

Kabobs, chicken, peanutty, 321
Key Lime Fruit Salad, 70, 71
Kielbasa and Sauerkraut Pizza, 123
Kitchen, tips for, 8–10

L

Lamb chops, mint-smoked, 336, 337
Lasagna, stove-top, 4, 94, 95
Latin Grilled Halibut with Green Sauce, 340, 341
Lemon(y)
 -Basil Chicken and Vegetables, 174, 175
 –cream cheese topping, ginger pancakes, 148
 -Dill Chicken, 158
 dried cherry-, scones, 383
 fish over vegetables and rice, 252, 253
 Glaze, 384
 -parsley tartar sauce, ranch halibut with, 255
Licorice Wands, 412, 413
Lime
 chili-, spread, grilled corn with, 374, 375
 dressing, 68
 dressing, spicy, 61
 Key Lime Fruit Salad, 70, 71
 tortilla chips, 46

M

Macaroni and cheese, easy, 106
Mango-peach salsa, strip steaks with, 196, 197
Maple-mustard sauce, asparagus with, 369
Maple-nut topping, pound cake with, 387
Maple-pecan syrup, spicy pumpkin pancakes with, 149

Marinara sauce, mozzarella and basil with, 44, 45
Marinara Shrimp and Vegetable Bowls, 268, 269
Marsala, chicken, 164, 165
Meat(s). *See also specific names*
 main dishes, 195–238
 meat loaves, mini, 209
 meat squares, spaghetti and, 213
 thawing timetable, 202
 tips for do-ahead cooking, 10
Mediterranean Couscous and Beans, 281
Mediterranean Skillet Chicken, 159
Metric conversion chart, 416
Mexican Beef and Black Beans, 212
Mexican dip, five-layer, 17
Mexican Fish in Foil, 344
Mexican skillet chicken, spicy, 163
Milk Gravy, 221
Minestrone Pasta Salad, 107
Mini Cookie Pizzas, 411
Mini Meat Loaves, 209
Mint-Smoked Lamb Chops, 336, 337
Mom's Best Waffles, 144
Monterey Skillet Hamburgers, 214, 215
Mostaccioli, Italian sausage and, soup, 48, 49
Mou Shu Vegetables with Asian Pancakes, 298, 299
Mozzarella and Basil with Marinara Sauce, 44, 45
Muffins
 double-corn, 382
 mini-, orange-almond, 380, 381
Mushroom(s)
 chicken and, Alfredo, 176

Mustard. *See also* Dijon mustard
 honey-, pork chops, 338
 honey-, turkey with snap peas, 188, 189
 maple-, sauce, asparagus with, 369
 portabella and bell pepper, grilled, sandwiches, 346, 347
 sauce, sweet, pork with, 220
 tomato and basil orzo pilaf, 349

N

Nacho bites, shrimp, 32, 33
Nachos, skillet, 286, 287
Nectarine, blueberry-, dessert tortillas, 398, 399
New England Baked Bean Stew, 58, 59
New Mexican Black Bean Burritos, 300
Noodle(s)
 chili beef 'n, 91
 orange teriyaki beef with, 92, 93
 soup, black beans and salsa, 50, 51
 soup, chicken, Oriental, 47
Nut(s)
 how to toast, 62, 88, 145
 maple-, topping, pound cake with, 387
Nutrition guidelines, 414–15

O

Oatmeal Pancakes with Strawberry Topping, 154
Old-Time Beef and Vegetable Stew, 200, 201
Olive, corn and, spread, 20
Omelet, salmon and cream cheese, 135
One-Pan Potatoes and Chicken, 181

Super Express Recipes

 = *super express* ready in 20 minutes or less

● = *super express* ready in 20 minutes or less

Complete your cookbook library
with these *Betty Crocker* titles

Betty Crocker's Best Bread Machine Cookbook
Betty Crocker's Best Chicken Cookbook
Betty Crocker's Best Christmas Cookbook
Betty Crocker's Best of Baking
Betty Crocker's Best of Healthy and Hearty Cooking
Betty Crocker's Best-Loved Recipes
Betty Crocker's Bisquick® Cookbook
Betty Crocker's Bread Machine Cookbook
Betty Crocker's Complete Thanksgiving Cookbook
Betty Crocker's Cook It Quick
Betty Crocker's Cookbook, 9th Edition – *The* **BIG RED** *Cookbook*®
Betty Crocker's Cookbook, Bridal Edition
Betty Crocker's Cookie Book
Betty Crocker's Cooking for Two
Betty Crocker's Cooky Book, Facsimile Edition
Betty Crocker's Cooking Basics
Betty Crocker's Diabetes Cookbook
Betty Crocker's Easy Slow Cooker Dinners
Betty Crocker's Eat and Lose Weight
Betty Crocker's Entertaining Basics
Betty Crocker's Flavors of Home
Betty Crocker's Great Grilling
Betty Crocker's Healthy New Choices
Betty Crocker's Indian Home Cooking
Betty Crocker's Italian Cooking
Betty Crocker's Kids Cook!
Betty Crocker's Kitchen Library
Betty Crocker's Living with Cancer Cookbook
Betty Crocker's Low-Fat Low-Cholesterol Cooking Today
Betty Crocker's New Cake Decorating
Betty Crocker's New Chinese Cookbook
Betty Crocker's A Passion for Pasta
Betty Crocker's Picture Cook Book, Facsimile Edition
Betty Crocker's Quick & Easy Cookbook
Betty Crocker's Slow Cooker Cookbook
Betty Crocker's Southwest Cooking
Betty Crocker's Ultimate Cake Mix Cookbook
Betty Crocker's Vegetarian Cooking